A Concise History
of Korea

A Concise History of Korea

From the Neolithic Period through the Nineteenth Century

Michael J. Seth

ROWMAN & LITTLEFIELD PUBLISHERS, INC.
Lanham • Boulder • New York • Toronto • Oxford

ROWMAN & LITTLEFIELD PUBLISHERS, INC.

Published in the United States of America
by Rowman & Littlefield Publishers, Inc.
A wholly owned subsidiary of The Rowman & Littlefield Publishing Group, Inc.
4501 Forbes Boulevard, Suite 200, Lanham, Maryland 20706
www.rowmanlittlefield.com

P.O. Box 317, Oxford OX2 9RU, UK

British Library Cataloguing in Publication Information Available

Library of Congress Cataloging-in-Publication Data

Seth, Michael J., 1948–
    A concise history of Korea : from the neolithic period through the nineteenth
century / Michael J. Seth.
        p.   cm.
    Includes bibliographical references and index.
    ISBN-13: 978-0-7425-4004-0 (cloth : alk. paper)
    ISBN-10: 0-7425-4004-9 (cloth : alk. paper)
    ISBN-13: 978-0-7425-4005-7 (pbk. : alk. paper)
    ISBN-10: 0-7425-4005-7 (pbk. : alk. paper)
    1. Korea—History. 2. Korea—Civilization. I. Title.
DS907.18.S4 2006
951.9′02—dc22
                                                                            2006010873

Printed in the United States of America

♾ ™ The paper used in this publication meets the minimum requirements of
American National Standard for Information Sciences—Permanence of Paper for
Printed Library Materials, ANSI/NISO Z39.48-1992.

Contents

Acknowledgments

I am indebted to the many people who have assisted me with this book. They are too numerous to mention here so I will just single out a few. I would like to thank the late Kim Chul-hee, who made my times in Korea comfortable, and my professor at the University of Hawaii, Yong-ho Choe, from whom I learned a great deal about Korean history. Many thanks to Edward Shultz and Donald Baker, who read the manuscript, offered many useful suggestions, and caught an embarrassing number of errors. Lisa Kuchy aided me in making the maps. The Korea Foundation and the Academy of Korean Studies have partially sponsored my visits to Korea. The patience and help of Jessica Gribble and the staff of Rowman and Littlefield walked me through the final stages of completing the manuscript. My colleagues in the area of Korean studies whose work is cited in the endnotes and bibliography of this book have done the hard research that this book is based on. My students at James Madison University have been guinea pigs for the early drafts of this text. Their questions guided me in deciding what to include and how to make it comprehensible to nonspecialists.

This book is the product of years of being around people who aided me in various ways in my pursuit of understanding Korean history. I want to express my gratitude to them, especially to the many Koreans who over the years have shared their love and knowledge of their culture and who have encouraged me to continue in my attempt to make Korea a bit better known to non-Koreans. To one Korean in particular, Choe Soo-ok, I owe a special thanks. Without her encouragement I would probably not have written this book.

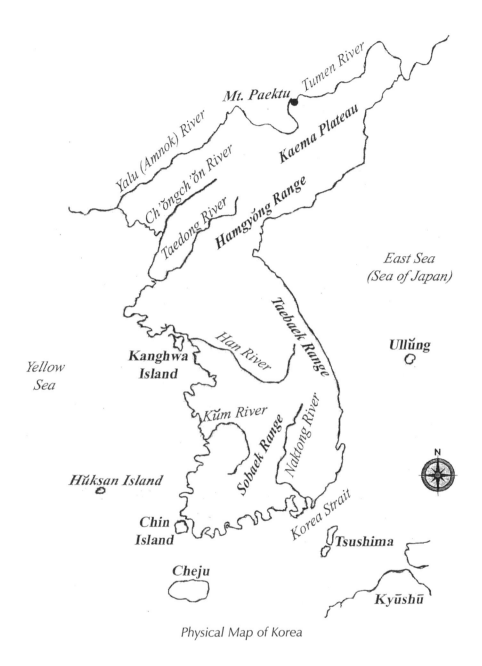

Physical Map of Korea

Physical Map of East Asia

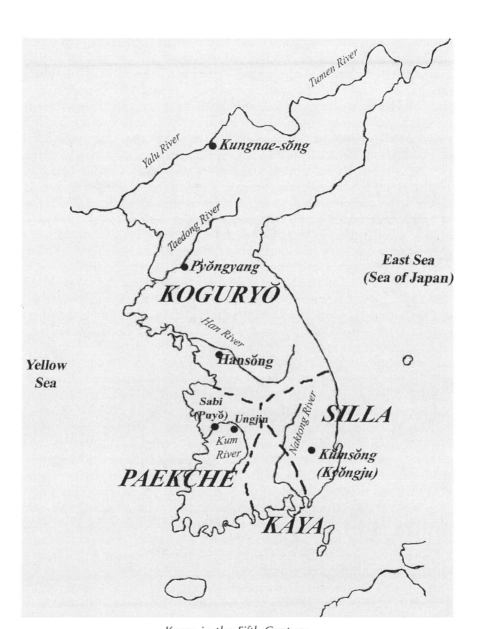

Korea in the Fifth Century

Silla and Parhae Kingdoms

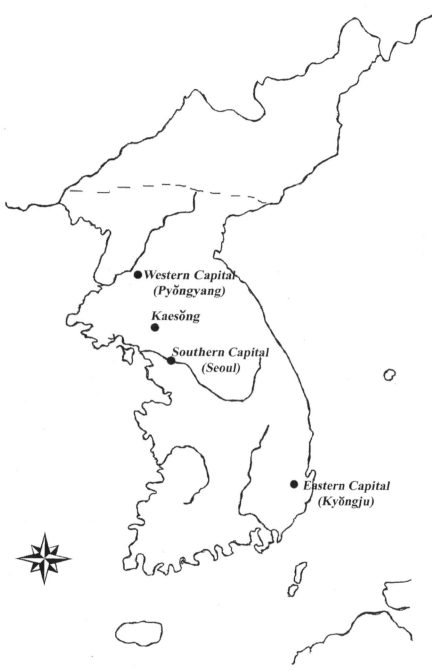

● Western Capital
(Pyŏngyang)

● Kaesŏng

Southern Capital
(Seoul)

● Eastern Capital
(Kyŏngju)

Koryŏ in the Eleventh Century

**HAMGIL
(Hamgyŏng)**

P'YŎNGAN

Hamhŭng

P'yŏngyang

HWANGHAE

Haeju

KANGWŎN

KYŎNGGI

*Hanyang
(Seoul)*

Wŏnju

CH'UNGCH'ŎNG

• *Kongju*

KYŎNGSANG

Taegu

Chŏnju

CHŎLLA

Tongnae

Chosŏn Korea

Introduction

Korea is a modest-sized country surrounded by much larger neighbors: China, Japan, and Russia. The fact that it has been lodged between the important and culturally rich Chinese and Japanese societies has meant that Korea is often overlooked. It has been difficult for Koreans to emerge from the shadow of their East Asian neighbors and to make their presence and their culture known to the rest of the world. Yet Korea, small as it seems next to its neighbors, is not all that small. The area of North and South Korea combined is 84,000 square miles, about the same as Utah. This sounds unimpressive, but it is also the same size as the United Kingdom and a little smaller than another peninsular society, Italy, which it roughly resembles in shape. In population today North Korea has about 23 million inhabitants and South Korea 47 million for a total of 70 million, a little larger than that of Britain, France, or Italy, and a little smaller than that of Germany.

Korean society emerged from varied peoples who gradually forged a society characterized by cultural homogeneity and political unity. Korea today is divided into two rival states, but this is a fairly recent development. Before being effectively partitioned by the United States and the Soviet Union in 1945, Korea had been one of the oldest continuously unified states in the world. The peninsular heartland of what is today Korea was united in 676, and except for one brief period, remained so until the end of the Second World War. It had also become one of the most homogeneous societies in the world. A number of peoples entered the peninsula in antiquity, but gradually all merged into a single ethnicity, sharing one language and participating in one political system. In modern times there have been no significant ethnic minorities. Binding Koreans together and distinguishing them from their neighbors has been their language. Korean, while showing some similarities to Japanese and to the Altaic languages of Inner Asia, is also quite distinct from them. In modern times all Koreans spoke the Korean language,

1

which since the fifteenth century has been written in a unique alphabet. Before the twentieth century, there were no significant Korean-speaking groups outside of Korea. Thus, Korea became one of the few lands where ethnicity, membership in a language community, and a state were coterminous. This unity and homogeneity that emerged over the centuries has become an important part of Korean identity.

Korea has been a part of an East Asian civilization centered in China. China was one of the earliest homes of agriculture, urbanization, state structures, and literacy. As long as three and a half millennia ago a culture emerged in northern China that was recognizably Chinese. This culture profoundly influenced its neighbors, Korea, Vietnam, and Japan, to the extent that the cultures of these societies can be viewed as offshoots of Chinese civilization. Literate states emerged first in Korea and then Japan in the early centuries of the first millennium C.E. From China the Koreans received their writing system. Although in the fifteenth century the Koreans invented their own unique alphabet, Chinese characters were the main means of writing until the twentieth century. The Korean language borrowed much of its higher vocabulary from Chinese, much as English borrowed most of its educated vocabulary from Latin and Greek. Koreans then brought literacy further castward to their Japanese neighbors. Written classical Chinese was studied by all educated Koreans before the twentieth century, and it served as the means for communicating with their Chinese, Japanese, and Vietnamese neighbors.

China provided the model for literature, art, music, architecture, dress, and etiquette. From China Koreans imported most of their ideas about government and politics. They accepted the Chinese world view in which China was the center of the universe and the home of all civilization, and its emperor the mediator between heaven and earth. Koreans took pride in their adherence to Chinese cultural norms. For most of the period from the seventh to the nineteenth century they accepted their country's role as a subordinate member of the international hierarchy in which China stood at the apex, loyal adherents of Chinese culture such as Korea ranked next, and the barbarians outside Chinese civilization stood at the bottom. Close adherence to civilized standards was a source of pride. But this did not result in a loss of separate identity. On the contrary, in adapting Chinese culture to their own society Koreans defined their own cultural distinctiveness. Nor did Korea's membership in the "tributary system" in which the Korean king became a vassal of the Chinese emperor mean, as was sometimes misunderstood by Westerners, that Korea was less than fully independent. In fact, Koreans were fiercely independent. Much of their history has been the story of resistance to outside intruders. Korea's position as a tributary state was usually ceremonial, and for Koreans it did not imply a loss of autonomy. Chinese attempts to interfere in domestic affairs were met with opposition.

Indeed, some today view the Korean past as a saga of the struggles of a smaller society to resist control or assimilation by larger, more aggressive neighbors: the Chinese, the Japanese, and the Inner Asian peoples that border them on the north, the Russians being the successors of the last.

Missionaries from China and Central Asia introduced Buddhism to Korea. For much of its history Korea was a Buddhist land. Millions of Koreans are still adherents to Buddhism, which until recently has been the most influential religious tradition. Buddhism originated in India from where it spread throughout most of Asia, coming to Korea via China. When it reached Korea it had absorbed a number of Chinese and other Asian traditions. Buddhism had a profound impact on Korean art, music, and literature. Buddhism inspired the earliest sculptures and the first monumental architecture other than tombs, and importantly, its missionaries brought literacy. It included the idea of reincarnation, that the suffering in life is inevitable, but escape from the cycle of births and rebirths is possible. For many Koreans it meant a hope for a future life of bliss through faith in the Buddha. It also taught a respect for all forms of life. Buddhist practices of meditation and the escape from daily concerns that temples provided were an important outlet for those who found the obligations and pressures of everyday life too strong.

Confucianism had an especially profound impact on Korean society, forming the basis for ethical standards, and for ideas about government, society, and family relationships. Confucianism was a tradition of thought in China, a dynamic tradition that evolved over the centuries. It taught that the world was a moral universe, that all humans were connected to the universe and to each other. For Koreans it was important in that it made the family, and the roles and responsibilities of each member of the family, the foundation for morality. Each individual had the duty to adhere to his or her role as mother, father, son, daughter, elder brother, and so on. These relations were given cosmic significance. At a political level Confucianism emphasized the importance of loyalty, hierarchy, and authority. It made obedience to a ruler a moral duty and correctly carrying out rulership a moral obligation. It also influenced the Korean concern for social rank. Koreans viewed the world as a hierarchical order in which everyone has a place. The young were subordinate to their elders, women to men, commoners to members of the upper class, and subjects to the ruler. Yet in each of these relations both were bound by moral obligations.

While Buddhism and Confucianism came to Korea from China, the Korean love and respect for nature has indigenous origins. Koreans have looked to the natural world—the mountains, rivers, trees, rocks, flowers, animals, and seashores—as sources of artistic and spiritual inspiration. The changing of the seasons and the beauties of nature have always been among the most popular topics of painting, poetry, and song. Prominent features of nature, especially mountains, but also rocks, trees, and rivers, have been seen as sources of spiritual power. This took the form of directly worshiping the spirits of nature, spirits that were not personified as gods and goddesses but accepted as part of nature. Nature worship blended with geomancy, the belief imported from China that certain topographical settings are auspicious. The location of buildings, the layout of cities and towns, and the placement of graves, as well as architecture and everyday activities, took note of their natural settings.

While in general, the Koreans adhered to Chinese models more closely than did the more distant Japanese, Chinese culture imports did not erase indigenous cultural traditions and beliefs. Shamanism and nature worship remained a strong component of religious life, particularly for the nonelite. Folk dances, folk art, and craft traditions drew upon domestic sources. Koreans often selectively borrowed and adapted from China. Korean homes, for example, with their heated paper floors, were unlike those of their neighbors. Their cuisine took on its own style, evolving into a highly spiced culinary tradition in sharp contrast to the blander fare of the northern Chinese and Japanese. The social system evolved differently from that of China. Korea retained a fairly rigid hierarchical tradition, with an aristocracy made up of families who often could trace their ancestries back many generations, in contrast to the Chinese ruling class with its greater social mobility and lesser stability. Yet the Korean aristocracy gradually moved from a warrior aristocracy to a civilian one that held military skills in contempt in contrast to the Japanese warrior elite. In many ways, such as ritual practices, marital customs, the role of women, the structure of the family, and the patterns of governance, Korean society provided a distinctive variant within East Asian civilization.

Another way Korean history was distinctive was its remarkable continuity. From the seventh to the twentieth century only three dynasties ruled Korea. The second ruled for almost five centuries and the third for more than five centuries; both were among the longest-ruling dynasties in history. The two dynastic changes that did take place did not bring about a vast upheaval. Elite families as well as institutions were carried over from one dynasty to another. This, along with a Confucian concern for examining the past, contributed to a strong sense of historical consciousness among Koreans.

Korea was a somewhat isolated society for most of its history; its contacts with its East Asian neighbors were often restricted, and those with the rest of the world limited and sporadic. It was one of the last non-Western societies in the world to be visited by Westerners. And even today it still is not well known. But in contemporary times Korea has played a much more important role in the world than it had in its past. North Korea has become one of the world's trouble spots, an impoverished, totalitarian society that is a threat to its neighbors and a major international security concern. South

Korea is a vibrant, economically dynamic society that has become a model of economic and social modernization for other developing nations and a major participant in the world economy. South Korea's success and North Korea's menace have helped attract more attention and interest in the peninsula. Most of this attention has been focused on recent events. Any understanding of the two Koreas today, however, must include an understanding of the past of this ancient, historically minded people.

This history traces the origins and development of Korean society from the varied tribal peoples who had settled in the peninsula and its northern borders to the formation and of a distinctive, homogeneous culture that had a long tradition by the nineteenth century. It generally follows a chronological pattern. The first chapter deals with the origins of the Korean people from the earliest human inhabitants to the emergence of indigenous literate states in the third century C.E. The second chapter deals with the "Three Kingdoms" period, in which three states—Silla, Paekche, and Koguryŏ—competed for supremacy in the peninsula and ends with the unification of most of the peninsula under Silla in the seventh century. The remaining chapters deal with the evolution of Korean society and culture under a unified state structure. The third chapter examines developments during United Silla (676–935); the fourth and fifth during Koryŏ (935–1392), the second dynastic state; and chapters six, seven, eight, and nine survey the social, political, and cultural evolution of Korea during the third and longest dynastic state, Chosŏn (1392–1910). The account ends in the late nineteenth century, approximately in 1876, when Korea centered into the Western-dominated world political and economic system, and became part of the emerging global society.

Any periodization that divides Korean history into "traditional" or "premodern" and "modern" carries the risk of implying too sharp a dichotomy between the two. Any decision as to where to mark the boundary between modern and premodern is to some extent arbitrary. However, the strong continuities in Korean history before the later nineteenth century and the profound changes that occurred afterwards make the 1870s a reasonable point to end this account of Korean history. It should be reemphasized that only by understanding the historical heritage of the Koreans can their modern experience be intelligently understood. Furthermore, the history of Korea to the nineteenth century is a fascinating tale of a rich cultural tradition. Our knowledge of it contributes to our understanding of East Asian and of world history.

1

The Origins

GEOGRAPHICAL SETTING

Most of Korea is a mountainous peninsula. The Korean term for peninsula is *pando*, literally, "half island." This term is especially appropriate for Korea, whose history has been so profoundly influenced by the fact that it is a geographic entity clearly defined by the long narrow piece of land that juts out of the great Eurasian continental landmass. The Korean Peninsula extends some 600 miles (1000 km) from north to south and is about 150 miles (240 km) in breadth at its widest. Its peninsular character sets it off from the continent of which Korea has never been fully a part of, and yet neither is it an island with indisputable geographical boundaries and the advantages that an oceanic moat can provide. The Yellow Sea to the west, the East Sea (Sea of Japan) to the east, and the Korea Straits to the south form natural boundaries. The northern border of modern Korea is a 300-mile (500 km) boundary with the Manchurian region of China and a short 25-mile (40 km) border with Russia. The Yalu and Tumen Rivers define most of this border. Paektu Mountain, the highest in Korea, forms the watershed between the two frontier rivers. This northern border was established in the fifteenth century and has seen only minor modifications since. The Korean peninsula gives the land distinctive boundaries marking it off from the mainland. It also acts as a bridge linking the Asian continent with the vast island archipelago along the eastern rim of Asia that begins with the Kurile Islands, runs through the Japanese chain, and extends to the Philippines.

Korea's climate is dominated neither by a continental nor by a maritime regime but by a combination of the two. In summer maritime breezes from the south bring warm, tropical air. In the winter cold, dry air comes down from the Mongolian plains. The growing season varies greatly with the latitude: forty-four weeks in the south and twenty-eight in the north. This reflects the peninsula's unusually wide variation in temperatures for such a small area. The January mean is a mild 6 degrees centigrade (43 degrees Fahrenheit) on the island of Cheju but only −19 degrees centigrade (−2 degrees Fahrenheit) in the bend of the Yalu River. Snow falls everywhere in winter except in the extreme south. Summers are hot and humid except in the northernmost part of the country.

Korea is a land of mountains. While the peninsular nature of Korea has given it a natural unity, the mountainous terrain has divided the country up into pockets and acted as an isolating and regionalizing factor. The mountains are not especially high, with only a few rising above 5,000 feet (1,600 meters); the highest peak, Paektu Mountain on the Korean-Manchurian border, is only 9,003 feet (2,744 meters). Though not high, many mountains are rugged, forming obstacles to easy travel within the country. They were not formidable enough to prevent the creation of a central state, but they did hinder internal transport and trade. Mountains dominate the land. No part of Korea is out of view of the mountains; there are no broad plains. Level land is at a premium, and the population has been densely concentrated in the narrow but agriculturally rich alluvial basins. The numerous mountains and lack of large plains as in China or even anything as large as the Kanto and Kansai Plains in Japan contributed to the modest size of its urban centers in premodern times compared to its two East Asian neighbors. Mountains have played an important part in Korean religion and in art. Koreans have worshiped the spirits of mountains, have sought refuge from everyday cares in them, and have admired their beauty. Especially admired have been the bell-shaped Diamond Mountains along the eastern coast. The narrowness of the peninsula has made access to the sea easy and provided coastal routes to link the various regions, partly compensating for the obstacles to regional integration created by the mountainous terrain.

The seas around Korea are rich in protein and have been a major source of sustenance, but they are rough and not ideal for navigation. The eastern coast has few harbors and only a narrow coastal plain and is cut off from the more inhabitable western part of the peninsula by the Taebaek Range. The western coast has among the world's highest tides, along with treacherous sandbars. Consequently, Koreans have not been a seafaring people. This has contributed to another geographic factor in Korean history: the remoteness of Korea. Although near the Chinese cultural heartland in the North China Plain, with easy access to Chinese cultural influences, Korea is far from the other major centers of world culture. It has not been located on major international trade routes, with the significant exception of those between China and Japan. As a result it has not been exposed to the variety of cultural influences and peoples that some other lands have. For most of its history Korea has been a land little known except by its immediate neighbors.

KOREA "IN EAST ASIA"

Korea occupies a central position in East Asia. It can be thought of as lodged between three cultural/geographical areas: China, the northern frontiers of Manchuria and Siberia, and Japan. To the west lie the fertile and densely populated plains of northern China, the cultural cradle and later political center of the vast Chinese empire. For most of its history Korea did not actually border China since the lands north of the Yalu River were not permanently incorporated in China until the seventeenth century and remained an ethnically non-Chinese frontier until the nineteenth. But whether by land or by sea China was not far. The Shandong Peninsula in China is only 120 miles away from the nearest point on the west coast. Throughout Korea's history its proximity to China has been a major factor in shaping its history. China was close enough to be make cross-cultural exchanges easy but at most periods was not an immediate threat. This enormous, ancient, wealthy, and powerful neighbor was the main source of ideas about government, scholarship, and cultural sophistication for Koreans.

To the east is the Japanese archipelago. Korea often acted as a bridge between China and Japan. It was through Korea that much of Chinese culture, including Buddhism and literacy, was transmitted. This was mostly a one-way exchange as Korea before the late nineteenth century borrowed little from Japan. Rather the Japanese with their military culture and pirates posed a constant threat to Korean security. Relations, however, were sometimes peaceful. At such times trade between the two northeast Asian societies flourished. The third side of the triangle that surrounds Korea was the northern forest and plains of Manchuria and adjacent Siberia. This region posed an even greater threat to Korean security. For this northern border marked the easternmost end of the vast Inner Asian realm of grasslands, forests, and deserts that stretches across Eurasia, and that was the home to the world's great nomadic empires. Repeatedly Korea faced the incursions, invasions, and threat of invasions from the warlike and mobile nomadic and seminomadic peoples of this region. The contact was not entirely negative, since the Inner Asian peoples were sometimes conveyors of new ideas and technologies from elsewhere, and sometimes immigrants into the peninsula.

A central fact of Korean history, however, is that it has been surrounded by larger societies that were some of the most militarily formidable peoples in history. Or as Koreans sometimes say, they have been a "shrimp among whales." Yet the land was more than a passive victim of larger forces but a part of a large interactive regional sphere that included China, Japan, and Northeast Asia. An understanding of Korean history sheds light on understanding these lands as well.

THE KOREANS

The Koreans today are one of the world's most ethnically homogeneous peoples. In recent times there have been no significant ethnic or linguistic minorities. Ethnicity is a very difficult term to define, but language is simpler. All Koreans speak Korean as their native tongue and all people who speak Korean as their first language identify themselves as ethnically Korean. No other language is known to have been spoken by any large group on the peninsula in recent centuries.

Korean is not closely related to any other language. Most linguists classify it as related to Japanese and remotely related to the Altaic languages of Inner Asia, which include Mongolian, the Turkic languages, and the Tungusic languages such as Manchu. Korean shares a grammatical structure with Japanese and the Altaic languages. All are agglutinative, that is, one adds components to a root to form words that are often long. This linguistic relationship, if accurate, is often interpreted as meaning that the ancient ancestors of modern Koreans came from central Asia and entered the peninsula through Manchuria, with some of them going on to occupy the Japanese archipelago. According to one current theory the ancestral Koreans spoke Proto-Altaic, one branch of which evolved into the Tungusic languages and another into Proto-Korean-Japanese, which eventually became the modern Korean and Japanese languages. The evidence of this, however, is less than irrefutable.[1] Even if in fact this is correct it does not imply that massive migrations took place. For example, a relatively small number of Proto-Korean speakers may have imposed their language on the preexisting peoples. Nor did this process need to have been violent; it may have been a slow, gradual mingling of peoples. Or it may not have taken place at all. The fact is, that in the two thousand years of Korean history that can be supported with written records no documented large-scale migrations of people into the peninsula took place.

Korean shares many similarities in sentence structure with Japanese and it is probable that the two languages are genetically related. This is probably because migrants from Korea influenced the development of the Japanese language. Yet, the unusual sound system of Korean and most of its native vocabulary are very different. Korean consonants make a distinction between aspiration and nonaspiration, and between tense and lax sounds, but do not make phonemic distinctions between voiced and unvoiced consonants. This means that Korean has no initial b, d, hard g, or j sounds but has three p, three t, three ch, and three k sounds. This plus the complex system of sound changes makes it a difficult language for most nonnative speakers to pronounce. It is highly inflected and has no tones. Although modern Korean is filled with many Chinese loanwords it does not resemble Chinese at all. The distinctiveness of Korean native vocabulary and phonology is a source of pride to some modern Korean nationalists who like to emphasize

Korean uniqueness. For the historian it presents a linguistic puzzle, making it hard to trace Korean origins. It should be added that historians do not know much about how the language sounded before the invention of the Korean alphabet in the fifteenth century and can only guess at its structure in ancient times.

EARLY INHABITANTS

Humans have lived on the Korean Peninsula since very early times. Remains of Paleolithic humans have been found at Kulp'ori in Unggi-gun in the extreme northeast of Korea that have been tentatively dated back four hundred thousand years. North Koreans have claimed to have found evidence of human habitation as early as six hundred thousand years ago. Stone implements and evidence of the occupation of caves by paleolithic people have been reported at a number of sites in South Korea. The dating of these early inhabitants is uncertain. It is also unclear if the peninsula was continuously inhabited since these early times. At the minimum, we can say that human activity in Korea goes back hundreds of thousands of years.

The search for the origins of Korean culture begins during the Post-Pleistocene climatic optimum, 6,000 to 2,000 B.C.E. This period of warming climate roughly coincided with the early Neolithic period in Korea. Our chief source of information on Neolithic peoples in Korea comes from pottery. The earliest pottery is found on top of layers of pre-pottery sites. This, along with a continuity in the stone tools, suggests that the pottery cultures may have emerged from the preexisting cultures rather than being the product of new peoples entering the peninsula.[2] The earliest pottery dates back to perhaps 6,000 B.C.E. and is found in connection with shell middens along the Korean coasts. This early pottery is known as *chŭlmun* or comb-patterned pottery (also known in Korean as *pitsal munŭi*) after the characteristic decorative pattern that consisted of incised parallel lines. The early forms show considerable regional variation. After 3500 B.C.E. the classic *chŭlmun* emerged in the Han and Taedong River basins on the west coast. Regional variations in pottery remained. Along the east coast a flat-based pottery has been found while on the south coast, pottery vessels are typically round-based vessels with wide mouths. The early cultures associated with these pottery remains appear to have had a subsistence base that was heavily dependent on fishing. In addition to shell middens, the importance of fishing is apparent from the abundant stone net sinkers and fishhooks that have been found at these early Neolithic sites.[3]

Villages associated with *chŭlmun* pottery resemble earlier ones, being small clusters of semisubterranean dwellings made by digging a pit into the ground and covering it with wood, mud, and thatch. A central hearth lined with stones provided heat. This was a practical adaptation to the climate since the homes would likely be cool in summer and relatively warm in winter. The complex relationship between the peoples of the peninsula and their relationship with their regional neighbors China, Manchuria/Siberia, and the Japanese archipelago are apparent in this early period. Pottery in Korea shows some similarity to that of Japan and the Yellow Sea region of China. Some scholars have also noted some resemblances in regional Korean styles to Siberian pottery. Similarity in pottery styles suggests these early inhabitants of Korea were part of a larger complex of Northeast Asian peoples and cultures. Some scholars see a distinctiveness in the pottery of Korea from what has been found in either the Asian mainland or in Japan. Others, however, find the evidence for a distinctive Korean culture at such an early date unconvincing.

The *chŭlmun* period, which lasted until about 2,000 B.C.E., is a period of transition from hunting, fishing, and gathering to agriculture as the basis of subsistence. To understand this transition, we can best see developments in Korea as part of a worldwide change in human patterns of existence. About ten thousand years ago people in various parts of the world shifted from economies based on specialized hunting with minor subsidiary gathering of plants and some fishing to a broad-spectrum strategy for existence. This involved hunting a wider variety of game, including many smaller animals, and relying more on fishing and on plant collection for food. In many parts of the world this was followed by the gradual domestication of plant and animals until societies became sedentary and once again specialized, relying on one to several species of cultivated plants or livestock. The reasons for this development remain somewhat mysterious, although the transition to agriculture is possibly related in some complex way to the end of the most recent glacial period about ten thousand years ago and the subsequent global warming.

Archaeological evidence shows Korea fitting very much into this pattern. During the Neolithic, the peoples of the peninsula lived by fishing; shellfish collecting; hunting deer, wild pigs, and oxen; and collecting wild plants. The forests of Korea, especially during the Post-Pleistocene climatic optimum from 6,000 to 2,000 B.C.E., contained great bounties of edible plants: acorns, chestnuts, arrowroots, turnips, green onions, garlic, and Japanese camellia. The stone implements left behind show that these foods became increasingly important in the diet.[4] In the fourth millennium the beginnings of agriculture appear. Millet, native to Korea, was probably the first major domesticated plant and by the end of the *chŭlmun* its cultivation was widespread, as was the domestication of the pig. Evidence for plant domestication is found in the existence of grinding stones, hoes, and stone sickles at archaeological sites. Agriculture is extremely important for historical development, for it makes possible dense populations of sedentary communities, transforms the landscape, and creates the possibilities for more complex forms of social organization to emerge. But agriculture developed slowly as the basis of subsistence, and settlements remained small. Hunting, fishing, and wild plant collecting were still important. The changes brought about by the *chŭlmun* peoples were laying the foundation for the future developments in Korea, but who these peoples were and what their relationship was to the peoples and cultures outside the peninsula or to the later Korean peoples are unclear.

THE AGE OF RICE FARMING BEGINS

Rice has been staple crop in Korea for the past several millennia.[5] Korea is well suited for rice cultivation. There are two main varieties of rice: *Oryza sativa indica* and *Oryza sativa japonica/sinica*, both of which were cultivated in the Yangzi basin in central China by the third millennium B.C.E. *Oryza sativa japonica/sinica* is best suited for Korea since its germinates and ripens at lower temperatures and is more resistant to cold weather. Rice can be grown on dry fields but the best yields are in wet paddies. During earlier times most rice was grown in dry fields, but after the sixteenth century wet rice farming emerged as the dominant form of agriculture in Korea. In wet rice farming, water is kept in small reservoirs or diverted from small streams to flow into fields. Rice seedlings are first planted in seedbeds and then transplanted into the main field. In Korea the transplanting is usually done in June just before the start of the summer monsoon season. Weather patterns in Korea are ideal for this type of rice cultivation. The summer monsoon brings most of the year's rainfall, which amounts to about sixty inches a year in the southern areas and about fifty inches in the central Han River basin and declines further as the monsoon proceeds northward. Rice grows fast in the Korea's warm, humid, tropical-like summers and ripens in the bright, cloudless, dry autumns that characterize the fall. Although there are no broad plains in Korea, the many river valleys provide rich alluvial soils, and the numerous streams that trickle down the mountainsides into the valleys make for a ready supply of water for the paddies.

A number of other crops, such as soybeans, barley, and millet, have been important components of the Korean diet, but rice occupies a place in the culture unrivaled by any other food source. The word for meal, *pap*, means cooked rice. Most Koreans from the beginnings of recorded history two thousand years ago until the mid-twentieth century were rice farmers. The rhythms of rice production have been dictated by the planting and harvesting or rice. Rice production has been the prime determinant of the population distribution. The majority of Koreans in historical times have lived in the warmer and moister regions of southern and central Korea; the northern regions, less suitable for rice, have been less populated and more marginal.

The elite derived their wealth primarily from their ownership of good rice lands and their control over those that farmed them.

It is not yet clear when rice farming began in Korea. Between 2,000 and 1,500 B.C.E. the *chŭlmun* pottery culture gave way to the *mumun* or plain pottery style, so named after the characteristic undecorated double-rimmed vessels. It was during this period that agriculture clearly emerged as the dominant way of life. During the early *mumun* culture hunting, fishing, and foraging were still important, and archaeological evidence suggests that cultivation of rice was not extensive until the first millennium B.C.E., indicating not an abrupt change but a slow transition as the peoples of the peninsula adapted to rice farming.[6] But by the late first millennium, a great transformation had taken place as rice cultivation was beginning to be the basis for the Korean way of life, as it would continue to be until the twentieth century. The impact of rice cultivation on the peoples and cultures of Korea was profound. Rice cultivation made it possible to support dense populations. It bound this expanded population to the soil and to the seasonal rhythms associated with the cultivation of rice. Collecting wild plants, the planting of a variety of vegetables, the raising of pigs and oxen, fishing, shellfish collecting, and the cultivation of barley and millet as secondary crops were also important, but only as supplements to rice farming.

Some archaeological evidence suggests that the early peoples of Korea were influenced by developments of China. Around 700 B.C.E. or perhaps a little earlier the use of bronze began in Korea. Western scholars impressed by the impact of technology on social and cultural change have tended to regard the arrival of bronze tools and weapons as of epochal significance. In the case of Korea, however, the appearance of bronze knives and tools was in itself probably of only minor significance. During the bronze age, some graves are accompanied by bronze mirrors, daggers, and bells, which are sometimes found in stone cists. These would appear to be precious goods, setting off their possessors from those whose graves had simpler, more common stone burial possessions. Characteristic among Korean bronze artifacts are the *p'ip'a* (Chinese lute)-shaped dagger and the multiknobbed mirror; both are found in adjacent areas of Manchuria, and the dagger is also found in Shandong and parts of northern China. Neither appear to be of Chinese origin, and these may be indicators of a broad Northeast Asia cultural zone.[7] Interestingly enough, not a single bronze ritual vessel, which is characteristic of China's bronze age, has been found in Korea. This suggests that although bronze metalworking most probably spread to Korea from China, where it developed around 1,800 B.C.E., Korea remained culturally different from the Chinese mainland. Also interesting is the fact that bronze was not associated with state formation in Korea as it has been elsewhere. Despite efforts by some nationalist Korean historians to claim bronze artifacts as evidence of early states, it is unlikely that any organization above the tribal level existed at this time. Iron also probably came to the peninsula from China sometime before 300 B.C.E. Iron is important not only because it is superior to stone for cutting trees, clearing fields, and eliminating enemies but also because it contributed to economic specialization and the development of trade. Both are key elements in the creation of complex societies.

Another artifact that suggests Korea was part of a northeast Asian cultural zone distinct from most of China is the megalith. About ten thousand dolmens have been found in Korea, most probably built in the first millennium B.C.E. These are not unique to Korea but are found in Manchuria, northern Shandong province of China, and northern Kyushu. They usually mark grave sites and consist of two basic types. The northern type, called *t'akja* (table) style, has typically three or four stones covered by a large stone; the southern *paduk* (Korean name for the game of *go*) type consists of a large capstone resting on a number of much smaller stones or directly on the ground. Less is known about them and the people who constructed them than is known about the more famous megaliths in Western Europe. The construction of elaborate stone megaliths suggests formation of social stratification and of social units larger than simple villages. Presumably it took large numbers of peoples, more than would inhabit a small village, to construct the megaliths, and burials there would be for persons of high or important status.[8] Many mysteries remain about the megaliths. For example, why do the artifacts found in stone cists and dolmens vary considerably? Do they represent different ethnic groups or social strata? If the latter, then why are bronze artifacts more likely to be found in the stone cists than in the more impressive dolmens?

Early peoples in Korea lived in small self-sufficient communities, originally hunting bands and later farming or fishing settlements. It was most probably only in the late first millennium B.C.E. that larger political units were formed. By the middle of the second millennium B.C.E. states appeared in North China. The formation of states and later empires in North China had a profound impact on Korea. The emergence of early kingdoms in Crete and mainland Greece was influenced by the more ancient societies of Egypt and the Near East. Likewise state formation in Northeast Asia—Manchuria, Korea, and Japan—occurred under the influence of the earlier and more complex societies of China. This, however, does not mean that Northeast Asian state formation was always and only the product of the direct impact of Chinese developments. For throughout the history of Korea cultural processes took place that were often very different from those in China, indicating a high degree of autonomous development based in part on cultural roots and ecological factors that were quite distinct. From the beginning of Korean history, proximity to the great Chinese civilization was one of the main determining factors in the evolution of Korean culture. Consequently, the absorption of Chinese cultural patterns and their adaptation to indigenous and non-Sinitic patterns have been a major part of the process that created a clearly definable Korean culture and society.

SOURCES FOR EARLY KOREA

Our knowledge of the early Korean states comes from several sources: written records, archaeological evidence, and myths and legends. The earliest Korean written sources are inscriptions; the earliest dates from 414 C.E. The most important written sources are two histories, the *Samguk sagi* (see chapter 4) and the *Samguk yusa* (see chapter 5). But these were compiled in 1145 and 1279 respectively, centuries after the events they describe. Although they are based on earlier, no longer extant sources and remain extremely important for our understanding of ancient Korean history, their usefulness is greatly enhanced when they can be confirmed and supplemented by other sources. Chinese sources also bring considerable light to early Korean history. During the Han dynasty, the first great dynasty that unified all of China on a long-term basis (202 B.C.E. to C.E. 220), the first detailed accounts of events on the Korean peninsula appear. The most important of these are the Chinese history *Shiji* (*Historical Record*), written by Sima Qian around 100 B.C.E., and the *Dongizhuan* (*Account of the Eastern Barbarians*) section of *Sanguozhi* (*Record of the Three Kingdoms*), compiled in 297 C.E. The latter is probably the single most important contemporary document on ancient Korean history. Archaeologists have also provided valuable information that is no less important in understanding this period. And although it seems unlikely that major new written sources will be found, new archaeological evidence is providing a continuously better picture of early Korea.

Still another source is the myths and legends associated with this period. The study of myths for historical information is a difficult and controversial field, but it too can yield clues about the past. The most famous myth is that of Tan'gun (see Tan'gun below). In this myth a celestial deity mates with a compliant bear who gives birth to Tan'gun (Sandalwood Prince), who in turn establishes the first Korean state of Chosŏn in 2333 B.C.E. While this story was not recorded until the thirteenth century, it is probably of much more ancient origin. It hints of animal totems; mountain worship, since most of the action takes place on a sacred mountain; and perhaps at the semidivine claims for early ruling families. In the twentieth century the Tan'gun myth would be interpreted by nationalist writers as supporting claims for the antiquity and uniqueness of the Korean people.

CHOSŎN

An early recorded name associated with Korea is Chaoxian (Korean: Chosŏn). The name is derived from the Chinese characters *chao*, meaning "dawn" or "morning," and *xian,* meaning "fresh" or "calm." Often translated in English as "Land of the Morning Calm," it is one of the names Koreans call their country. The name comes from the geographic position of Korea in relation to China. Korea was to the east of China; hence it was an early morning country in the same way that Japan still farther east was later designated Riben (anglicized as Japan) or "sun origin" land. By the second century B.C.E., Chinese works such as the *Zhanguoce* and the *Shangshu dazhuan* refer to an area called Chaoxian. Although some later Korean histories would assert that the state was founded by Tan'gun in 2333 B.C.E., the earliest uncontested date for a political entity called Chosŏn is 109 B.C.E.[9] At that time the Chinese under Emperor Han Wudi attacked and conquered Chaoxian or Chosŏn. Almost everything about the origin and nature of this Chosŏn is obscure. It was likely to have been more a tribal federation than a state. Perhaps originally located in southern Manchuria, it fell after the Chinese besieged a fortress located in northern Korea, probably near P'yŏngyang.[10] The people of the Chosŏn were most likely illiterate. Modern Koreans see ancient Chosŏn as an ancestor to their nation but there is no clear evidence linking it with any particular ethnic group or culture. Its chief historical importance is that it brought the Chinese into direct involvement in Korea.

In 221 B.C.E. the Qin unified all China for the first time, although only briefly. After 210 B.C.E. the Qin empire began to fall apart and in the struggle for power that ensued Liu Bang emerged and reunified China, establishing the Han dynasty that lasted from 202 B.C.E. to C.E. 220, an empire comparable to its contemporary, the Roman Empire, in area and population. Liu created a number of *wang* (kings) to function as vassals; the king of Yan was one of these. In 195 B.C.E. the Yan king revolted and went over to the Xiongnu, a steppe nomad people. One of his lieutenants, Wiman (Chinese: Weiman), is recorded in the *Shiji* as having fled with a thousand followers to Chosŏn where the ruler Chun appointed him a frontier commander. Wiman, however, seized power, with the aid of Chinese who had already settled in Chosŏn, and set himself up as king. This was sometime between 194 and 180 B.C.E. His descendants ruled until 108 B.C.E.

Wiman and his successors probably served as foreign vassals of China, perhaps acting as middlemen between the tribal peoples in the area and the Chinese. But if this was so, Chosŏn's relationships with China were often uneasy. It had become a place of exile for dissidents in the northeastern part of the Empire. The rulers of Chosŏn also blocked attempts by tribal groupings in the area to directly contact and trade with tribal peoples to the south. When the Han emperor Wudi (141–87 B.C.E.) sought to bring the frontier regions of his empire under direct control, he conquered this troublesome neighbor. During 109–108 B.C.E. Wudi launched a land and sea invasion. Following initial setbacks the Chinese occupied the Chosŏn capital of Wanggŏm and the last king, Ugŏ, a grandson of Wiman, was killed by his own ministers. For the next four centuries a northwestern part of the Korean peninsula was directly incorporated into the Chinese empire, the first and only time the Chinese exerted direct rule in Korea.

THE CHINESE COMMANDERIES

The Chinese, having conquered Chosŏn, set up four administrative units called commanderies (Chinese: *jun;* Korean: *kun*). The Taedong River basin, the area where the modern city of P'yŏngyang is located, became the center of the Lelang (Korean: Nangnang) commandery. Three other commanderies were organized: Xuantu Korean: Hyŏndo), Lintun (Korean: Imdun), and Chenfan (Korean: Chinbŏm). The locations of these commanderies are not altogether certain, but most likely Xuantu was on the northeast coast, and Lintun was just south of it in the area inhabited by a people known as the Okchŏ. The site of Chenfan is less easy to determine but was probably south of Lelang. After the Han Emperor Wudi's death in 87 B.C.E. a retrenchment began under his successor, Emperor Chao (87–74 B.C). The remote Chenfan commandery was abandoned in 82 B.C.E., the Lintun commandery was merged with Xuantu in 75 B.C.E., and Xuantu in the same year was relocated further east, most probably in the Yalu River basin. Thus the history of the Chinese presence in Korea was mainly the story of Lelang and Xuantu, with the former being the more populous and prosperous of the two outposts of Chinese civilization.

The creation of the Chinese commanderies is important in the development of Korean history. It brought the peoples of the peninsula into direct contact with the advanced civilization of the Chinese, launching the process of the sinification of the Korean peoples. With the establishment of the commanderies, the various peoples of the peninsula became involved in a web of trade and cultural ties that connected them with the vast empire of the Han. The Han Empire radiated out from its base in the North China Plain to the Yangzi and southward to Vietnam, and from the Pacific coast to the oases of Central Asia. Thus Korean history became a part of a larger history of East Asia.

These Chinese commanderies have been likened to colonies. However, the commanderies were not foreign territories, but were an integral part of the Han Empire with the same administrative structure that characterized the rest of China. The inhabitants included many Chinese settlers. Just how many is not known, nor is it possible to estimate the percentage of the population that was ethnically Chinese. In any case a good deal of intermarriage and cultural assimilation is probable. The Chinese presence was not a sudden break in the history of the region, for Chosŏn had already absorbed Chinese refugees, and the ruling house of Chosŏn was, at least according to the recorded accounts, of Chinese descent. The Lelang commandery produced textiles and fine Chinese ceramics locally. It imported silk, lacquerware, jade, and gold and silver jewelry, and the elite rode in carriages made from imported equipment. The way of life maintained by the elite at the capital in the P'yŏngyang area, which is known from the tombs and scattered archaeological remains, evinces a prosperous, refined, and very Chinese culture.[11] The existence of imported goods in large numbers from all over the Han Empire testifies to the prosperity of Lelang.

The prosperity of the commanderies was derived from trade. Lelang, and to a lesser extent Xuantu, sat in the center of a network of trade that incorporated the peoples of Manchuria and of northeastern Korea and the tribes in the southern peninsula, and even extended to the peoples and polities of the Japanese archipelago. Bronze mirrors, silk brocade, jade, vermillion, and gold seals from China were exchanged for the hardwood timber, fish, salt, iron, and the agricultural produce of the region. Many of the imports into Lelang from the surrounding peoples were locally consumed, but the wealth of goods that were imported from the Chinese mainland suggests that any local products may have been re-exported to the rest of China. Many of these goods were of symbolic nature: caps, robes, seals, and precious items that were status goods enhancing the prestige and authority of native elites. This policy was termed *heqin*, "peace and kinship," buying peace with nomadic and settled peoples along the frontiers with entertainments and sumptuous gifts.[12] In the time-honored practice of successful imperialists, the Chinese extended their authority beyond the territory they physically occupied by incorporating surrounding indigenous peoples into the imperial system. Tribal and clan leaders received prestige goods, along with Chinese titles and symbols of authority, and were able to engage in a profitable trade in return for their loyalty and cooperation. In this way most of the peoples of Korea became tied to the Han Chinese imperial system.

Economic considerations may have entered into the original conquest; however, it seems clear that the primary concern was strategic, to protect the eastern flank of China's northern frontier with often warlike and aggressive tribal peoples. Tribal leaders were required to come to the Xuantu or Lelang capitals to "pay tribute," that is, to trade and receive the caps, gowns, seals, and titles that were bestowed upon them by Chinese officials as vassals of the emperor. Throughout Korean history this use of the Chinese emperor as a source of authority would prove mutually advantageous to the Chinese and to Koreans. In return tribal leaders were called upon to aid in fighting other tribal groups beyond the control of the Chinese. In the southern part of the Korean peninsula, tribal groups appear to have generally been militarily less formidable and perhaps less organized. Their relationship with the Chinese may have been more ruthlessly exploitative, and tribute goods, food, timber, iron, and other resources may have been forcefully extracted from local peoples. But even if this was the case, the tribute relationship still held many of the same advantages for the elite groups among the southern peoples.

CHINESE COMMANDERIES AND THEIR NEIGHBORS: THE NORTHERN PEOPLES

Chinese sources from the time of the commanderies provide us with the earliest written descriptions of Korean societies and cultures. What is now Korea was inhabited by a confusing array of tribal groups who had not merged into a single culture. The Chinese sources refer to the Dongyi (the "Eastern Barbarians"), a general term for the non-Chinese people of the northeast region. According to the third-century *Sanguozhi* there were nine Dongyi: Puyŏ (Chinese: Fuyu), Okchŏ, Ŭmno (Chinese: Yilou), Ye (Chinese: Hui), Koguryŏ (Chinese: Gaogouli), the three Han tribes of southern Korea, and the Wa of Japan. The actual classification of peoples is a complex matter, as different tribes were called by different names, peoples moved about, and groups split off from other groups. Trying to sort out these groups and their relationships to each other has been a problem for historians of early Korea.

Along the northern borders of the Chinese commanderies were several major groups, among which the Puyŏ were the first to be recorded by the Chinese. The Puyŏ who attracted the notice of the Chinese in the third century B.C.E. lived in the plains and valleys of the upper Sungari River basin in central Manchuria. Although very much on the fringe of the Chinese world, they were influenced by Chinese culture and often served as allies against the warlike Koguryŏ who lived south of them. They were not organized as a state but were ruled by tribal chiefs who apparently met to elect a supreme chieftain for all the Puyŏ. This Puyŏ tribal confederacy emerged by the second century B.C.E. as the most powerful force in the region.

South of the Puyŏ lived the Koguryŏ, a people who according to the Chinese spoke a similar language and had similar customs but who differed from the Puyŏ in their emotional and volatile temper. Koguryŏ may have originally been a branch of the Puyŏ who settled further in the southern Manchuria in the region of the Yalu headwaters. Not only were they linguistically and culturally related to the Puyŏ, but their legends as well suggest Puyŏ origins. Unlike the Puyŏ, the Koguryŏ appear in Chinese records only in 12 C.E., by which time a long-standing client relationship had been established between them and the commandery of Xuantu. Living in marginal lands less suitable for agriculture than the fertile plains the Puyŏ occupied, the Koguryŏ were more dependent on hunting for their livelihood and maintained a more aggressive and warlike way of life that caused considerable concern for the Chinese. In fact, the principal function of the Xuantu may have been to attempt to control the Koguryŏ. The Koguryŏ were in frequent conflict with the Chinese after 12 C.E., which no doubt accounts for the more negative assessment of them as an emotional and volatile people.

From 75 B.C.E. to 12 C.E. the Koguryŏ paid tribute to the Chinese. Then they established a tribal federation, in the Hun River, a tributary of the Yalu; and the ruler began to call himself *wang* or king, a sign that he no longer accepted subordinate status as a mere marquis but wished to be treated as the ruler of a sovereign state.[13] The Koguryŏ began a territorial expansion that included establishing a suzerain relationship with the Okchŏ on the eastern coast of Korea. From there they launched frequent raids against their neighbors, including many clashes with the Chinese. Our information on the culture of the Koguryŏ in this period is limited. The religion of the Koguryŏ appears to have had an astral element similar to that of more nomadic steppe peoples from which they themselves were most probably descended. It also included a "Spirit of the Underground Passage," and worship of rivers and other natural features. We also know that they were divided into five main tribes or clans: the Yŏnno, Chŏllo, Sunno, Kwanno, and Kyeru. The next several centuries saw the gradual evolution from a loose confederacy of these five tribes into a centralized state (see next chapter).

In terms of the future history of Korea the Koguryŏ were by far the most important of the northern peoples; however, several other groups played an active role during this period. The Ŭmno were a people subordinate to the Puyŏ who never organized themselves into a state. From their home in Manchuria, they conducted raids during the summer into northeastern Korea; the peoples along the coast appear to have been their chief victims. Famed as archers and as pig breeders, the Ŭmno were probably less closely related to modern Koreans. They may have been related to the Suksin (Chinese: Suzhen), another people based in Manchuria who earned a reputation for their use of poison arrows. Two other groups that lived in what is now Korea were the Yemaek and the Okchŏ. Most of these people were associated with Manchuria as much as they were with the modern boundaries of Korea.

CHINESE COMMANDERIES AND THEIR NEIGHBORS: THE SOUTHERN PEOPLES

To the south of Lelang were the Han tribes.[14] Present-day South Koreans generally trace their ancestry to the Han tribes. In South Korea the official term for the Korean nation is Han'guk, "country of the Han." Since they were further away from the center of Chinese civilization, less was recorded about these peoples. Much of the knowledge we do have about them comes from the *Sanguozhi*, written at the end of the third century. It describes the

Samhan (the three Han): the Mahan, the Chinhan, and the Pyŏnhan. These terms refer not to states or organized groups but to three related peoples that lived in different regions of Korea south of the Han River. Collectively their homeland roughly covered the area of modern South Korea. They were organized into what the Chinese called *guo* (countries), petty statelets of varying size, ruled by chiefs. By the middle of the third century the Mahan inhabited the rich farmlands of the southwestern part of Korea, which has been the rice basket of Korea. Not surprisingly they were listed as the most numerous of the Han, constituting fifty-four "*guo*" or "countries." The *guo* varied in size. Some were reported as having up to ten thousand households, and the total number of households was said to be one hundred thousand.[15] The Chinhan, who lived in the middle and upper Naktong basin and occupied most what is now Kyŏngsang Province, constituted twelve *guo*. Along the lower Naktong River basin and along the southeast coast were the Pyŏnhan, who also lived in twelve *guo*.

It would be inaccurate to regard the *guo* as states. Their small size and the lack of any clear archaeological evidence of organized states confirm the observations made by the ancient Chinese that the rulers of the *guo* were not *wang*. Most probably these were chiefdoms, that is, small polities ruled by hereditary chiefs who controlled at least a few villages but lacking any state administrative structure. Although most were farmers, an elite stratum existed who, the Chinese recorded, wore silk garments and leather shoes, in contrast to the common people who wore hemp clothes and straw shoes. The elite were also fond of earrings and necklaces. The Mahan, who lived in earthen huts, were an agricultural people. As with most agricultural peoples they held festivals in the spring and at harvest time in which sacrifices were made. The Chinese sources describe the Mahan as backward people who did not value horses or money. The Mahan traded with an island people called Hoju who lived on a large island in the western sea, perhaps referring to Cheju Island.

The Chinhan lived in settlements, the Chinese reported, enclosed by wooden stockades, practiced sericulture, and used oxen and horse carts. Of particular note is that they traded in iron, which appears to have been an important export from the southeastern region. The Chinhan were reported to have been fond of dancing and drinking, an observation that has been made by many subsequent foreign observers to the Korean countryside. The Mahan and the Chinhan spoke the same (or similar) languages, but the Pyŏnhan, who shared the same dwellings and customs as the Chinhan, were said to have spoken a different language.[16] The general assumption has been that the languages spoken by the Samhan were directly ancestral to the modern Korean language. And while there is no proof of that assertion, it seems a reasonable one. Thus in terms of ethnicity and language the Samhan can be said to be early Korean peoples. Most lived in semisubterranean homes in little villages near river terraces where they were able to grow rice, barley, and other crops. These villages were likely to have been largely self-sufficient. Sustained contact with the Chinese commanderies was probably a key factor in stimulating organizational development among the people of the peninsula, especially the southern folk.

Further to the south of the Han were the T'amna of Cheju island, cattle and pig breeders who spoke a language different from the Samhan. Further still were the Wa peoples, long considered to be the earliest reference to the Japanese. The first contact with the Wa was in C.E. 57 when an embassy arrived in Lelang. Another was recorded in 107 and four were recorded from 238 to 248. Evidence indicates that the Wa had close connections with the Pyŏnhan and probably imported iron from the Kimhae area. A regular trade between the Korean peninsula and the Japanese archipelago must have existed, since Korean and Chinese artifacts from this period are frequently found there. The first detailed description of both the Samhan and the Wa, the *Sanguozhi* makes a clear distinction between the two peoples, whose customs are described as very different. Who were the Wa? In traditional accounts they are simply equated with the Japanese. It is highly unlikely, however, that a definable Japanese ethnic group existed at such an early date. Rather, the peoples of both the peninsula and the archipelago consisted of various tribal cultures. The Wa probably lived in western Japan and perhaps on both sides of the Korean Strait. Just as tribal peoples in southern Manchuria and Korea overlapped, so the peoples along the southern coast of Korea were probably linked with those of western Japan. Only later did separate and distinct Korean and Japanese peoples emerge.

POLITICS OF THE THIRD CENTURY

The fortunes of the Chinese commanderies fluctuated with those of the Chinese heartland. Toward the late second century the Later Han dynasty went into decline. In 220 C.E., the Han empire broke up into three states. Wei, the northernmost, controlled the North China Plain, the heartland region of ancient China and the region closest to Korea. As part of the efforts by the Wei to consolidate their power, they launched a series of campaigns against the belligerent peoples of the northeast from 238 to 245, which became one of the most impressive displays of Chinese power in the history of Korea. A main target of the campaign was Koguryŏ, which the Chinese defeated, destroying its capital in 244. The revival of Chinese authority, however, did not last long, and the Jin dynasty that temporarily reunited the Chinese empire rapidly declined in the early fourth century. A civil war broke out in North China in 301. In 311, the Xianbei, a steppe nomad people, sacked the imperial Chinese capital, Luoyang. Six years later the Jin relocated their capital to the lower Yangzi region and all effective administration in northern China collapsed. This inaugurated a period of Chinese history whose troubled nature is exemplified in the convention of referring to it as the Period of the Five Dynasties and the Sixteen Kingdoms (317–589).

The Lelang and Taifang commanderies, cut off from the rest of China by a series of nomadic intruders who had overrun northern China, continued a shadowy existence. By tradition Lelang was conquered by a resurgent Koguryŏ in 313 and its southern outpost Taifang by the emerging kingdom of Paekche in 316. It appears, however, that some sort of rule by local Chinese elites continued well into the fourth century.[17] After four centuries the Chinese presence in Korea disappeared. One reason for the lack of a continued Chinese presence was the geographic remoteness of Korea. The commanderies in Korea were distant outposts of the empire that could not be maintained in troubled times. With the withdrawal of China, the people of the Korean peninsula had several centuries to develop their societies without direct Chinese intervention. It was during these centuries that the first literate indigenous states emerged.

The Tan'gun Myth

The Wei shu tells us that two thousand years ago, at the time of Emperor Yao, Tan'gun Wanggŏm chose Asadal as his capital and founded the state of Chosŏn. The Old Record notes that in olden times Hwanin's son, Hwanung, wished to descend from Heaven and live in the world of human beings. Knowing his son's desire, Hwanin surveyed the three highest mountains and found Mount T'aebaek the most suitable place for his son to settle and help human beings. Therefore he gave Hwanung three heavenly seals and dispatched him to rule over the people. Hwanung descended with three thousand followers to a spot under a tree by the Holy Altar atop Mount T'aebaek, and he called this place the City of God. He was the Heavenly King Hwanung. Leading the Earl of Wind, the Master of Rain, and the Master of Clouds, he took charge of some three hundred and sixty areas of responsibility, including agriculture, allotted life spans, illness, punishment, and good and evil, and brought culture to his people.

At that time a bear and a tiger living in the same cave prayed to Holy Hwanung to transform them into human beings. He gave them a bundle of sacred mugworts and twenty cloves of garlic and said, "If you eat these and shun the sunlight for one hundred days, you will assume human form." Both animals ate the species and avoided the sun. After twenty-one days the bear became a woman but the tiger, unable to observe the taboo, remained a tiger. Unable to find a husband, the bear-woman prayed under the altar tree for a child. Hwanung metamorphosed himself, lay with her, and begot a son called Tan'gun Wanggŏm.

—From the *Samguk yusa* 1:33–3][18]

Tan'gun later was often considered the first Korean and/or founder of the first Korean state. This account goes on to say that in the "fiftieth year of the reign of Emperor Yao," on a date calculated as October 3rd, 2333 B.C.E., Tan'gun was said to have established the state of Chosŏn. This date has become a national holiday in South Korea. Koreans today often refer to the "five thousand years of Korean history," a phrase based on this legendary date.

NOTES

1. Gari Ledyard, "How the Linguist's Tail Wags the Historian's Dog: Problems on the Study of Korean Origin," *Korean Studies Forum* 5 (Winter–Spring 1978–1979): 80–88; For an example of linguistic evidence used to explain the origin of the Korean peoples, see Roy Andrew Miller, "Linguistic Evidence and Japanese Prehistory," in *Windows on Prehistoric Japan*, ed. Richard J. Pearson et al. (Ann Arbor, MI: University of Michigan, 1986), 101–20.

2. Sarah M. Nelson, "The Politics of Ethnicity in Prehistoric Korea," in *Nationalism, Politics, and the Practice of Archaeology*, ed. Philip L. Kohl and Clare Fawcett (Cambridge, UK: Cambridge University Press, 1998), 218–31.

3. Sarah Nelson, "Korean Interpretations of Korean Archaeology," *Asian Perspectives* 27, no. 2 (1990): 185–92.

4. Choe Chong-pil, "Origins of Agriculture in Korea," *Korea Journal* 30, no. 11 (November 1990): 4–14.

5. Choe Chong-pil, "The Diffusion Route and Chronology of Korean Plant Domestication," *Journal of Asian Studies* 41, no. 3 (May 1982): 513–18.

6. Martin Bale, "The Archaeology of Early Agriculture in the Korean: An Update on Recent Developments," *Indo-Pacific Prehistory Association* 21 (2002): 77–84.

7. Sarah Nelson, "The Neolithic of Northern China and Korea," *Antiquity* 64, no. 2 (June 1990): 234–48.

8. Sarah Nelson, "Social Dimension of Burials in Prehistoric Korea," in *Proceedings of the Seventh International Symposium on Asian Studies 1985* (Hong Kong: Asian Research Service, 1986), 247–56.

9. This ancient Chosŏn state, usually called Old Chosŏn, is not to be confused for the official name of the Korean state from 1392 to 1910 (see chapter 6).

10. Gina L. Barnes, *State Formation in Korea: Historical Archaeological Perspectives* (London: Curzon Press, 2000), 14–15.

11. Barnes, *State Formation in Korea*, 19–20.

12. Gina L. Barnes, "Early Korean States: A Review of Historical Interpretation," in *Bibliographical Review of Far Eastern Archaeology 1990: Hoabinhian, Jomon, Yayoi, Early Korean States* (Oxford: Oxbow Books, 1990), 125.

13. Kenneth H. J. Gardiner, *The Early History of Korea: The Historical Development of the Peninsula up to the Introduction of Buddhism in the Fourth Century C.E.* (Honolulu: University of Hawaii Press, 1969), 29.

14. Written with a different character from the Chinese Han, the latter a name derived from the Han dynasty.

15. Barnes, *State Formation in Korea*, 27–31.

16. Yi Ki-moon, "Language and Writings Systems in Traditional Korea," in *The Traditional Culture and Society of Korea: Arts and Literature*, ed. Peter H. Lee (Honolulu: Center for Korean Studies, 1975), 16.

17. Gardiner, *Early History of Korea*, 42, 52–58.

18. Peter H. Lee and William Theodore De Bary, eds., *Sources of Korean Traditions,* vol. 1, *From Early Times Through the Sixteenth Century* (New York: Columbia University Press, 1997), 5–6.

2

The Fourth Century and the Emergence of the Three Kingdoms

The fourth century is an important period for Korean history. It was a time when the welter of peoples, polities, and imperial outposts that had characterized Korea was replaced by three large, well-developed states: Koguryŏ, Paekche, and Silla. The next three centuries saw the development of Korean society and culture within the frameworks of these three states and their struggle for the mastery of the peninsula.

The term "Three Kingdoms" is somewhat misleading, for in addition to Silla, Koguryŏ and Paekche, there were a number of small states in the southeast that are collectively known as Kaya. However, the states of Kaya failed to consolidate themselves into a centralized political unit and as a result were swallowed up one by one by their northern neighbor Silla, a process that was completed in 562. For about a century there were only three states on the peninsula. In 660, Silla and its Chinese ally conquered Paekche, and in 668 Silla and the Chinese destroyed Koguryŏ. Silla then drove the Chinese out of southern Koguryŏ and by 676 emerged as the sole peninsular power.[1] The origins of the three kingdoms are somewhat obscure. The traditional dates for the founding of the Three Kingdoms as recorded in the *Samguk sagi*, the oldest extent Korean history, are 57 B.C.E. for Silla, 37 B.C.E. for Koguryŏ, and 18 B.C.E. for Paekche. And these dates are dutifully given in many textbooks and published materials in Korea today, but their basis is in myth; only Koguryŏ can be traced back to a time period that is anywhere near proximity to its legendary founding.

THE EMERGENCE OF THE THREE KINGDOMS

The Koguryŏ peoples were most probably a branch of the Puyŏ who from 75 B.C.E. to 12 C.E. were living in the Hun River basin just north of the

Yalu. The early Koguryŏ kingdom was more of a tribal federation than a centralized state. From 12 to 207 C.E. it was independent of China, and it was a formidable military power that conducted frequent raids on its neighbors. In 207, after suffering a series of retaliatory attacks by the Liaodong commandery, Koguryŏ relocated to the Yalu valley. Its leaders set up a stone-walled capital at Hwando (Chinese: Wandu) in the Tonggou region of what is now Jilin province in Manchuria. From there the kingdom expanded to the mouth of the Yalu, gaining an access to the Yellow Sea. When China in the third century became divided into three rival dynasties, Koguryŏ carried out diplomatic relations with the southern dynastic rivals of the northern Chinese state of Wei. In retaliation the Wei state of north China destroyed the capital in 245. After disappearing from the historical record Koguryŏ reemerged as a strong state during the reign of King Ŭlbul (reigned 300–330).[2] The rise of Koguryŏ at this time coincides with the decline of Chinese power in the region, and the two are no doubt related. Koguryŏ's rise was probably aided by the fact that it was able to move into a power vacuum that existed at the time.

Paekche emerged from the area of the Mahan in southwestern Korea. According to tradition, it was founded in 18 B.C.E. by the two sons of Chumong, Onjo and Piryu, who were given some land by the Lord of Mahan. Onjo then became the first king of this new state, and his descendants ruled until 660 when the last king Ŭija went down in defeat by his Silla rivals and their Chinese allies. The foundation legend places the founding of Paekche much too early; nonetheless, many historians assume that Paekche grew out of one of the fifty-four *guo* mentioned in the *Sanguozhi,* although the ruling family may have been of Manchurian Puyŏ origin. Evidence suggests that there may have been a migration into the Mahan region by some Puyŏ or related Manchurian peoples; however, the links between the Paekche and Puyŏ are not well understood. Whatever its origins, unlike Koguryŏ, Paekche appears rather suddenly in the historical records with the reign of Kŭnch'ogo (r. 346–375), who ruled a state that inaugurated diplomatic relations with the Chinese state of Jin in 372. The first capital of Paekche was Hansŏng, believed to have been in the Han River area.[3] This served as the capital until 474. The inhabitants of Paekche were probably ethnically and linguistically Han and thus more closely related to the people of Silla and Kaya then to Koguryŏ or Puyŏ. But it is hard to untangle the ethnic and tribal links between the peoples within the peninsula and the peoples in Manchuria and the Japanese archipelago at this time.

The emergence of the Paekche kingdom coincides with the crumbling of Chinese power in Northeast Asia. The Chinese appear to have conducted a divide and rule policy in the peninsula, bestowing honors and status on local chieftains but intimidating them from extending their power. The collapse of Chinese authority led to a power vacuum, in which indigenous polities were left to contend for mastery of the region. In the decades after 290 when the Chinese position in Korea began to decline consolidation of Korean states preceded rapidly, with Koguryŏ in the north making a strong revival after 300. Quite possibly the rise of Paekche begins at this time as well.

Located in the southeastern part of the peninsula farthest from direct contact with China, Silla was last to receive influences from the continent, and its institutional development showed a time lag compared with Koguryŏ and Paekche. But Silla was the state that unified of most of the Korean peninsula and whose language, customs, and institutions dominated the subsequent historical development of Korean society and culture. The Silla state began in the Kyŏngju basin, a small fertile area sheltered by surrounding hills. The nucleus of the state was Saro, one of the twelve Chinhan *guo*. According to tradition, Silla was founded in 57 B.C.E. by Pak Hyŏkkyŏse, who was miraculously born from an egg. His name Pak was perhaps derived from *palk*, meaning bright, since sunlight shone from his body. In the recorded legend, Saro had prior to Pak been made up of six villages. It was their headmen who unanimously chose this strange youth as their leader.[4] Subsequently, the villages were under his united rule. The date 57 B.C.E. is far too early for the likely founding of the Silla state. It is of symbolic importance for later Silla historians who established this traditional chronology because it makes their state older than its two neighbors. The date itself is derived by counting back twelve sixty-year cycles (these cycles were the principal unit of measuring years in East Asia) from 663 C.E., the year that Paekche was finally destroyed.

The legend does suggest that Saro was formed by a voluntary union of the six villages/descent groups: Kŭmyang, Saryang, Ponp'i, Maryang, Hanji, and the Sŭpp'i. The Pak kings came from the Kŭmyang, and the queens, starting with Pak Hyŏkkŏse's bride Aryŏng, came from the Saryang. This legend would appear to hint that the founder of Saro or at least its first major ruler was an outsider, since he arrived mysteriously when an egg was discovered. His supernatural birth could also be a means of justifying the elevated status of the later rulers of Silla, since they could lay claim to being descendents of no ordinary men. The Paks, however, were not the sole ruling family for the Sŏk, and the Kim families supplied rulers as well. The Sŏk founder was also born from an egg and is reported to have come from the east coast. When in the fourth century Silla emerges as a fully historical state the ruling family was from the Kim clan and would remain so until the tenth century. This royal Kim clan (the Kyŏngju Kim) is still a major Korean clan. The Kim rulers chose their consorts from the Pak clan.

The first fully documented ruler of Silla was Naemul (r. 356–402), who held the title of *maripkan*, a word that denotes an elevated ridge.[5] In 377, Silla is recorded as having sent envoys who accompanied a Koguryŏ embassy to the Qin rulers of northern China. It is not clear, however, how far state development had proceeded in Silla at this time, or to what extent it ruled or dominated the former Chinhan territories. The adoption of a new title (previous Silla rulers are said to have called themselves *isagŭm*, "successor princes"), and its active role in international politics, would suggest that Silla was undergoing a new phase in its history. Most probably Silla was still in the process of completing its consolidation of the former Chinhan *guo* in the late fourth century. As it did so it began associating itself with Koguryŏ and competing with Paekche and the Kaya states for mastery of the entire Samhan region, roughly the region that makes up what is now South Korea.

The fourth century also saw the emergence of a loose federation of small states collectively known as Kaya. The Kaya states may have evolved out of the Pyŏnhan peoples who inhabited the fertile middle and lower Naktong basin and the southeast coast. They actively engaged in commerce and iron production. Despite their prosperity and apparent commercial sophistication, the Kaya states were never consolidated into a large kingdom. The price they paid for this was their gradual annexation and absorption by Silla. Yet, Kaya had a distinctive culture that exerted considerable influence on its neighbors, as illustrated by its pottery, which became the basis for both Silla pottery and Japanese *sue* ware, as well as the *kayagŭm*, a kind of zither, that is still one of the most popular of traditional Korean musical instruments. There were six main loosely confederated Kaya polities. The two most important were Pon Kaya (original Kaya) and Tae Kaya (Greater Kaya). Pon Kaya, also known as Kŭmgwan Kaya, was located near Kimhae. Iron slags dating to at least the first century B.C.E. testify to the long importance of this area as a center of commerce and industry. Tae Kaya was located in the rich farmlands of the middle Naktong River valley.

The origins of the Kaya states are best known from the eleventh-century work *Karak Kukki*. In the legend it records, the kings of the Kaya states emerged from golden eggs that descended from heaven to Mount Kuji (Turtle Mountain) during a festival. This occurred as local chieftains sang a song about a turtle at the command of a strange voice from the mountain. As with Silla we have dynastic founders emerging from supernatural origins (eggs again).[6] The Kaya had close connections with the Wa of Japan, probably involving trade based on the Kaya area's rich iron deposits. Recent archaeological excavations of the royal tombs of Tae Kaya reveal a wealthy state. The size of the mounded tombs and the considerable wealth of the royal family indicate a highly developed society where the kings were not merely local chieftains but rulers of exalted status with considerable power to command labor and resources.[7] The fertile rice land, the existence of iron deposits, and its location on an ancient trade route that reached from central Japan to northern China were the sources of this wealth. Despite their prosperity the Kaya states were too small to remain viable political entities. Consequently, they fell victim to an expanding Silla that absorbed Pon Kaya in 532 and Tae Kaya in 562.

THE WA AND MIMANA

Another political presence in fourth-century Korea was the Wa. If little is known for certain about the formation of states in Korea before the late fourth century, even less is known about what transpired in Japan. The peoples of Japan were an important factor in northeast Asian politics even in this early period, yet information about them is sparse and almost anything that is said is bound to be caught up in controversy. Both the Japanese and Korean peoples are proud of their uniqueness and concerned about their origins. Furthermore, the bitter legacy of Japan's twentieth-century conquest of Korea has made the study of the relationship between the two peoples an emotionally laden topic. In the late nineteenth and early twentieth centuries Japanese expansionists cited the evidence that Wa peoples were in Korea to support their claims that in ancient times Korea was ruled by Japan. Much of this was based on the existence of the territory of Mimana, also identified with Kaya. According to the eighth-century Japanese history *Nihon shoki* Empress Jingu in the fourth century conquered a region in southern Korea and set up the Mimana territory, which was administered by a Japanese official. Later the territory was turned over to Yamato's ally Paekche and then lost to Silla. Japanese imperialists used this historical claim to justify imperialist expansion into the peninsula. When the Japanese annexed Korea in 1910 they could claim to be "restoring" the ancient unity of the two countries.

Most historians today regard the story of Empress Jingu's conquests with skepticism, and many question whether Mimana ever existed at all. Some scholars have suggested that rather than Japanese peoples conquering Korea, horse riders from the peninsula invaded and subdued the peoples of Japan.[8] The "horse rider theory" has been used to account for the appearance of weapons, armor, and tomb decorations found in Japan from the fourth and fifth century that are similar to those found in Korea. More likely, the peoples on both sides of the Korea Straits were related and interacted with each other.

Evidence suggests that between 300 B.C.E. and 300 C.E. large numbers of peoples migrated from the Korean Peninsula to the Japanese archipelago, where they introduced rice agriculture, bronze and iron working, and other technologies. Thus rather than the existence of Korean and Japanese peoples there was a continuum of peoples and cultures. The Wa of Western Japan, for example, may have lived on both sides of the Korean Straits, and they appeared to have close links with Kaya. It is even possible that the Wa and

Kaya were the same ethnic group. The fact that Japanese and Korean political evolution followed similar patterns is too striking to be coincidental. On both sides of the straits the collapse of Chinese authority at the end of the third and early fourth century was followed by the formation of large and durable states. In Japan the rise of Yamato apparently began during or shortly after the formation of the three kingdoms. Its rise was probably related to influences, and possibly migrations, from the peninsula. Northeast Asia formed an interacting and intermingling complex of peoples and cultures. The task of historians to sort out the links and patterns within this complex has been made more difficult by the strong nationalist sentiments that prevail in the region today, and by the tendency to project modern notions of national and ethnic identity anachronistically onto these early times.

Thus by the second half of the fourth century a number of clearly defined states emerged. These are no longer tribal units or chiefdoms but strong centralized states that were ruled by kings who governed through administrative officials and who were cut off from ordinary subjects by their supernatural origins and their exalted status. They possessed considerable territory and something else as well: literacy. For in the confusion that entailed the fourth-century collapse of Chinese authority north of the Yangzi River valley, Chinese scribes and officials found their way into the courts of these "barbarian" states. They supplied a veneer of sinification (Chinese cultural influence) as they tutored their masters in the use of Chinese characters, a development that would ensure that these newly rising states and their successors would have the means of sophisticated recordkeeping that is needed by advanced civilizations. The use of Chinese characters as the basic form of writing also meant that the Korean people would be linked by a shared written medium with the civilization of China.

KOREA AND NORTHEAST ASIA IN THE FOURTH AND FIFTH CENTURY

Events of the Korean peninsula were set in the larger context of fourth-century Northeast Asia and beyond. For reasons that historians are still trying to determine, the fourth century was a period of profound upheavals in much of Eurasia. In Europe, the Roman Empire, weakened by demographic and economic decline, split into two halves, abandoned its traditional panoply of gods, and adopted a new religion of otherworldly salvation: Christianity. In the next century it saw its western half crumble and lapse into semibarbarism. The other great Eurasian empire, the Chinese, similarly went into economic and military decline and saw half its empire, the northern half, collapse under the strain of nomadic invaders who like their European equivalents set up a number of ephemeral semibarbarian successor states. And the Chinese too accepted a foreign religion of otherworldly salvation: Buddhism.

The collapse of the Chinese imperial authority in the north gave the peninsular peoples breathing space for purely indigenous forces to come to play; this led to the rise of large-scale centralized native states. The process was assisted by the diaspora of Chinese who, fleeing turmoil in north China or its northeast Asian commanderies, took refuge in the newly emerging Korean kingdoms. Korean rulers, in turn, sought the Chinese's skills as a means of strengthening their own states. Although there was no direct Chinese intervention into Korea for several centuries, all three states sought trade and diplomatic support from the various states of divided China during this period. They were also greatly influenced by Chinese culture. The chief avenue for Chinese influences was Buddhism. Buddhist missionaries from China converted all three kingdoms. In 372, the Eastern Qin sent a monk, Sŏndo, to introduce Buddhism to the Koguryŏ court, and Buddhism became a state religion. Buddhism was adopted by Paekche in 384 when the Southern Jin state of China sent the Indian monk Marananda to the Paekche court. In more remote Silla another century and a half would pass before the rulers converted to Buddhism.

Koguryŏ was a Manchurian-based power that moved into the peninsula in the fifth century. Under Kwanggaet'o (r. 391–413), Koguryŏ won an impressive series of victories known chiefly through the Kwanggaet'o Inscription, a stele put up by his son and successor Changsu (r. 413–491) in 414 to commemorate his father's achievements.[9] This is the earliest dated Korean inscription. Kwanggaet'o defeated the Murong tribal people that had emerged as a power in Manchuria, expanded his domain to the Liao River, conquered the Yilou, a tribal people in the northeast, and captured 64 walled towns and 1,400 villages. He also boasted of inflicting a defeat on the Wa. Kwanggaet'o, whose name means "broad expander of the realm," took on a reign title, Yŏngnak ("Eternal Rejoicing"), an act that symbolically placed himself on terms of equality with the rulers of China since in Chinese practice only the Chinese emperor could hold a reign title. His successor, Changsu ("Longed Lived"), under pressure from the Sino-Turkic states of northern China moved the Koguryŏ capital from the Yalu to P'yŏngyang on the Taedong River in 427, and thus planted the center of the kingdom firmly in the Korean peninsula. This provided Koguryŏ with a large area of fertile rice lands as a reliable economic base. Changsu continued to press southward, and in 474 Paekche was forced to move its capital from Hansŏng on the Han River south to Ungjin (modern Kongju) in Ch'ungch'ŏng Province. Koguryŏ then gained control of the Han River basin.

The expansion of Koguryŏ threatened the survival of the southern states and led to the alliance betwen Paekche and Silla in 433. The next 120 years was largely the drama of Paekche and Silla fighting the attempts at further southern encroachments by Koguryŏ. Despite this alliance, Paekche, which experienced the main brunt of the Koguryŏ advance, suffered a series of setbacks, including the death of King Kaero (r. 455–474) in battle as Changsu took Hansŏng. But by the sixth century it was Silla that began to go on the offensive. The period from the middle sixth century until 676 saw Silla's emergence as master of the Korean peninsula.

CULTURE AND SOCIETY OF
THE THREE KINGDOMS

During the period from the late fourth to the mid-fifth century a process of political and cultural change occurred in each of the Three Kingdoms. Selectively borrowing from the states that ruled China, the Korean states carried out administrative reforms, adopted Buddhism as a state protective cult, and acquired bits of Chinese cultural forms and learning. Chinese models were adopted because these were the only models of state organization available to the peoples of the region. These proved useful to the growth of state power and appealed to the elites as forms of cultural enrichment. Yet Chinese culture was introduced to Korea at a time when China itself was politically weak and divided and much of the northern heartland was ruled by alien dynasties of Inner Asian origin. Chinese states were useful sources of cultural ideas and practices, but during this period of political disunity in China they were not in a position to threaten the existence of the Korean states. Nor was there any great empire with universalistic pretensions and the ability to dazzle its neighbors with its cultural brilliance or intimidate them with its military might. As a result, the process of state building during the Three Kingdoms period was largely an indigenous development, and Chinese cultural borrowing was done on a purely voluntarily basis. A process of sinification occurred, but the native institutions and cultural forms were still dominant in this period.

Another feature of this time was the armored mounted warrior. In East Asia, the appearance of these horse-riding warriors with coats of bone or iron, similar to the medieval knights of the West, began around the fourth and fifth centuries. Impressive bone armor has been discovered in Paekche and elaborate iron armor has been uncovered in Kaya dating from at least the fifth century.[10] Surviving depictions of Korean warriors show them formidably outfitted in armor and deer antler helmets. Armored warriors fought for all three kingdoms, and this style of warfare spread to Japan where it formed the basis for the elaborately attired horse warrior of medieval Japanese samurai lore.

The earliest of these three kingdoms, Koguryŏ was a society dominated by a warrior aristocracy. Rulers and high-ranking nobility built elaborate tombs during this time, which are one of the main sources of information about this period. Most of Koguryŏ's tombs have been looted, but tomb paintings provide some information about this society. One of the best-known of these is the Ssangyŏng-ch'ong (Tomb of the Twin Pillars) that depicts broad streets, and rouge-faced ladies dressed in skirts and three-quarters-length coats engaged in conversation with upper-class men. Other tombs show hunters, mounted archers, dancers, and wrestlers engaged in what appears to be an early form of *ssirŭm*, Korean-style wrestling. Paintings show people in the kinds of activity expected to be found in a warrior aristocracy: horse-riding, hunting, vigorous sports, and warfare. This artistic style, so different from later Korean art, shows less Chinese influence; instead it shares more traits with the art of the peoples of Central Asia, Manchuria, and Siberia. The murals such as those in the Tomb of the Four Spirits in South P'yŏngyang Province, which contains pictures of a dragon, tiger, phoenix, tortoise, and snake, were probably of religious and cosmological significance. Interestingly, tomb paintings show little Buddhist influence. The name of one Koguryŏ artist, Tamjing, who went to Japan has been recorded; but generally the producers of some of the most splendid works of art in Korean history are anonymous. The Koguryŏ are recorded to have been fond of music and dance. The most renowned of Koguryŏ musicians was Wang San-ak, master of the *hyŏnhakkŭm* (black crane zither), a modified Chinese seven-string instrument.

Buddhism was the official state religion, but its influence on Koguryŏ society was initially limited as indicated by the tomb murals. By the sixth century, however, the dominant Vinaya (Rules) school of Buddhism had become a major institution that provided learned advisors to Koguryŏ rulers. In the sixth century Koguryŏ was able to act as a point of dispersal for the spread of Buddhism. In 551, a Koguryŏ monk was appointed by the king of Silla to head that kingdom's monastic organization, and in 594, the monk Hyeja went to Japan, where he became an advisor to Prince Shotoku. A generation later, in 628, the monk Hyegwan introduced the important Samnon (Japanese: Sanron) school of Buddhist philosophy to Japan. No Koguryŏ Buddhist temples have survived, but a gilt bronze statue of Tathagata Buddha and a gilt bronze half-seated Maitreya testify to the high level of Buddhist art that flourished by the sixth century.

Koguryŏ gradually adopted elements of Chinese culture in a pattern that Paekche and Silla repeated. To promote learning and train government clerks an official academy, the Taehak, was established in 372, where the curriculum included the study of Confucian learning. This is the first known center where Confucianism was studied in Korea. The Han histories *Shiji* and *Han-shu* were studied as well as the Chinese literary anthology the *Wenxuan* (*Literary Selections*). Knowledge of the Chinese literary tradition may not have been very deep or profound, but the aristocratic class had some exposure to it. Little is known of the popular religion or customs except that the tenth lunar month was a time of harvest festivals, as it was in all three kingdoms. Although the aristocracy practiced Buddhism, it probably remained only a marginal part of the spiritual life of the people, who sought shamans rather than monks when dealing with the supernatural. One Koguryŏ institution worthy of notice was the *kyŏngsang*, communal bodies of unmarried men, presumably of aristocratic background, who were organized in each locality, trained in archery, and given instruction in Chinese texts.

Paekche too was a state dominated by a warrior aristocracy and a monarch who had by the end of the fourth century developed a centralized administration. As with the case of Koguryŏ much of what we know of Paekche culture comes from the tombs of Paekche rulers and high-born aristocrats. Paekche tombs show a strong affinity with those of Koguryŏ that may be due to the fact that both were derived from the Puyŏ or perhaps from the geographic proximity of Paekche to Koguryŏ. By the fifth century, large mounded tombs with horizontal passageways leading to stone-walled high-ceiling burial chambers were constructed. Since these proved rather easy to pillage, the contents have long since been looted. The discovery of the undisturbed Tomb of Muryŏng (r. 501–523) in the 1970s near Kongju, however, provides a glimpse of the splendid and refined culture of the Paekche kingdom. The tomb murals are more refined and less animated than those of Koguryŏ. They were a product of a gentle culture more removed from the rough nomadic influences of Manchuria and Central Asia and in closer maritime contact with the courts of southern China. Paekche bronzes, with their thin, elongated bodies, are perhaps the most famous product of the kingdom's artistic tradition. The best example is the Kudara (Paekche) Kannon in the Horyuji temple in Nara Japan. The cultural high point of Paekche is considered the reign of King Sŏng (r. 523–553). It was at this time that the famous Paekche mission to Japan took place (either in 538 or 552) that has traditionally been attributed with introducing Buddhism to that country.

Buddhism played the same role in Paekche as it did in Koguryŏ, as a state protective cult patronized by the court. The most influential form of Buddhism before the seventh century was Vinaya, which emphasized monastic discipline and, as its meaning ("rules") implies, systematic organization. The Vinaya-trained monks offered an array of practical information about administration, law, and systematic procedure as well as knowledge of literacy and the traditions of other lands. This was a valuable aid to early Korean rulers as they attempted to consolidate their rule and strengthen their states. Our knowledge of Buddhist architecture in the Three Kingdoms period is limited, but we do know that Paekche pagodas were highly regarded in medieval times. Of the many Buddhist temples that must have dotted the landscape only a few stone pagodas remain; the most famous was the Nine

Story Wooden Pagoda of the master craftsman Abiji that was destroyed by the Mongol invasion in the thirteenth century. As with Koguryŏ it is questionable how deeply the influence of Buddhism penetrated among the peasant majority, but at least among the court it was profound. Paekche king Pŏp (r. 499–500) went so far as to ban killing animals and hunting. He ordered the release of all domestic animals and the destruction of hunting weapons. Not surprisingly, he was shortly deposed. It is clear, however, that by the end of the fifth century Buddhism as a way of life was being taken seriously by some.

Although the last to emerge in recorded annals, Silla is today the best known of the Three Kingdoms for it was Silla that unified the peninsula and implanted its language and culture as the dominant element in the evolution of Korea. Most of our knowledge of this period comes from histories written by later historians who saw themselves as heirs to the Sillan tradition. As a result there is an inherent pro-Silla bias in most Korean history. Also, because Silla became the dominant power its traditions have been best preserved and have served as the models for later Koreans. Thus more is known about Silla and its culture than of Paekche and Koguryŏ. It would be wrong, however, to regard Silla as the most advanced of the states; rather the opposite is closer to the truth. Archaeological evidence suggests that Silla, tucked in the southeast corner of the Korean peninsula out of direct contact with the East Asian heartland, developed somewhat later than Koguryŏ and Paekche in terms of social stratification, the creation of institutions of a centralized state, and the adoption of literacy. And it maintained its indigenous cultural traditions longer. Compared to Koguryŏ, Silla was very much a latecomer as an organized state, and compared to Paekche, Sillan culture was less refined and sophisticated. Yet this does not mean that Silla remained a primitive backwater, for it developed into one of the medieval world's more sophisticated societies. Its cultural legacy, which can be seen today in the museums of South Korea, is impressive by any standard. The Sillan mounded tombs, a prominent feature of modern Kyŏngju, differed somewhat in their design from Koguryŏ and Paekche mounded tombs.[11] This indicates the cultural autonomy of Silla, that appears in general to show less pronounced Manchurian influences. These tombs were less easy to loot, and as a result, vast cultural treasures have survived to the present. Not all tombs have been opened by modern archaeologists, but those that have reveal a splendid artistic heritage.

As with Paekche and Koguryŏ a major theme in the early history of Silla was the emergence of a centralized monarchical state. The concept of kingship had to contend with strong local, tribal, and aristocratic traditions. Buddhism was important in strengthening the power of the early kings. Under Pŏphŭng (r. 514–540) Silla adopted Buddhism. Silla resisted the alien religion long after Buddhism had been accepted in Koguryŏ and Paekche, a testimony to the comparative remoteness of the state and the strength of its indigenous culture. In 527, a local noble, Ich'adon, was martyred for his beliefs. According to later tradition a set of miracles followed this event and the Silla king converted to Buddhism, adopted the name Pŏphŭng ("rising of the dharma"), and officially sponsored the new faith. Buddhism was initiated by the Silla monarchs, as it provided a source of religious sanction to the monarchy and an impressive ritual tradition that when closely aligned with its royal patrons served to greatly enhance the majesty and prestige of the royal house and of the state. In Silla, Buddhism would retain a close association with the state.

Silla kings borrowed Chinese institutional practices to add to their power and prestige. Pŏphŭng's reign also saw the first code of administrative law, issued in 520. The content of this code is unknown but it is believed to have included a seventeen-grade official rank system with different ranks distinguished by distinctive attire. The *kolp'um* or bone-rank system, the basis of Silla's social structure, may have been formalized around this time. To further add to monarchical prestige Pŏphŭng in 536 took on an independent era name, "Kŏnwŏn" (Initiated Beginning). In the Chinese tradition an era name was given only to the emperor and it signified his role as a mediator between heaven and earth. An era name by a ruler other than the Chinese emperor was a declaration of equality. In times when China was united and strong this would be a direct challenge to the authority of the Chinese emperor. At this time of course, China was politically divided; nevertheless, the adoption of an era name was at the very least a sign of the growing influence of Chinese culture and the pretensions of the Silla monarchs.

Pŏphŭng expanded his domain by conquering Pon Kaya, the largest of the Kaya states, in 532. His successor, Chinhŭng (r. 540–576), expanded the state further, making Silla a serious contender for control of the entire peninsula. With Silla's ally Paekche, Chinhŭng launched an invasion of the Han River basin during the years from 551 to 554. Under his general Koch'ilbu, the Silla forces and their Paekche allies were successful in driving Koguryŏ out of the Han valley. Then turning against his erstwhile partner and severing a 120-year alliance, Chinhŭng attacked Paekche, whose King Sŏng perished at the battle of Hwansan in 554. The Han River basin was now part of the Silla state. This gave Silla access to the Yellow Sea and brought Silla into direct contact with China. It also separated Paekche from Koguryŏ, making cooperation between the two states more difficult. Perhaps most importantly, the Han River basin with its rich farmlands and its iron deposits enriched the kingdom. Chinhŭng then conquered Tae Kaya in 562, ending the independent existence of the Kaya states and bringing all of the Naktong valley under Sillan control. This step excluded direct Japanese influence in Korea for over a thousand years. Silla forces then invaded the former territory of the Eastern Ye along the Hamgyŏng coast, inflicting another defeat on Koguryŏ. Chinhŭng celebrated his military triumphs by erecting what are known as the Four Chinhŭng Stelae. These were placed at strategic points in his domain at Ch'ungnyŏng Pass, at Pukhansan in north Seoul, and in the Hwangch'o and Maŭn Passes in Hamgyŏng Province and have survived to the present, providing us with among the earliest Sillan written documents.

THE BONE-RANKS, THE HWABAK, AND THE HWARANG

Silla's strength was drawn in part from its three prominent social and political institutions: the bone-rank system, the *Hwabaek* (Council of Notables), and the *hwarang* (flower boys). The *kolp'um* (bone-rank) was a system of hierarchical ranks in Silla corresponding to hereditary bloodlines. Each rank conferred a variety of special privileges such as qualification for office or the right to possess certain kinds of material goods.[12] The two top bone-ranks were the *sŏnggol* (sacred bone), that was confined to the main branch of the royal Kim clan, and the *chin'gol* (true bone), whose members were the cadet branches of the royal family, members of the Pak and Sŏk royal consort families, and the royal house of Pon Kaya. These made up the highest level of the aristocracy. Originally the *chin'gol* may have been formed by those lineages that were related to the royal family through marriage and were probably expanded to include the Kaya royal clans that were absorbed into the bone-rank system. The *chin'gol* held the highest offices and served on the *Hwabaek* council. The *sŏnggol* line, however, became extinct when King Chinp'yŏng left no male heir and was succeeded by his sister Sŏndŏk (r. 632–647) and his daughter Chindŏk (r. 647–654). Thereafter the royal family was drawn from the *chin'gol* line. The name *sŏnggol*, which can be translated as "hallowed" or "sacred," implies a sacred or priestly authority for the Silla kings, a role that is also hinted at by the term *ch'ach'aung*, used by an early ruler and believed to refer to a shaman or priest. It is possible that the Silla royal line may have been evolving in a pattern similar to the imperial line of the Yamato in Japan where the ruling family took on a sacerdotal (priestly) function. With the extinction of the royal line the Silla kings became merely first among *chin'gol* equals. Silla kings after 654 were frequently challenged by powerful aristocrats, their throne never entirely secure. The extinction of the sacred bone line then may have been a factor contributing to the less exalted status of the Silla and later Korean kings. Throughout Korean history the position of monarchs was more humble than in many premodern Asian societies.

Beneath the two bone-ranks was a system of *tup'um* (head-ranks), of which there were theoretically six; but only the head-ranks six, five, and four, the three highest, appear to have functioned as meaningful groupings. The most important was the *yuktu-p'um* (head-rank six), which was the highest aristocratic ranking after the *chin'gol*. Head-rank-six members held many of the middle-level offices and provided a sizeable portion of the country's scholars. The bone-rank system was an early manifestation of the propensity toward hierarchical social structure with sharply defined status distinctions and a stress on hereditary bloodlines that were to characterize Korean society throughout its history. While little is known about women in this period, in later Silla at least, social status was determined by the maternal as well as the paternal lines and women of the upper classes appeared to have considerable freedom of movement. Burials also suggest the Silla queens had high social status and perhaps wielded considerable power.[13]

A Silla institution of particular importance was the *Hwabaek* or Council of Notables. The *Hwabaek* was a council headed by the single aristocrat who held "extraordinary rank one" and was composed of those of "extraordinary rank two," all of whom are thought to have been of true-bone lineage. Its function was to deliberate on the most important matters of state, such as succession to the throne and the declaration of war. The decision to formally adopt Buddhism also was made by the *Hwabaek*. The principle of unanimity governed the *Hwabaek*, which convened at four sites of special religious significance around Kyŏngju. Significantly, the *Hwabaek* typified another feature of the political process of Silla that was to characterize most Korean governments: political decision making by councils of high aristocrats. Throughout most of Korea's history rulers shared power with aristocratic families who governed through various councils or committees.

Another key Silla institution was the *hwarang*, military bands of aristocratic youth that served as elite units in the Silla army. The *hwarang* were originally connected with shamanist rituals. Pre-Buddhist religious practices remained a part of their ceremonies. Boys just beyond puberty would meet at sacred sites outside the Silla capital, swear oaths of loyalty to each other, and participate in initiation ceremonies. According to a later recorded tradition they were selected for their beauty, and painted their faces.[14] Whatever the sexual connotations these ceremonies may have had, it is clear that they served primarily a military and political purpose. Only sons of the elite could be *hwarang*. These young men traveled around the country getting to know the land and each other before later serving as the elite warrior-aristocrats who would govern the state. Silla's aristocrats were first of all warriors, and the greatest honor for a parent was to have a son die a hero in battle. An example of this is the story of General P'umil, whose sixteen-year-old son Kwanch'ang, later venerated as an exemplary youth, died in battle against Paekche. Upon hearing of his son's death the general is reported to have remarked that he regretted having only one son to give his kingdom. Most of the prominent military and political figures of Silla, such as the famed general Kim Yu-sin, served in their youth as *hwarang* warriors. There may have been shamanist and later Buddhist rituals associated with these gatherings of youths, but this is not clear from the surviving evidence. Twentieth-century Korean nationalists would later glorify the *hwarang* and the *hwarangdo* (the way of the *hwarang*) as an example of dedication to the nation.

The bone-ranks, the *Hwabaek,* and the *hwarang* do not appear to have been unique to Silla; similar institutions are known to have existed in Koguryŏ and Paekche. Each was dominated by warrior-aristocracies ranked in sharply defined status hierarchies. The *Hwabaek* had its parallel in the Paekche *chŏngsa-am,* and councils of high aristocrats are known to have made decisions in Koguryŏ. The *hwarang* had a parallel in the *kyŏngdang* of Koguryŏ. But less is known about these social institutions. It is principally in Silla that we see clearly the patterns of rigid status hierarchy and councilor governance that characterized later Korean social and political history.

Silla kings and queens were buried in luxurious style. There is no sign of human sacrifice as in ancient Chinese royal burials, although royal members were interred with the emblems of their authority. These included the Silla crown, whose shape is derived from deer antlers, and the *kogok* or curved jewel, stylized bear claws that also served in Japan as symbols of royal authority. Both the crowns and the *kogok* suggest totemism and Manchurian and Siberian religious influences. In addition to the tombs, a gilt bronze statue of a meditating half-seated Maitreya Boddhisattva shows a more linear style of sculpture than the more famous Paekche statue. Painting was apparently prized, and the names of a few masters have survived but not their works. In Kyŏngju, the stone-brick pagoda of the Punhwang-sa temple and the Ch'ŏmsŏngdae observatory hint at the architecture of this period, but not enough has survived for us to make sound evaluations of the nature of Silla architecture.

One of the main purposes of the Silla state was to make war, so it is not surprising that the military organization of the state was well developed. Each of the six *pu* contained a *chŏng* (garrison) headed by a general of the *chin'gol* bone-rank. In 583 a more centralized *sŏdang* (oath banner) system was organized. Somewhat resembling the banner system of later Qing China, the *sŏdang* were named after the different-colored fringed banners that each of the six military groups had. Each banner had specialized units of armored troops, catapult teams, ladder teams, teams for breaching walls, composite bow units, and crossbow units. After Silla's conquest of Paekche and Koguryŏ, three additional banners were formed containing troops of those former kingdoms. Commoners were allowed to serve in the banners, and they swore an oath to its commanders.

THE CHANGING ENVIRONMENT OF THE
LATE SIXTH AND SEVENTH CENTURIES.

The late sixth and seventh centuries saw important changes throughout East Asia. In 589, after more than three centuries of division, China was reunified under the Sui dynasty. The new Chinese rulers sought to strengthen the tributary system. Under the imperial order of the Han the tributary system was fully developed and functioned in East Asia as the main method of handling foreign affairs. According to the usual practice, foreign peoples would be granted permission to establish trade and diplomatic and cultural contact with China on the condition that their ruler or the ruler's representatives demonstrate their subservience to the Chinese emperor by personally bearing him tribute. This was usually in the form of local products or of rare precious goods. The presentation of tribute was accompanied by ceremonies in which the ruler or his representatives offered to accept Chinese suzerainty in an exchange of seals and patents of authority, and he was presented with a Chinese calendar that symbolically incorporated his state into the Chinese cosmological scheme. The seals of ranks, robes, caps, and paraphernalia of authority were important symbols of the tributary's legitimacy and status. New rulers, when they came to power, were expected to present themselves or their representatives to the imperial court to be formally enfeoffed. Besides the symbolic value this offered them, the tributaries received permission to trade. Much of this trade under the guise of an official exchange of gifts, but in practice this often amounted to a lucrative trade for the tributary state. It also provided an opportunity to travel and study in China and participate in China's rich cultural life. During the fourth through sixth centuries the Korean states regularly sent tribute missions to states in China. While this in theory implied a submission to Chinese rulers, in practice it was little more than a diplomatic formality. In exchange Korean rulers received symbols that strengthened their own legitimacy and a variety of cultural commodities: ritual goods, books, Buddhist scriptures, and rare luxury products. Different Korean states, however, had paid tribute to different Chinese states. Now the Sui wanted to bring all of the peninsula into its diplomatic orbit.

The second Sui emperor, Yangdi, was determined to bring the northeast frontier under control and to match the achievements of the Han by controlling all the lands that were once part of the Han Empire, including Liaodong and northern Korea. But Koguryŏ was an obstacle to a resurgent Chinese empire's expansionary plans. Yangdi directed his attention at subjugating the northern Korean state. In 612, after an unsuccessful naval attack, he embarked upon a major campaign against Koguryŏ. This was a large-scale undertaking that involved forces and resources from across the Chinese empire. A confident Yangdi, fresh from successful campaigns against the

Turks, sent a reported 1,130,000 men 1,000 *li* into Koguryŏ.[15] About 300,000 troops were detached from the main force and unsuccessfully besieged P'yŏng-yang. On their return they were ambushed by Koguryŏ general Ŭlchi Mun-dŏk at the Salsu (Ch'ŏngch'ŏn) River, a defeat which only 2,700 Chinese forces are reported to have survived. The size of the forces and the magnitude of the defeat were recorded by Tang China historians, who no doubt inflated these figures to discredit their Sui predecessors. Nonetheless, Koguryŏ won an impressive victory that became part of Korean legend. Ŭlchi Mundŏk later became a symbol of national resistance for modern Koreans. Yangdi made two more unsuccessful attempts on Koguryŏ in 613 and 614, and those costly defeats were a major factor in the collapse of the Sui and the rise of the Tang.

The newly established Tang (618–907) dynasty, one of the most brilliant in Chinese history, inherited the same foreign policy objectives of its predecessors—to secure the northern frontier and bring all the former Han lands under its control. When in 628 the Tang defeated the Turks it began to reconsider Silla appeals for assistance. Silla, seeing an opportunity to deal a fatal blow to its northern rival, justified its need for Chinese intervention in much the same way that Han chieftains may have called for Han help in overcoming the Wiman Chosŏn's blockade of the overland route to China. Tang emperor Gaozong attacked Koguryŏ and was defeated at Ansi-sŏng fortress by Koguryŏ general Yang Man-ch'un. Gaozong was again defeated in 648, and his successor, Tang Taizong, launched unsuccessful attacks in 655 and in 658–59. Koguryŏ's consistent success against the world's mightiest military force was an impressive achievement in Korean annals. It also shielded the states of Paekche and Silla from the brunt of Chinese expansionism, allowing them time for autonomous development.

While Koguryŏ was engaged in its wars of resistance, Paekche fought Silla. In 642, it seized forty border forts. Silla, seeking assistance, sent the official Kim Ch'un-ch'u on diplomatic missions to Japan, to Koguryŏ, and twice to China. In 650 he presented the Tang emperor with a poem written by Queen Chindŏk requesting Tang military aid against Paekche. At the same time Silla sought to move culturally closer to Tang. In 649, the state adopted Tang court dress and in 651, it reorganized administration closer to the Chinese model. This cooperative policy toward China continued when in 654 Kim Ch'un-ch'u was elected by the *Hwabaek* as king and reigned under the name Muyŏl (r. 654–661).

THE UNIFICATION OF KOREA UNDER SILLA

In 660, the Tang, frustrated by their inability to overcome Koguryŏ resistance, decided on a plan to invade Paekche by sea, and after subduing Paekche, to invade Koguryŏ from the south. This plan was implemented, with Admiral Su Dinggang, who had recently defeated the Turks, leading the Chinese forces. His ships sailed up the Kŭm River while Silla forces under General Kim Yu-sin crossed the Sŏbaek range that separates the Kyŏngsang heartland of Silla from the Chŏlla and Ch'ungch'ŏng regions of Paekche. Then on the Hwangsan Plain the Paekche forces under General Kyebaek were defeated. Paekche king Ŭija surrendered at Ungjin, and by July of 660 the Tang forces were in control of most of Paekche.

Tang now concentrated on its major goal of destroying Koguryŏ. In 668, Tang land and naval forces, and Silla forces under Kim In-mu, captured P'yŏngyang. As a result Koguryŏ fell. It was clear that Tang efforts were now aimed at directly controlling the entire Korean peninsula, with the former Koguryŏ and Paekche territories to be directly incorporated into the empire and Silla to survive only as a satellite state. The Chinese emperor proposed that Silla become the Great Commandery of Kyerim—in essence a Chinese territory—and offered to appoint the Silla king as its head. The Silla monarch Munmu rejected the offer and instead invaded the Chinese-controlled territory in Paekche. Sillan forces drove out the Chinese by 671, and then moved north into Koguryŏ. In a series of battles in the Han River basin in 676 Silla forced the Tang into retreat, gaining control of all the territory south of the Taedong River, that is, almost all of peninsular Korea. Although Chinese and Korean accounts of this period vary, it is clear that Silla emerged as the victor.[16] Most of the peninsula was now under Silla's control. The Korean peninsula, and Silla especially, proved too much of a logistical problem for permanent occupation by China. China had a hard time supplying its troops in the peninsula. Silla had provided its Chinese forces with food. Once Silla turned against them the logistical problems proved too much for the Chinese, contributing to their defeat and withdrawal. Tang settled for the destruction of a strong Koguryŏ contiguous to its northeast frontier and ceased further efforts to intervene militarily in the peninsula. To further secure their frontier, the Chinese set up a small puppet state of Lesser Koguryŏ in the Liaodong region of Manchuria.

Silla's victory in unifying most of the peninsula can be attributed to several factors. The political and military institutions of the kingdom proved capable of providing a stable and effective government that could successfully carry the country's expansion. The kingdom itself enjoyed considerable prosperity, and had an economic base and a system of extracting the surplus from that base sufficient to support large military undertakings. Nonetheless, it is not certain that this was any less the case with its rivals. Most probably it was geography that provided the greatest opportunities for the kingdom. Koguryŏ had to wage wars on its northwestern and southern boundaries, and Paekche was vulnerable to Koguryŏ to the north, Silla to the south, and China from the sea. Silla in the southeast corner of Korea, however, had easier boundaries to defend and was out of reach of direct assault by China. China assisted in the unification, but unintentionally since its motive was to establish control over Korea, not to create a strong united state there.

The unification of most of the peninsula by Silla in 676 was a pivotal event in Korean history. From the late seventh century to the twentieth, a single state dominated the peninsula, including most of the agricultural heartland of what was to become Korea. Gradually within the framework of the peninsular state a culturally well-defined and ethnically homogeneous Korean society emerged. This process, however, was only beginning in the seventh century.

Origins of the Hwarang[17]

The *wŏnhwa* ["original flowers"; female leaders of the *hwarang*] were first presented at the court in the thirty-seventh year [576] of King Chinhŭng. At first the king and his officials were perplexed by the problem of finding a way to discover talented people. They wished to have people disport themselves in groups so that they could observe their behavior and thus elevate the talented among them to positions of service. Therefore two beautiful girls, Nammo and Chunjŏng, were selected, and a group of some three hundred people gathered around them. But the two girls competed with one another. In the end, Chunjŏng enticed Nammo to her home and, plying her with wine till she was drunk, threw her into a river. Chunjŏng was put to death. The group became discordant and dispersed.

Afterward, handsome youths were chosen instead. Faces made up and beautifully dressed, they were respected as *hwarang*, and men of various sorts gathered around them like clouds. The youths instructed one another in the Way and in rightness, entertained one another with song and music, or went sightseeing to even the most distant mountains and rivers. Much can be learned of a man's character by watching him in these activities. Those who fared well were recommended to court.

Kim Taemun, in his *Annals of the Hwarang* [*Hwarang segi*], remarks: "Henceforth able ministers and loyal subjects shall be chosen from them, and good generals and brave soldiers born therefrom."

—From *Samguk sagi* 4:40

King Hŭngdŏk's Edict on Clothing, Carts, and Housing[18]

There are superior and inferior people, and humble persons, in regard to social status. Names are not alike, for example, and garments too are different. The customs of this society have degenerated day by day owing to the competition among the people for luxuries and alien commodities, because they detest local products. Furthermore, rites have now fallen to a critical stage and customs have retrogressed to those of barbarians. The traditional codes will be revived in order to rectify the situation, and should anyone transgress the prohibition, he will be punished to the law of the land.

—From the *Samguk sagi* 33:320–326

NOTES

1. This statement needs some qualification, for most of the old Koguryŏ state became part of the state of Parhae; but Parhae was more of a Manchurian power than a peninsular one.

2. Kenneth H. J. Gardiner, *The Early History of Korea: The Historical Development of the Peninsula up to the Introduction of Buddhism in the Fourth Century A.D.* (Honolulu: University of Hawaii Press, 1969), 31–34.

3. Gina L. Barnes, "Early Korean States: A Review of Historical Interpretation," in *Bibliographical Review of Far Eastern Archaeology 1990: Hoabinhian, Jomon, Yayoi, Early Korean States* (Oxford: Oxbow Books, 1990), 137–38.

4. Kenneth H. J. Gardiner, "Beyond the Archer and His Son, Koguryŏ and Han China," *Papers on Far Eastern History* 20 (September 1979): 57–82.

5. The term *"kan"* here may be of Central Asian origin and related to the later term *"Khan"* used by the Mongols and others.

6. Russell J. Kirkland, "The 'Horserider' in Korea: A Critical Evaluation of a Historical Theory," *Korean Studies* 5 (1991): 109–28; Obayashi Taryo, "The Ancient Myths of Korea and Japan," *Acta Asiatica* 61 (1991): 68–82.

7. J. H. Grayson, "Excavations of Late Kaya Personal Tumuli in Koryong, Korea: Chisan-dong tombs 32–35 and Associated Burials," *Indo-Pacific Prehistory Association Bulletin* 5 (1984): 64–73.

8. Namio Egami, "The Formation of the People and the Origin of the State in Japan," *Memoirs of the Research Department of the Toyo Bunko* 23 (1964): 35–70; see also Wontack Hong, *Paekche of Korea and the Origin of Yamato Japan* (Seoul: KudaraInternational, 1994).

9. Hatada Takeshi, "An Interpretation of the King Kwanggaet'o Inscription," *Korean Studies* 3 (1979): 1–17.

10. Gina L. Barnes, *State Formation in Korea: Historical Archaeological Perspectives* (Richmond, Surrey: Curzon Press, 2000), 134–142.

11. Barnes, *State Formation in Korea*, 195, 209–11.

12. Ki-dong Yi, "Shilla's Kolp'um System and Japan's Kabane System," *Korean Social Science Journal* 11 (1984): 7–12.

13. Sarah Nelson, "The Queens of Silla: Power and Connections to the Spirit World," in *Ancient Queens: Archaeological Explorations*, ed. Sarah Nelson (Walnut Creek, CA: Altamira Press, 2003), 77–92.

14. Richard Rutt, "The Flower Boys of Silla," *Transactions of the Korea Branch of the Royal Asiatic Society* 37 (October 1961): 1–66.

15. The *li* was the principal unit for measuring distances in East Asia; its length varied with time and place but a rough rule of thumb is three *li* to one mile.

16. John Charles Jamieson, "Collapse of the T'ang-Silla Alliance: Chinese and Korean Accounts Compared," in *Nothing Concealed: Essays in Honor of Liu Yu-yun,*

Occasional Series No. 4, ed. Frederick Wakeman (Taipei: Chinese Materials and Research Aids Service Center, 1970), 81–94.

17. Peter H. Lee and William Theodore De Bary, eds., *Sources of Korean Traditions.* vol. 1, *From Early Times Through the Sixteenth Century* (New York: Columbia University Press, 1997), 55.

18. Lee and De Bary, *Sources of Korean Traditions,* vol. 1, 27.

3

United Silla

THE PENINSULAR KINGDOM

Silla's victories created a kingdom that controlled most of the Korean Peninsula. Historians often refer to the period from 676 to 935 C.E. as United Silla. This unification of Korea needs some qualification. Although Silla ruled most of the agricultural heartland of Korea it did not control the northern third of the modern boundaries of Korea. It is also somewhat controversial to speak of a single Korean state after 676 since the demarcation between Korea and Manchuria was not well defined, and a northern kingdom, Parhae, emerged in the early eighth century that occupied much of the former Koguryŏ. Nor was there a single "Korean" ethnic group. Over the centuries, however, under the peninsular kingdom of Silla and its successor states an increasingly well-defined Korean culture and society emerged. For the next twelve centuries from 676 to 1876, Korea underwent two major political reformations, suffered several assaults from the outside, and experienced continual sociocultural evolution. In the process it developed a society that possessed a strong sense of its own identity and historical continuity. Then after 1876, Korea entered the emerging Western-dominated global civilization, and the Korean people faced the challenge of adapting their culture and applying their historical experience to the modern world.

During the twelve centuries of the premodern peninsular kingdom, historical events can be put into context by placing them within several broad patterns of change. First, the kingdom became increasingly homogeneous. In terms of language, cultural identity and shared values and traditions, the Koreans became one people. Second, the peoples of Korea continued absorbing Chinese notions of government, religion, ethics, art, music, family structure, and fashions. Chinese-derived cultural values and habits penetrated further down the social hierarchy. As this happened Koreans combined these with indigenous traditions and developments. Thus Korea was able to become a full participant in, and at the same time a distinctive component of, the cosmopolitan East Asian civilization centered in China. Third, the kingdom gradually expanded in population and wealth. It expanded internally by absorbing more marginal lands and internal frontiers into its sociopolitical system, while externally there was a slow, fitful extension of its northern frontiers until by the middle fifteenth century they were stabilized at their present Yalu and Tumen river boundaries.

The periodization of Korean history generally follows dynastic demarcations. From 676 to 935 there was the Silla state that was ruled by the Kyŏngju Kim kings from the southeastern capital of Kyŏngju. From 935 to 1392 the kingdom, renamed Koryŏ, was governed from Kaesŏng under the Wang family, and from 1392 to 1910 the Yi dynasty governed the state, renamed Chosŏn, from Seoul. Within this chronological outline, it is helpful to see Korea as undergoing several stages and transitions. From 676 to the late eighth century the state under Silla experienced a period of growth and consolidation accompanied by an artistic and literary efflorescence. The period after 780 to the end of the ninth century was one of political if not socioeconomic and cultural decline. The tenth century was truly a transitional period that saw the disintegration of Silla, a brief period of political disunity, and the reformulation of the kingdom under the early Wang kings. Their Koryŏ state lasted nearly five centuries until another transitional period in the fourteenth century saw the establishment of the remarkably durable and stable Chosŏn state of the Yi dynasty, which survived to the annexation of Korea by Japan in 1910.

CONSOLIDATION OF CENTRAL MONARCHICAL RULE UNDER SILLA, 676–780

Silla's rulers sought to consolidate their power and create a centralized state. This proved difficult because the society was dominated by powerful aristocratic families, especially those of the highest true-bone rank. The true-bone aristocrats monopolized higher political offices, possessed private armies, and through the *Hwabaek* chose the king and participated in policy making. In 654, Kim Ch'un-ch'u succeeded to the throne as King Muyŏl (r. 654–661) and began a line of kings that remained on the throne to 780. These Silla rulers struggled to establish a centralized state under monarchical control. The task was made more difficult by the fact that the *sŏnggol* (sacred-bone) line died out with Queen Chindŏk (r. 647–654). Although Muyŏl's mother was of the royal Kim clan and his primary queen was the younger sister of Kim Yu-sin and a member of the Kaya royal family, Muyŏl and his descendants were of *chin'gol* (true-bone) rank, that is, of the same rank as the great aristocratic families. This meant that in terms of caste they were merely first among equals. The term sacred-bone implies a magicoreligious function that may have contributed royal authority. It is not clear if, in fact, the early rulers actually possessed priestly functions; it is apparent, however, that the status of the Silla kings after Muyŏl was far from secure and they had to struggle to maintain their supremacy. Because of this they were eager to seek alternative sources of legitimacy.

The chief rivals of the Silla kings were other higher aristocrats of true-bone rank who were represented in the *Hwabaek* and who held the top administrative posts. Muyŏl was challenged by the *sangdaedŭng,* as the chief of the *Hwabaek* was called, a man named Pidam, and later by another *sangdaedŭng,* Alch'ŏn. Another king, Sinmun (r. 681–692), was challenged by Kim Hŭm-dol, the father of his first queen, and purged another *sangdaedŭng,* Kun'gwan, forcing him and his son to commit suicide. To secure his authority Sinmum reorganized the army to bring it under closer royal control. The *yukchŏng* (six garrisons) were replaced by the *sŏdang* (oath banner) system as the main military force. Recruits were selected from Koguryŏ, Paekche, and from the Malgal tribes along the northern border. He placed these under direct royal authority. This was supplemented by the *sip chŏng* (ten garrisons). These forces, primarily concerned with internal security, were stationed outside the capital, Kyŏngju. One garrison was placed in each province with two in the capital area, and two in Hanju, the strategic province between the Han and Taedong Rivers. Since earlier Silla armies are believed to have been headed by powerful aristocrats, and perhaps organized along clan lines, the new royal forces marked the beginning of a truly centralized military. Meanwhile, the *hwarang* continued to exist as an organization of aristocratic youth. Sinmun also attempted to strengthen the fiscal basis of the state by reforming the tax system.

Under Sinmun the regional administration was reorganized, and in 685 nine *chu* (provinces) were created: three out of the Silla homeland, three out of the former Paekche, and three out of former Koguryŏ territories; while at the same time five secondary capitals were created, a measure important in controlling the country since the capital Kyŏngju was awkwardly situated in the extreme southeastern corner of the country. Following Chinese practice each province was subdivided into *kun* (prefectures), which totaled over one hundred, and into *hyŏn* (smaller counties) of which there were more than three hundred. At the lowest level of administration were *ch'on* (villages) headed by village chiefs. An elaborate administrative hierarchy of governors, prefects, and county magistrates administered the country. There were also subcounty units called *hyang* and *pugok* that were places of settlement for outcaste groups.

On the surface Silla appeared to be an impressively centralized state with royal administration penetrating down to smaller units of administration, much like, on a bigger scale, Tang China. In reality, however, Silla functioned more as an alliance of powerful families in the capital and prominent provincial families. Royal authority was limited by the fact that the top officialdom was recruited from a small segment of the aristocracy, the true-bone aristocrats of the Kyŏngju area. Local elites were appointed to serve as functionaries in the local administrations, perhaps a recognition of the need to rule with the support of these prominent families. To insure the loyalty of non-Sillan and other local elites a hostage system was believed to exist in which family members served at court on a rotation basis (this was later dubbed the *sangsuri* system). In the capital a complex central bureaucracy existed headed by the *Chipsabu* (Chancellery Office), which had been created in 651 and was headed by a *chungsi* or chief minister.[1] Eleven ministries, a Board of Censors, and hundreds of departments administered the court and the state. It is generally believed that after unification the *Hwabaek* declined in importance and the royal bureaucracy under the *Chipsabu* administered the kingdom.

SILLA AND THE CHINESE MODEL

Silla, a close ally of Tang and an exemplary tributary in many ways, modeled itself on Tang China. Yet for all the adoption of court robes and rituals; Chinese legal concepts and administrative nomenclature; and the careful study of Chinese literature, art, and philosophy, Silla maintained some distinctive features. This is evident in its administration. Tang China was administered by three chancelleries and six ministries: revenue, rituals, military, personnel, justice, and public works, a system later adopted by the Koryŏ state. In contrast, Silla's bureaucratic structure included many different ministries, including a Ministry of Horses and a Ministry of Marine. There were also on paper at least, hundreds of departments, including offices that dealt with monasteries, astronomy, medicine, and translation. There was even an office of water clocks. It is not clear how many of these offices functioned or whether they existed only on paper. Many or most may have been sinecures for the well connected. Provincial administration was based on the nine *chu* (Chinese: *zhou*) of the ancient Zhou dynasty, not the circuits (Korean: *to*; Chinese: *dao*) of Tang. Silla's society was also evolving differently from China's. While the Tang state was gradually reducing the hereditary aristocracy's control over government posts, despite efforts by monarchs to assert their personal authority, the aristocracy's monopoly of government was strengthened under Silla. In fact, it can be argued that Silla was not so much a centralized state as a coalition of local and central elites. Furthermore, while anti-Buddhist sentiment asserted itself in late Tang, the links between Buddhism and the state remained strong in Silla. Thus, while the Silla state faithfully adopted much of Chinese culture and nomenclature, it was not a miniature Tang China.

SUPPORTING THE SILLA STATE

As with other premodern states, Silla consisted of a small elite of officials and courtiers on top of a mass of farmers. To support itself, the state exacted tribute from its peasants and fishers to feed and clothe its officials and their retainers. How this taxation was organized during the Three Kingdoms period is not clear, but by the seventh century we have enough information to give a general description. *Sigŭp* (tax villages) were granted to prominent members of the elite as a reward for their services to the state. Apparently the owners of these estates were free to extract what produce and labor they could. It is not known how often this was done or how much of the country-side was controlled in this manner. The famous general Kim Yu-sin was granted five hundred households and six horse farms, but as he was a national hero this might not have been typical. Most officials were supported by *nogŭp* (stipend villages), which are believed to have included the right to collect a stipulated grain tax and perhaps corvée labor (use of labor service as a form of taxation) on the part of the recipients. In 687, a new system, the *chikchŏn* (office-field), was introduced, which assigned land to specific offices and entitled the officeholder only the right to collect the grain tax. Two years later the stipend village system was abolished. Both moves were an apparent attempt to gain greater control over the nation's resources by the state. The office-field system was abandoned in 757, and the *nogŭp* restored. More ambitious was the *chŏngjŏnje* ("able-bodied land system") that was initiated in 722. Based on the Chinese term "equal field" (Chinese: *juntian;* Korean: *kyunjŏn*), this was an attempt to establish state control over all land and periodically redistribute it to individual households, the amount depending upon the number of able-bodied adult males each contained. Upon the death of an adult male, his portion of land reverted to state control and was redistributed. This would insure that the state had access to the sur-plus produce and labor of its peasantry, and would prevent great landowners from controlling these resources and denying the state access to them. This too was abandoned; just when is not known. Along with the failure of the *chikchŏn*, the failure of the "able-bodied land system" indicates the limits of the state's control over its aristocracy and peasantry.

However, a chance discovery of four village registers found in the form of a wrapper over another document in the Shosoin Imperial Repository in Nara, Japan, in 1933 belies this impression of limited government control. This fascinating peak into Silla administration, while highlighting the frag-mentary knowledge of this period of Korean history, also testifies to the ingenuity of historians who have managed to derive a wide range of insights and interpretations of Korean history from a single scrap of documentation. The document contains portions of a census register of four villages near modern Ch'ŏngju. The dating of this document is given in a sexagesimal cycle year used in East Asia to count by giving each year in a sixty-year cycle a name. The year name given is generally believed to refer to 755, although 815 is a possibility. With surprising detail the villages were classified into nine grades of households based on the number of able-bodied adults and others available for corvée duty. Fields were divided into paddies, dry fields, and hemp fields. Horses, oxen, and mulberry, pine nut, and walnut trees were all listed. Certain fields appear to have been set aside for the support of village heads. There are other categories of fields of uncertain purpose.[2] These were perhaps office lands in accordance with the *chikchŏn* system, that is, for the support of the state officials.

All this would indicate that the Silla state made a considerable effort to consolidate its control over the peasantry and its resources, and possessed an impressive level of administrative organization and recordkeeping. An important form of taxation was corvée. Peasants were required to work on major public construction projects. Skilled workers owned or controlled by the state provided it with services and needed goods that were produced in state workshops. Metalsmiths, leather workers, butchers, guards, spinners and weavers of cotton and hemp, makers of medicinal goods, temple officials, street cleaners, and bookkeepers worked for the state in varying degrees of servitude. The state's ability to extract taxes and labor was the key to its effectiveness as a political institution. Potential revenues were lost to grants of tax-free land given as rewards, such as the impressive grant to Kim Yusin. Buddhist temples owned farmland that was also exempt from taxes. How much land was owned by temples is not clear, but it may have been considerable. Revenue gathering reached its peak efficiency in the late seventh and eighth centuries as monarchs consolidated their power. In the ninth century, especially in the latter half, there appeared to have been a sharp drop-off in state revenues, and a concomitant decline in the power of the Silla monarchy.

At the apex of the state was the monarch. The king, however, had to compete for authority with the great landowners for revenue, who were generally the high-born aristocrats. To shore up their legitimacy Sillan kings made use of the Chinese tributary system. The Chinese emperor was recognized as the Son of Heaven, and the Silla king as his enfeoffed representative on the peninsula. The Chinese imperial calendar was official, and in the eighth and early ninth centuries each king sought to confirm his position by sending an envoy to the Tang capital upon coming to the throne.

Kings also used Confucianism to strengthen state authority. Confucianism was a line of teachings derived from the Chinese philosopher Kongfuzi, known in the West as Confucius (551–479 C.E.). In Silla times its most important teachings were its emphases on filial piety, loyalty to the ruler, and respect for authority, all useful for the state. Confucian ideas would gradually penetrate Korean culture until by the fourteenth or fifteenth century they became the principal basis for moral, social, and political philosophy. In Silla times, however, Confucianism was primarily useful for training literate and loyal officials. The full implications of this school of thought were not felt until much later. As early as 636, Queen Chindŏk appointed scholars to teach the Confucian classics. Her successor, Queen Sŏndŏk, followed Koguryŏ and Paekche practice by designating certain scholars as *paksa* (erudites). In 682, a *Kukhak* (National Academy) along Tang lines was established to promote the study of the Chinese classics. This institution was open to sons of aristocratic families between eighteen and thirty years of age. In 717, portraits of Confucius and the "ten philosophers" and seventy-two worthies were brought back from Tang China, and in 750, the National Academy was reorganized as the *T'aehakkam* with a curriculum based on Confucian works. Examinations on Chinese classics were held to select worthy officials. Confucianism, however, was strictly secondary to Buddhism as a source of moral and political authority. It is also unlikely that the examinations were more than a short-lived modest experiment. Only later with the reintroduction of the civil examinations in the Koryŏ state did the Chinese practice of selecting officials by examination begin to play a significant role in Korean political culture.

A number of scholars trained in the Chinese classics served that state. Some were historians. Historical compilation played an important role in Silla society as it did throughout Korean history. Two erudites of history served the Sillan kings. The most distinguished historian was Kim Tae-mun, active in the early eighth century, who authored a history of the *hwarang*, the *Hwarang segi* (Chronicles of the Hwarang), *Kosŭng chŏn* (Biographies of Eminent Monks), the *Kyerim chapchŏn* (Tales of Silla), and the *Hansan ki* (Record of Hansan). Unfortunately none of these have survived. The men like Kim Tae-mun who served as officials became the forerunner of the Confucian scholar-bureaucrat who would characterize later Korean history. Another early scholar official was Kangsu (d. 692), who, as with most of the men of Chinese learning, came from the lower head-rank aristocracy (see below). Most famous of the early masters of classical Chinese learning was Sŏl Ch'ong, a contemporary of the historian Kim Tae-mun. Son of the Silla monk Wŏnhyo by a Silla princess, Sŏl Ch'ong (c. 660–730) was one of the outstanding learned men of Silla. He served as a royal advisor, and his letter to the throne *P'ungwang so* (Parables for the King) urged monarchs to renounce pleasure seeking and strictly observe moral standards. This is one of the earliest examples of the Confucian moralistic admonitions to the monarch that would remain a major feature of premodern Korean politics. Sŏl

Ch'ong was also incorrectly credited with inventing the *idu* (or *kugyŏl*) transcription system used to facilitate the reading of the Chinese classics, but he may have standardized it.

A distinction existed between these men of the head-rank-six class, who were generally better educated so they could carry out the clerical functions of the state, and the higher aristocracy of the true-bone that monopolized the top posts. Many of the early Confucian scholars such as Kangsu and Sŏl Ch'ong were locally educated men, and their knowledge of the Chinese classics was still a rare and valuable skill. By the ninth century a large number of men who had studied in Tang and were fluent in Chinese emerged to take an increasingly active part in government serving the kings. They were mostly from the lower aristocratic head-rank-six class. These educated head-rank-six officials insisted, as men of learning and merit, on the right to serve government at the higher levels despite their lower rank. Ch'oe Ch'i-wŏn was the most famous of these. Ch'oe went to Tang China in 868 where he studied Chinese classics and literature. He distinguished himself in the Tang examinations in 874 and served in the Tang bureaucracy. After returning to Korea in 885, Ch'oe served as an advisor to Queen Chinsŏng (r. 887–897), to whom he submitted a number of memorials proposing reforms. The content of those proposals has not survived, but he is believed to have been an early champion of the employment of the Chinese civil examination system. When his proposals were not adopted, he retired to self-imposed exile, setting a pattern for many subsequent scholars and reformers. Ch'oe Ch'i-wŏn was regarded in his day as an outstanding poet and essayist both in China and in Korea. A collection of his writings, the *Kyewŏn p'ilgyŏng chip (Plowing the Laurel Grove with a Writing Brush)*, has survived. They represent the earliest extant collection of literary works of an individual Korean author. He was also highly thought of as a calligrapher and samples of his calligraphy have survived in the "four mountain inscriptions."[3]

Daoism (Taoism) was another school of thought that shaped Korean culture at this time, albeit to a much lesser extent than Buddhism or Confucianism. The Daoist classic, the *Laozi*, was known in Koguryŏ. Religious Daoism was actively promoted as an alternative to Buddhism by the state in the seventh century. Even earlier references to the *Laozi* and the *Zhuangzi*, the other great Daoist classic, appear in Paekche. In Silla, the official transmission of Daoism came in 738 when the Tang envoy presented King Hyosŏng with a copy of the *Laozi*. It was, however, only during the period of decline during the eighth and ninth centuries that Daoism had a significant influence in Korea.

SILLA SOCIETY

Silla's elaborate formal government apparatus was imposed over a society structured along hereditary class lines. Bureaucratic positions were limited to corresponding hereditary ranks. At the top was the *chin'gol* (true-bone) aristocracy. The true-bone aristocrats, for the most part, resided in the capital and monopolized the first five of the seventeen bureaucratic ranks, including the highest position, the *sangdaedŭng;* the *yŏng* (heads) of the ministries; the provincial governors; and the generals. Many of these high-ranking aristocrats possessed private armies of armed retainers. According to one Chinese source these private armies numbered as many as three thousand men.

Below the true-bones were the *tup'um* (head-ranks). The *yuktup'um,* the topmost head-rank six, formed the second tier of the aristocracy. Also primarily residents of the capital Kyŏngju, they played an increasingly significant political and cultural role. The head-rank-six members held positions of lesser bureaucratic rank and provided the state with many of its scholars and court scribes. Beneath the aristocratic class were commoners. We hear little of these people who probably made up the majority of the population. One historical problem has been whether the peasantry was free or in some state of servitude. Evidence is too fragmentary to make conclusions as to whether they were free to move or to buy and sell land. In view of the powerful grip the aristocracy had on society, it is not likely that peasants possessed much freedom of movement. That peasants enjoyed at least some rights and privileges is implied by the fact that they were distinguished from people of more servile status. Free or not, in Silla's hereditary class-based society the opportunity to rise in status, serve in government, or change occupation was at best extremely limited.

Koreans adopted the Chinese classification of nonelites into *p'yŏngin* ("good people") and "mean" or "base" people. The *p'yŏngin* lived in villages (*ch'on*) and were subject to the supervision of village elders, farming their own fields as well as those designated for government and elite support. "Mean" people ranged from skilled craftsmen and specialists to chattel slaves. While slavery certainly existed, it does not appear to have been the primary economic basis of society. There appears to have been no large landed estates, only scattered parcels of land that could have been worked by slaves; public construction, however, was carried out by peasant corvées, not slaves. But that slaves were probably fairly numerous and could be held by commoners is suggested by the few records that have survived.[4] The four village census registers list twenty-five slaves among the 442 members of the agricultural communities.

Available evidence indicates that Silla was a rigidly hierarchical society where rank, status, and privilege ran along hereditary class lines. Incidences of social mobility, if it existed, must have been rare. Strict sumptuary laws reinforced class differences. Clothing, footwear, utensils, the size of houses, the designs on tiles, size of carts, and room sizes were all regulated. Commoners were forbidden from having big entry gates to their homes and could have no more than three horses in their stables. Nevertheless, commoners could become wealthy, and the flourishing maritime trade of late Silla must have afforded many opportunities for lower-ranked merchants to amass wealth and influence. The records state, for instance, that in 834, King Hŭng-dŏk issued an edict prohibiting the possession of luxurious foreign goods by commoners because this was leading to confusion in social ranks. Family descent was extremely important as was true of Korea in later periods. The main kinship organization was the *chok,* a large descent group. Later Koreans would have family shrines and elaborate rituals honoring their ancestors, but this was probably not the case in Silla.[5]

The status of women in Silla was higher than in subsequent periods or perhaps in Paekche and Koguryŏ. Much of our knowledge of Silla's family structure and the role of women, however, remains a matter of speculation. It is believed that the status of women was high compared to most contemporary Asian societies, that men and women mingled freely and participated together in social functions, and that families traced their ancestry along both their father's and mother's line. Women were able to succeed as the family head, and failure to produce a son was not grounds for divorce. Three women ascended to the throne—the last was Chinsŏng (r. 887–897)—although only when there was no male heir. Among royalty, about whom much more information is available, girls married between sixteen and twenty, and there was often a considerable difference in ages between partners. No strict rule seems to have existed concerning the use of paternal surnames. Succession was not limited to sons, but also included daughters, sons-in-law, and grandsons by sons and daughters. Equal importance was given to the rank of the father and the mother in determining the status of the child.[6] Kings selected their queens from powerful families. A careful reading of the historical records that were edited in later times suggests that Silla queens may have exercised considerable authority.[7]

In all these ways Korean society at this time differed from later periods in which the position of women weakened considerably. If the above represents an accurate picture of Silla society, then the pattern of the next one thousand years of Korean history is one of a steady decline in the status of women, of the greater segregation of sexes, and of a shift to a more patrilineal society.

Agriculture was the basis of the economy and the vast majority of the population lived in small villages and hamlets where they farmed rice, barley, and vegetables. Little is known about farming methods in this period, but enough surplus was produced to support a sizeable urban population. Kyŏng-ju was the largest city. The thirteenth-century history *Samguk yusa* states that at one point it had 178,936 households. The city is said to have had 1,360 residential quarters in its fifty-five wards, thirty-five great private estates, and four royal palaces, one for each season. While these figures no doubt are greatly exaggerated, archaeological evidence suggests that it was indeed a sizeable city, among the major urban centers in Asia. It was apparently a prosperous city of parks, bridges, and large official markets. The *Samguk yusa* records that when King Hŏn'gang (r. 875–886) looked out from his palace he could see "homes with tiled roofs in rows from the capital to the seas, with not a single thatched roof in sight."[8] Historical demography for Korea is still largely undeveloped, but Korea under Silla probably had a population of at least two million, possibly twice that, making it one of larger states in Eurasia.

Religion and Aristocratic Culture

Silla was a Buddhist kingdom. The religion had taken deep roots, at least among the ruling class, by the time of unification. Both kings Chinhŭng and Pŏphŭng, for example, abdicated late in their reigns to be ordained as monks.[9] Originally from India, Buddhism eventually spread across most of Asia. Through Buddhism Korea was linked to the wider world that included not only China and Japan but the Buddhist lands in Central Asia, Southeast Asia, and India. A few Korean monks even journeyed to India in search of Buddhist teachings. Best known was Hyech'o (704–?), who described his pilgrimage to India in *Wang och'ŏnch'ukkuk chŏn (Record of a Journey to the Five Indian Kingdoms)*. The basic teachings of Buddhism included the ideas that the world was full of suffering, and that this suffering was the result of karma or deeds done in this or past lives. The goal of Buddhism was to break the cycle of births and rebirth and achieve Nirvana, a state of nonexistence that was free from suffering. The forms of Buddhism that reached Korea had undergone considerable change from the original teachings that had emphasized moderation and avoidance of excessive attachment to worldly affairs. These modifications were, in part, due to the Chinese practice of *ge-yi,* that is, finding suitable Chinese equivalents to Indian Buddhist terms, a process that did much to reinterpret and perhaps dilute the original meanings. Chinese Buddhism during the Tang also reflected the influence of Daoism and other indigenous beliefs. In Silla Buddhism was a source for legitimizing authority, adding to the prestige of the monarchy, and providing the state with scribes and advisors. It was especially, perhaps principally, valued for the supernatural aid it provided. This role gradually declined with the absorption of Chinese secular learning, especially Confucianism, and with the consequent growth of a literate segment of the aristocracy trained in the Chinese classics and in Chinese principles of law and government. Yet, Buddhism still provided the chief source of artistic inspiration, continued to attract many of the best minds in Korea, and pervaded all aspects of secular culture. It was the fundamental belief system of the dominant groups of society. The Buddhist scholarship produced during this period was one of the finest outpourings of intellectual creativity in Korean history.

Tang Buddhism was characterized by its division into many doctrinal sects. Most were named after a particular sutra that was regarded by the sect as the embodiment of the true essence of Buddha's teachings. Korean Buddhism inherited this multiplicity of doctrines and the focus on certain sutras from Tang. It also shared, if not inherited, the Chinese practice of doctrinal tolerance and the absence of sectarian strife as well as a tendency toward syncretism. Sects tended to borrow from one another so that distinctions between them gradually became blurred.

One of the most important sects was Hwaŏm (Flower Garland). Named for the *Avatamsaka (Flower Garland) Sutra,* this sect tried to incorporate various doctrines by classifying them into varying degrees of truth. The tenets of Hwaŏm were complex and intellectually demanding, making little concession for the follower who was unable to devote his life to them. It appealed to the small number of monks of aristocratic background who spent their lives mastering esoteric knowledge and thereby gaining awe and respect. It also appealed to other members of the elite who were attracted to its rich rituals and ceremonies, and who could afford to finance the construction of temples, perform elaborate ceremonies and prayers, and support monks who could study on their behalf. Ŭisang (625–702), founder of the Hwaŏm school in Korea, was one of the major intellectual figures of Korean history. Ŭisang went to China at sixteen where he studied under the Hwaŏm master Zhiyan, along with Fazang, who became one of China's seminal Buddhist thinkers. Among Ŭisang's many disciples were Simsang, who later propagated the doctrine in Japan. Ŭisang's later reputation was such that he was credited with saving Silla from an invasion by Chinese emperor Tang Gaozong. He emphasized strict learning, the performance of rituals, and monastic life. In this, he typified the Korean Buddhism of his age.

While Silla kings did not abandon the patronage of Buddhism or its use as a source of legitimacy, Silla Buddhism became less court centered and at the same time less confined to the aristocratic elite. Newer, less esoteric forms of Buddhism with simpler doctrines appeared that did not require constant sponsorship of costly ceremonies. A precursor of this popular Buddhism came with Wŏnhyo. Wŏnhyo (617–686) was one of the major Buddhist thinkers of Korea.[10] He preached to the common people at a time when Buddhism was confined mainly to the court and the aristocracy. Most of the eminent monks of Silla derived their fame from introducing some new teaching from China. Wŏnhyo, however, did not journey to China. Instead he traveled throughout the countryside as an act of penance after having broken his vows and sired a son, Sŏl Ch'ong, by a Silla princess. He was also the founder of the Pŏpsang (Dharma-nature) school of Buddhism, sometimes called the Haedong (Korea) school since it was the only indigenous sect. Wŏnhyo's aim was to create a school of Buddhism that would harmonize the doctrines of the various other schools. He would be the first major figure in a distinctively Korean tendency to seek a unifying school of doctrine and practice.

Two forms of Buddhism that appeared in Silla times had their major impact on Korean religious beliefs later on: Pure Land Buddhism and Meditative Buddhism. The Pure Land sect centered around devotion to Amitabha (Amit'a-bul) who helped the troubled reach Happy Land (Sukhavati). This belief spread among those of humble status as early as the mid-eighth century, becoming of greater importance in subsequent centuries. Sŏn (called Chan in Chinese but better known in the West by its Japanese pronunciation Zen) was first introduced by Pŏmnang (c. 632–646) after returning from Tang. Another monk, Sinhaeng (d. 779), founded one of the world's oldest extant Sŏn temples. Sŏn became important in the ninth century with the teachings of Toŭi (d. 825), the first major figure in that tradition, and it had a profound impact on Korea during the Koryŏ period.

Buddhism was the inspiration for much of the art of this period. The most outstanding examples are the Pulguk-sa temple and the Sŏkkuram grotto. Pulguk-sa, built near Kyŏngju in the mid-eighth century, is still one of the great architectural monuments of East Asia. Of special interest is the Muyŏng-t'ap (Pagoda that casts no shadow), built in 751. During its reconstruction in 1966 a dharani, a magical formula, was found that was apparently placed in the pagoda at the time of its construction. This is the world's oldest known printed document. The justly famed Sŏkkuram Grotto, located in a mountain near Kyŏngju facing the East Sea, contains among its many excellent carvings an exquisite eleven-foot stone Buddha that is situated so that it catches the first rays of dawn as the sun rises above East Sea. The bronze Buddhas and Boddhisattvas are of a high standard and were never equaled in Korea. Also impressive are the bronze bells. The Samwŏn-sa bell, cast in 725, the oldest extant, weighs fifteen hundred kilograms. The Pongdŏk-sa bell, cast in 770, is the second largest in the world. Silla bells were decorated with delicate bas-reliefs of flowers, clouds, and flames. Most famous of all is the Emille Bell in Kyŏngju.

Beneath the Buddhism of the Silla was a rich and complex tradition of indigenous religion and practices. We know little of these, however, because they did not leave behind written records. The peoples of Korea worshiped the spirits of mountains and rivers and of various natural features. Dragon spirits were worshiped. The popularity of the cult of Mirŭk, the Buddha of the future, may have been linked to dragon worship since the word for dragon is the same in Korean. A chilling hint of indigenous beliefs is the story of the Emille bell. According to legend the craftsman who cast the magnificent bronze bell was successful only after sacrificing his daughter by throwing her into the molten metal. The cry of her name could be heard, it was said, calling out when the bell was rung.

Silla rulers continued to construct tombs in the Chinese manner. A distinct feature of these tombs, not found on the mainland, is the zodiacal animal deities bearing weapons. One of the interesting surviving monuments from Silla is the Ch'ŏmsŏng-dae, a bottle-shaped granite tower in the ancient Silla capital of Kyŏngju, often cited as the world's oldest astronomical observatory. According to the *Samguk yusa*, the Ch'ŏmsŏng-dae was built during the reign of Queen Sŏndŏk (632–647). Its original purpose is not clear but it is widely believed that it served as an observatory, and it has been suggested that its shape was designed to hold a large armillary sphere. If so, it is the world's oldest extant observatory.[11] Due to the central role that Buddhism played as a state protective cult it has been suggested that the tower was built as a replica of the holy Mt. Sumeru, and that it was a place where praying and incantations took place. It is known that astronomy was an important science for compiling the calendar and for prognostication. One eighth-century astronomer, Kim Am, enjoyed a high reputation. Kim studied in China and was also remembered as a master of military science and of yin-yang theory.

Educated members of the elite wrote poetry in Chinese, and some of their works have survived in Chinese anthologies. The great anthology of Chinese literature, the *Wenxuan,* was taught in Korea; and the Tang poets Bo Juyi and Du Fu were highly esteemed by the educated elite, while some Korean writers in Chinese, such as Ch'oe Ch'i-wŏn, were highly admired in Tang. Ch'oe was considered a master of poetry and parallel prose. A collection of his writings was compiled in 886 and published in both China and Korea. In general, Koreans used Chinese characters (called *hanmun* or *hanja* in Korean) for writing, although, of course, they spoke one of the several dialects of Korean used in the peninsula during that time. All three kingdoms apparently employed systems for writing in their native languages using Chinese characters. One method of writing in the vernacular was called *idu.* *Idu* used *hanmun* sentences and placed them in Korean syntax by using certain characters to indicate grammatical markers. Another system, *Kugyŏl* or *t'o,* also employed a system of markers and was used as an aid in reading Chinese. Writing Korean in Chinese characters presented problems, as can be seen in the Oath Inscription of 612 where Chinese characters are put in Korean word order. The complicated sound system of Korean made development of a phonetic script difficult, and it was not until the fifteenth century that the Korean alphabet *han'gŭl* was developed (see chapter 7).[12]

Koreans in Silla times also wrote poetry in Korean. In the late ninth century an anthology of hundreds of vernacular Korean poems, the *Samdaemok* (*Collection from the Three Kingdoms*), was compiled, but it has been lost. Much Korean poetry was written in a system called *hyangch'al,* which was devised to transcribe entire Korean sentences with Chinese characters. Using this system, Korean-language poems known as *hyangga* were composed. Unfortunately few *hyangga* have survived (see below). Although we have the titles of many *hyangga,* only twenty-five *hyangga* now exist: fourteen dating to Silla times are in the *Samguk yusa;* the other eleven, attributed to the tenth-century monk Kyunyŏ, are in the *Kyunyŏ chŏn* (*Tale of Kyunyŏ*). These poems provide us with the earliest forms of purely Korean literature. They are invaluable in providing a window into the language and indigenous poetry of the period. Seventeen are Buddhist in inspiration and content; others show a shamanistic influence. Among the latter the "Song of Ch'oyŏng" is probably the best known. This eight-line poem refers to the legend of Ch'oyŏng, one of the seven sons of the Dragon King of the Eastern Sea, who married a beautiful woman. Seeing that the wife was extremely attractive, an evil spirit transformed himself into a man and attacked her in her room while Ch'oyŏng was away. But Ch'oyŏng returned, and witnessing the scene, he calmly sang the words of the poem, which so moved the evil spirit that it went away. The Ch'oyŏng mask was later used to exorcize evil spirits, usually on New Year's Eve. It is apparent that many of the *hyangga* were to be accompanied by music and dance. Indigenous religious undertones are strong in surviving Silla literature. Even many of the Buddhist poems appear to have been Buddhified shamanistic invocations to mountain spirits and other nature deities and are perhaps of remote origin.

Saenae-mu, mask dances, were performed on festival days such as the three-day *T'aep'o* (Festival of Wine), which was imported from China. The first was recorded in 615. In 746, at a *T'aep'o* given by King Kyŏngdŏk, a general amnesty was declared, and 150 novices were ordained monks. This was celebrated in Kyŏngju, which was the great center for aristocratic life. In fact, there appear to have been no significant regional cultural centers, and to a much greater degree than in later Korea, the higher culture was confined to the aristocratic elite living in the capital. An inkling of what this life may have been like is revealed in the Imhae-jŏn (Pavilion on the Sea) banquet hall, which was built over the man-made Anapchi Lake and in the P'osŏkchŏng. The latter was a slightly winding water channel carved out of stone in which wine cups were floated. Revelers took turns composing verse before the wine cups floated down to them. Little is known, however, of the art, music, and festivities of the nonelites.

Silla and its Neighbors

Silla relations with Tang began to improve in the eighth century. There were several reasons for this. After the reign of Gaozong the expansionary phase of Tang was largely over, and fear of a direct invasion lessened. Furthermore, the creation of Parhae, a new state in Manchuria, acted both as a buffer between Silla and Tang and as a mutual enemy. It controlled part of what is now Korea, posing a threat to its southern neighbor. An alliance between Tang and Silla against Parhae in 733 brought a long period of amiable relations between the two. Tang's interests in the Korean peninsula were largely strategic, and as it became obvious that Silla posed no threat to its security, relations warmed. China found instead that its policy of using trade and cultural exchanges and offering legitimacy and prestige to the Silla monarchy was effective in keeping Silla safely in the tributary system. Indeed, the relationship that was worked out in the late seventh and early eighth centuries can be considered the beginning of the mature tributary relationship that would characterize Sino-Korean interchange most of the time until the late nineteenth century.

Cultural relations with China were significant. Forty-five of the fifty Silla monks known to have traveled to China did so after unification. Many Korean students studied in Tang. There is no way of knowing how many, but it must have been a considerable number, for in 844, 105 Koreans who were studying at the national academy were sent back to Silla. Eighty-eight Sillans passed the highly competitive and prestigious civil examination during the Tang. A few Koreans even rose to high office in China. Koreans who succeeded academically or who achieved fame in China returned to the homeland as celebrated heroes. In addition to students, frequent embassies were exchanged. One Chinese embassy is said to have had eight hundred members. The resultant process of sinification among the elite was profound. Silla courtiers wore Chinese dress, aristocrats wrote verse in the best Chinese, and Chinese fashions in eating, drinking, music, and imported luxuries of all sorts were necessary accoutrements to high-born status. It is not certain how far Chinese cultural influences penetrated down the social scale. Most probably, the interest in Chinese culture was largely confined to the elite.

In contrast to those with China, relations between Silla and Japan were often hostile. In 733, the Yamato government participated in an alliance with Parhae and sent ships to attack Korea. Japanese leaders hoped to gain a foothold on the Korean peninsula. Attacks by the Japanese from the sea were a threat in early Silla. In 746, three hundred Japanese ships are reported to have attacked Silla. This was followed by a treaty of amity that initiated a period of peaceful exchange. Good relations with Silla served the Japanese well because during the next century the chief maritime route to China passed along the south coast of Korea. A Bureau for Silla was established in Dazaifu in Kyushu in Western Japan, and embassies were exchanged. One Japanese embassy had a reported 204 members. During 761–764, during the An Lushan rebellion in China, a Japanese court official, Fujiwara no Nakamura, planned another invasion; but this was called off by rivals at court and no further organized invasions of Korea took place for the next eight centuries. Instead, it was Sillan pirates who plagued the Japanese coast in the ninth century.

Silla was also tied to its neighbors by trade networks. This included the official tribute given to Tang and the "gifts" received in return. A great deal of private trade flourished as well. Silla silver and gold wares were prized in

China. Especially famous were silver and gold basins that became known in China through Song times as "Silla" and copper basins that were called "copper Silla." Silla silver and gold gained a reputation as far as the Middle East where early Arab references to al-Sila describe it as rich in precious metals.[13] Silla exported silver and gold bullion, textiles, and ginseng, for which Korea has always been famous in East Asia. Sometimes Silla took advantage of its location to reexport Chinese goods and furs and horses from the tribal peoples on its northern border to Japan. From China books, tea, textiles, swords, a variety of ceremonial goods such as court robes, and various luxurious goods were imported. Chinese coins were also imported; they served as a medium of exchange since Silla did not mint coins. Some of these goods were reexported to Japan, where they were traded along with Silla crafts for pearls, fans, and screens.

Silla was the greatest period of maritime activity in Korea's history. Koreans dominated the commerce of Northeast Asia in the eighth and ninth centuries; most of the commerce between Korea, North China, and Japan was carried out in Korean ships. Koreans established communities in the port of Dengzhou, the historic gateway into north China from Korea, and in Lianshui and Chuzhou on the Huai River. Korean ships sailed to Yangzhou at the junction of the Yangzi River and the Grand Canal, but did not generally venture into southern China where international commerce was dominated by Arabs. In the ninth century Japanese going to China sailed on Korean vessels, and the account of one these travelers, the monk Ennin, provides a valuable description of Korean maritime activities and of the Korean naval commander Chang Po-go (note hyphen).

Chang Po-go's career illustrates this interesting chapter of Korean history. Born on Ch'ŏnghae (Wando) Island off Korea's southwestern coast of humble family background, Chang Po-go emigrated to Tang, where he became a military officer in the lower Huai River basin. Chang returned to Korea and gained royal permission to establish the Ch'ŏnghae Garrison on his home island in 828 by arguing for the need to control Chinese piracy and to protect Korean trade and travelers. From his stronghold he operated a private navy that was a major power in the Yellow Sea. According to the Japanese monk Ennin in his *Account of a Pilgrimage to Tang in Search of the Law*, which tells of his 840 voyage to Tang China in one of Chang Po-go's ships, the Korean commander operated a large Buddhist temple in Shandong Province with twenty-eight Korean monks and nuns.[14] Chang Po-go's maritime trade and connections were so extensive that he was called "King of the Yellow Sea." According to Korean accounts he was given command of the Ch'ŏnghae Garrison because he wanted to end the marauding of pirates who were kidnapping Koreans and selling them as slaves. However, this official position was probably just an official acknowledgment of his already accumulated power. Chang supported Kim U-jing in his successful bid for the throne in 839, when he became King Sinmu. When the newly installed king died the same year Chang attempted to marry his daughter to King Sinmu's son and successor King Munsŏng. For an islander and a man outside the aristocratic elite of Silla, this bid for influence was a bold move, which failed when a member of the capital aristocracy assassinated him in 846. The Ch'ŏnghae Garrison was abolished in 851. Chang Po-go's rise from a maritime trader to a major power broker in late Silla was unusual but probably indicative of the growth of maritime lords during this period. Two other maritime lords were Wang Pang-gyu in Chinju and Wang Kŏn, the Koryŏ founder, who came from a maritime family in the Kaesŏng area. Korea's dominance of Northeast Asian sea lanes ended after the ninth century.

PARHAE

Silla was not the only state to occupy the Korean peninsula. To the north was the state of Parhae. After the collapse of Koguryŏ, remnants from that state and a number of Manchurian tribal peoples set up a state in southern Manchuria at the end of the seventh century that dominated most of Manchuria and the northern third of Korea for two centuries. From 713 to its destruction by the Khitans in 926, Parhae was a formidable power. Its relations with its neighbors were often tense. Parhae, an extensive state, was strong enough to launch a naval raid on the Chinese port of Dengzhou in 732. Despite the tense relations with Tang, Parhae was quickly brought into the Chinese cultural orbit, modeling its administrative structure, its laws, and its literature after its giant neighbor. In general the Parhae administrative structure conformed more closely to the Tang model than to Silla. The state impressed the Chinese enough to earn from them the sobriquet the "flourishing land in the East." A high-water mark of its wealth and power was reached under the tenth king, Sŏn (r. 818–831).[15] Sŏn expanded the kingdom to the Amur River.

For Silla Parhae was a menacing neighbor. This was heightened when the second king, Tae Hŏm-mu, known also as King Mu (r. 720–738), completed the tasks of subjugating the western Manchurian tribes and then turned south to subdue the Okchŏ and establish control over the Hamhŭng plain and the Hamgyŏng coast. In 721, Silla was forced to construct what is recorded as a wall but was more likely a chain of fortifications along its northern border that extended from the mouth of the Taedong to Wŏnsan Bay on the East Coast. In terms of geopolitics, Parhae occupied the former position of Koguryŏ. With the consolidation of the Parhae state under Mu, Silla found itself in the same position that it was in in the 660s when, after the fall of Paekche, it allied itself with Tang to remove the threat in the northern part of the peninsula. But the Tang-Silla military campaign of 733 was no repeat of 668. Half the Sillan army, including two sons of Kim Yu-sin, perished in the snows of the northern mountains. Parhae remained a powerful state that outlived by a couple of decades Silla's effective control over most the peninsula. The war did bring one benefit for Silla. Tang, in return for its support against Parhae, recognized Silla's sovereignty over all the territory south of the Taedong. Again in 762, during the An Lushan rebellion in China, Silla felt compelled to fortify its northern border in anticipation of a joint Parhae-Japanese invasion. Relations between the two states, however, were not always hostile, and diplomatic missions to Parhae are recorded for 792 and 812. Trade also was carried out between them, and there is a reference to thirty-nine stations along a trade route stretching from the Parhae city of Tonggyŏng to Silla.

Parhae's relations with Japan were of a much more consistently friendly nature. For two centuries the two nations exchanged diplomatic embassies. Parhae dispatched thirty-five embassies to Japan and the Japanese court sent thirteen embassies to Parhae.[16] A lively trade existed between the two, Parhae selling furs for Japanese textiles. Parhae also acted as an important avenue for the transmission of Chinese culture into Japan, assuming the role formerly played by Koguryŏ. The Japanese were impressed by the cultural attainments of Parhae's envoys; surviving poems composed by Parhae diplomats for the Japanese hosts remain the only extant examples of Parhae literature. Twice in 733 and again in 762 joint attacks on Silla were planned, the second one abortive. And when the Parhae state fell to the seminomad Khitans, a last embassy came in 929 unsuccessfully seeking assistance in restoring the kingdom. In the early eighth century Parhae also sought alliance with the Tujue (Turkish) confederation that arose in Mongolia, briefly making Korea the focal point of a vast East Asian military alliance system that pitted Tang and Silla against Parhae, the Tujue, and Japan.

Only fragmentary knowledge has survived about Parhae society and culture. The economy was based on agriculture with the rich central Manchuria plains supporting a population that according to one Chinese source consisted of one hundred thousand households or about half a million people. Ethnically the population was a mix of various Manchurian peoples of Tungusic linguistic stock along with possible admixtures of Koguryŏ-speaking people. Recently archeological work in Manchuria has begun to give us a glimpse of an amalgamated cultural style of Chinese, Korean, and indigenous elements. Interestingly an *ondol* system for heating homes characteristic of Korean houses was used. Many Parhae students studied and sat for the examinations in Tang, where the Chinese diplomatically admitted the same number of Sillan and Parhae applicants to the exams. But the Chinese were not always so even-handed and gave Sillan envoys a higher place in imperial audiences. Since only a few fragments of literature have survived, little can be said except that the elite at least had absorbed a great deal of Chinese culture and wrote eloquent Chinese verse. Buddhism was patronized and a purple porcelain was produced that gained a high reputation in Tang.

Since the eighteenth century many Korean historians have considered Parhae part of Korean history, which has led some historians to regard the united Silla period as the "two Kingdoms period."[17] The implications of this for Korea are significant. Considering Parhae part of Korea history strengthens the argument of those modern Korean nationalists who seek to incorporate much of Manchuria within the historical homeland of Koreans, and it provides support for modern ultranationalists who hold irredentist claims for all or portions of Manchuria. For contemporary Koreans it also provides an historical echo for their current north-south division. Still the questions remain: Was Parhae a Korean state? And what role does it play in Korean history? It did occupy the northernmost parts of what is now Korea, including the modern Hamgyŏng province, and its ruling dynasty of non-Korean ethnic origins proudly laid claim to Koguryŏ's heritage. The rulers of Parhae often referred to their state as the successor to Koguryŏ, and many of the leading families traced their ancestry to that state. But Parhae's population was predominately of groups different from those that evolved into modern ethnic Koreans. Furthermore, unlike Koguryŏ its population base and its primary capital (as well as three of four of its secondary capitals) lay outside the Korean peninsula. In short, Parhae was first of all a Manchurian state with a southern foothold in northern Korea and some ethnic and cultural affiliations with the peoples of the peninsula. Its role in Korean history is important because for all its tensions with its southern neighbor, Parhae acted as a protective barrier both from Tang and from potential seminomadic invaders. That is, Parhae stabilized the always troublesome northern frontiers of Manchuria and Siberia and enabled Silla to enjoy two centuries of relative peace and prosperity. This, perhaps, was Parhae's most important contribution to Korea's historical development.

THE DECLINE OF SILLA

After the mid-eighth century Silla began a political decline. The central government became weaker, powerful local warlords emerged, and the countryside was plagued by banditry. In part this was related to the changes in its international environment. Throughout East Asia the eighth century was a period of cultural brilliance and prosperity while the ninth century was a time of decline. All three cultural/geographical areas that surround Korea—China, the northern frontiers of Manchuria and Siberia, and Japan—experienced troubles. The Tang empire, after reaching a political and cultural apogee under Xuanzong (r. 712–756), began to weaken. By the late ninth century China saw internal rebellions and intrusions by tribal invaders, and at the beginning of the tenth century the Chinese Empire broke up into smaller rival states. The Manchurian state of Parhae was weakened by external pressures from seminomadic neighbors. In Japan, Nara was abandoned in 784 and the capital moved to Heian a decade later. While the early Heian period was one of cultural creativity, the central Japanese state declined and effective power gravitated toward regional warlords. Contacts between Japan and China diminished, hurting Korea since it had benefited as an intermediary in Chinese-Japanese trade. In the south, Annam (Vietnam) became restless, and in the tenth century it broke free from Chinese rule. Tribal peoples along the northern borders of the East Asian cultural realm became increasingly powerful, with the Khitans (or Qidans) emerging in the ninth century as the most formidable in the northeast. In the early tenth century they contributed to the fall of the Tang, destroyed Parhae, and threatened the Korean Peninsula with invasion. It is important to see the weakening of central authority in Silla, the rise of local warlords, and the resultant civil disorder within the context of the great fragmentation of authority and breakdown in order that characterized all of East Asia at this time. But the Silla state's decline was also part of the internal pattern. After 780, local landed aristocrats consolidated their landholdings, built *sŏngju* (walled towns), and commanded private armies. These local aristocrats in effect became warlords, even styling themselves as *changgun* (generals). Eventually these warlords formed alliances and competed with each other for power.

THE LATER THREE KINGDOMS

Toward the end of the ninth century the central government's control over most of the peninsula disintegrated. During Chinsŏng's reign (887–897) the bandit Kihwŏn overran much of south-central Korea. Yanggil, another bandit, controlled much of the north-central region; a third, Ch'onggil, lorded over parts of the south and central areas, while a group known as the Red Pantaloons terrorized the southeast and raided the outskirts of Kyŏngju in 896. Eventually three separate states emerged, so that the period from 901 until 936 is known as the Period of the Later Three Kingdoms. It became another three-way struggle for the mastery of the Korean Peninsula. Later histories portrayed the struggle for the mastery of Korea among three personalities, Wang Kŏn, Kyŏnhwŏn, and Kungye, whom one scholar has called respectively the good, the bad, and the ugly.[18] Kyŏnhwŏn, the bad one, a son of a farmer, served in the coast guard in southwest Korea, was commissioned as an army officer, and with his private army occupied the provincial capital of Muju, installing himself as military governor in 892. Initially he was still an officer in the Silla army, but then he aligned himself with the rebel-bandit Yanggil before setting himself up in 900 as the King of Later Paekche.

Kungye, the ugly one, according to traditional sources was either born from a liaison between King Kyŏngmun and a woman outside his court or was the son of a low-ranking concubine of King Hon'an (r. 857–861); the accounts vary. A Silla prince, as a victim of a power struggle he was exiled from the court, and eventually became a supporter of the bandit-rebel Kihwŏn and later of another rebel leader, Yanggil. As one of Yanggil's commanders in northern Silla he is said to have brought large areas of Kyŏnggi, Kangwŏn, and Hwanghae provinces under the former's control. In 901, after having killed Yanggil, Kungye established the Later Koguryŏ at Songak (Kaesŏng). He renamed his state twice; it is best known as Later Koguryŏ. As leader of one of the Later Three Kingdoms he engaged in a three-way power struggle with Later Paekche and Silla. Kungye is depicted in Korean histories as cruel and tyrannical with a deep hatred of Silla. Announcing "revenge on Silla for the fall of Koguryŏ" and declaring Kyŏngju the "City of Destruction," he is said to have killed anyone who ventured into his kingdom from the old Silla heartland, although his staff included Silla aristocrats. In an effort to sanctify his rule he claimed to be the Maitreya Buddha, proclaimed his sons bodhisattvas, dressed himself and his sons in colorful garb, and composed sutras. He rode on a white horse preceded by youths and maidens burning incense, followed by two hundred monks chanting mantras. Kungye, claiming to have the power of mind reading, carried out frequent purges of his officials whose disloyal intentions he could read.[19] In 918, he was murdered by one of his commanders, Wang Kŏn, the good one, and the founder of Koryŏ.

Silla was the weakest of the three states. The monarchy's control was limited to the extreme southeast corner of the country. Internal instability is suggested by the fact that between 912 and 927 three monarchs came from the ancient Pak consort line. In 921, the weakened Silla state allied itself with Wang Kŏn and his renamed Koryŏ state, a move possible only with the death of Kungye. Silla paid for this alliance with a devastating attack by Kyŏnhwŏn in 927 in which Kyŏngae (r. 924–927) committed suicide and Kyŏngju was sacked. A member of the royal Kim clan was then placed on the throne as Kyŏngsun (r. 927–935). Wang Kŏn, whose base of support appeared to be maritime, captured the islands off the west coast of Korea. But these early victories were followed by two decades of stalemate during which Silla just managed to survive and gradually came under the protection of Koryŏ. In 930, Wang Kŏn defeated Later Paekche at Mt. P'yŏng north of Andong; a year later he visited Kyŏngju and probably effectively controlled that state from then on. In 932, he was recognized as Korean ruler by the Later Tang dynasty that ruled northern China. His position was also strengthened by the arrival of refugees from Parhae including the crown prince, Tae Kwanghyŏn, in 934.

Later Paekche, increasingly isolated, was defeated at Ungju in 934 and lost all land north of the Kum River. Kyŏnhwŏn sought unsuccessfully to obtain military support from Japan in 935. In the end his older son Sin'gŏm murdered his younger son Kŭmgang, whom Kyŏnhwŏn had set up as his successor, and imprisoned his father. Escaping, the aging Kyŏnhwŏn marched with Wang Kŏn's army to Ilsŏn-gun. There Wang Kŏn, now able to act as an avenger for unfilial conduct, defeated the Later Paekche forces at Ilsŏn-gun in September 936. Sin'gŏm surrendered and died a few days later. The previous year, 935, the last Silla king, Kyŏngsun, abdicated and recognized Wang Kŏn as his successor. Thus Korea was reunified by Wang Kŏn and the Koryŏ period began.

Our information on this period comes from official sources written in the twelfth century under the sponsorship of the dynasty that Wang Kŏn founded. Much about the events remains unclear. For example, how did Silla manage to survive so many years? Why did Kyŏnhwŏn not annex it in 927? What were the bases of support for Kyŏnhwŏn, Kungye, and Wang Kŏn? Was the conjuring up of the names Paekche and Koguryŏ indicative of a resurgence of regional/ethnic sentiment in those regions? And, if so, does this mean that the unification of Korea under Silla was far from complete at the end of the ninth century? Or was the use of these names simply part of the search for sources of legitimacy by the rebel leaders? None of the answers to these questions are clear.

Silla rulers had only limited success in establishing a centralized polity. Powerful true-bone aristocrats resisted attempts to create a more Chinese-style centralized bureaucracy. After 780 real power seems to have slipped from the king and his officials in the capital to aristocrats in the countryside. By the end of the ninth century the king could no longer maintain control much beyond the capital, and a power struggle emerged among regional warlords. The use of the old names of Paekche and Koguryŏ suggests that the Korean peninsula was not as homogeneous as it later became; regional loyalties were still considerable. Evidence indicates that people in different areas probably still spoke distinctive languages. They also probably possessed local and ethnic identities apart from and/or stronger than any shared Korean/Sillan identity. Much of this is not yet understood. Whatever the reasons for the creation of the later three kingdoms, they were short-lived. Most of the Korean peninsula was soon reunited, and would remain united until the division of the peninsula by the United States and the Soviet Union in 1945.

Sŏl Kyedu[20]

Sŏl Kyedu was a descendant of a Silla official. Once he went drinking with his four friends, each of whom revealed his wishes. Sŏl said, "In Silla the bone rank is the key to employment. If one is not of the nobility, no matter what his talents, he cannot achieve a high rank. I wish to travel west to China, display rare resources and perform meritorious deeds, and thereby open a path to glory and splendor so that I might wear the robes and sword of an official and serve close to the Son of Heaven."

In the fourth year, *sinsa*, of Wu-te [621], Sŏl stealthily boarded an oceangoing ship and went to T'ang China.

—From the *Samguk sagi* 47:436

Great Master Kyunyŏ: Eleven Poems on the Ten Vows of the Universally Worthy Bodhisattva[21]

Worshiping and Honoring the Buddhas

I bow today before the Buddha,
Whom I draw with my mind's brush
O this body and mind of mine,
Strive to reach the end of the dharma realm

He who is in every mote of dust;
He who pervades every Buddha field;
He who fills the realm of dharma—
Would that I could serve him in the nine time periods.

Ah, idle body, mouth, and mind—
Approach him and be with him, unimpeded.

Rejoicing in the Merit of Others

The truth of dependent origination tells me
That illusion and enlightenment are one.
From the buddhas down to mortal men,
The other and myself are one.

Were I able to practice his virtues,
Were I able to master his ways,
I would rejoice in the merit of others;
I would rejoice in the good of others.

Ah, were I to follow in his footsteps,
How could the jealous mind be aroused?

Transfer of Merit

Would that all my merit
Might be passed on to others,
I would like to awaken them—
Those wandering in the sea of suffering.

When we attain the vast realm of dharma,
Removed karmas are jewels in dharmahood;

Since aeons ago
Bodhisattvas, too, have devoted their merit to others.

Ah, he whom I worship and I are one,
Of one body and one mind.

—From the *Kyunyŏ chŏn* 7, in Korean Tripitaka 47:260c–261b

NOTES

1. The translations of the names of Korean institutions in this text generally follow those in Ki-baik Lee, *A New History of Korea*, trans. Edward W. Wagner with Edward J. Shultz (Cambridge, MA: Harvard University Press, 1984).
2. Chin Kim, "The Silla Village Registers and Korean Legal History: A Preliminary Inquiry," *Korean Journal of Comparative Law* 7 (November 1979): 99–127.
3. Ki-baik Lee, *A New History of Korea*, 109.
4. Kim Chong Sun, "Slavery in Silla and Its Sociological and Economic Implications," in *Traditional Korea—Theory and Practice*, ed. Andrew Nahm (Kalamazoo: Center for Korean Studies, Western Michigan University, 1974), 29–43.
5. Martina Deuchler, "Thoughts on Korean Society," in *First International Conference on Korean Studies*, Ch'ŏngsin Munhwa Yon'guwŏn (Yongnam, Republic of Korea: Ch'ŏngsin Munhwa Yon'guwŏn, 1980), 643–52.
6. Martina Deuchler, *The Confucian Transformation of Korea: A Study of Society and Ideology* (Cambridge, MA: Council on East Asian Studies, Harvard University, 1992), 81.
7. Werner Sasse, "Trying to Figure Out How Kings Became Kings in Silla," *Cahiers d'Etudes Coreenes* 7 (2001): 229–41.
8. Peter Lee, ed., *Sourcebook of Korean Civilization*, vol. 1 (New York: Columbia University Press, 1993), 209.
9. Robert E. Buswell, Jr. "Imagining Korean Buddhism" in *Nationalism and the Construction of Korean Identity,* ed. Hyung Il Pai and Timothy R. Tangherlini (Berkeley: Institute of East Asian Studies, University of California Press, 1998), 73–107.
10. Ik-jin Koh, "Wonhyo and the Foundation of Korean Buddhism," *Korea Journal* 21, no. 8 (August 1981): 4–13.
11. Nha Il-Seong, "Silla's Cheomseongdae," *Korea Journal* 41, no. 4 (Winter 2001): 269–81.
12. Yi Ki-moon, "Language and Writing Systems of Traditional Korea," in *The Traditional Culture and Society of Korea: Art and Literature*, ed. Peter H. Lee (Honolulu: The Center for Korean Studies, University of Hawaii, 1975), 15–32.
13. William E. Henthorn, *A History of Korea* (New York: Free Press, 1971), 65.
14. Edwin Reischauer, *Ennin's Travel in T'ang China* (New York: Ronald Press, 1955).
15. Song Ki-ho, "Current Trends in the Research of Palhae history," *Seoul Journal of Korean Studies* 3 (December 1990): 157–74.
16. William H. McCullough, "The Heian Court, 794–1070," in *Cambridge His-*

tory of Japan, vol. 2, *Heian Japan,* ed. John Whitney Hall et al. (Cambridge, UK: Cambridge University Press, 1988), 20–96.

17. The relationship between Parhae and Korea is not fully understood. In the eighteenth century Korean scholar Yu Tŭk-kong in his *Parhae ko* argued that Parhae was a successor state to Koguryŏ and a part of Korean history. Since then, many Korean historians have regarded the eighth and ninth centuries as the period of the "Two Kingdoms."

18. C. Cameron Hurst, "The Good, the Bad and the Ugly: Personalities in the Founding of the Koryo Dynasty," *Korean Studies Forum* 7 (Summer–Fall 1981): 109–25.

19. Kenneth H. J. Gardiner, "Korea in Transition: Notes on the Three Later Kingdoms (900–935)," *Papers on Far Eastern History* 36 (September 1987): 139–61.

20. Peter H. Lee and William Theodore De Bary, eds., *Sources of Korean Traditions,* vol 1., *From Early Times Through the Sixteenth Century* (New York: Columbia University Press, 1997), 27.

21. Lee and De Bary, *Sources of Korean Traditions,* vol. 1, 114–16. Kyunyŏ (923–973) was a monk who revived the Flower Garland school of Buddhism. His collected works include eleven poems written in the *hyanch'al* system and are among the surviving twenty-five poems in this early form of writing in Korean.

4

Koryŏ

THE NEW KORYŎ STATE

The disunity of Korea in the tenth century was short-lived and soon the peninsula was reunited under the Wang Kŏn. He named the state Koryŏ after Koguryŏ, the ancient state that ruled the northern part of the peninsula as well as parts of Manchuria. The English name Korea is derived from Koryŏ. The Wang dynasty he founded in 918 ruled all of the peninsula for the better part of five centuries from 935 to 1392, making it among the longer-reigning dynasties in world history and inaugurating a sense of stability and continuity in Korean history. Under Koryŏ the peoples of Korea became integrated into a single, distinctive culture and society to a far greater extent than under Silla. In fact, it may not be too much to say that a truly Korean society and ethnicity that was coterminous to the state emerged during this time.

Toward the end of the ninth century and the early tenth century as centralized rule broke down, Korea became in effect a land where local military warlords ruled. Considering the rugged mountainous terrain of Korea, the strength of local traditions, and the great difficulty that even the ablest of Silla's rulers had in trying to create a centralized state in the face of powerful aristocratic clans, the disintegration of the Silla is not surprising. What is more surprising is how quickly Korea was reunified in the tenth century under Wang Kŏn. Several factors help explain this. Silla left a two-century legacy of unified, bureaucratic government that may have become accepted as the norm. Furthermore, under the Silla a strong cultural unity among the peoples of the peninsula emerged, although it is difficult to gauge its extent or depth. Korea was also influenced by outside events. The nomad threat posed by the Khitans (or Qidan), a proto-Mongol group that emerged as dominant in Manchuria in the tenth century, made the need for a centralized authority more obvious. Korea may have also been influenced by the model of a strong unified state that Tang presented, a model reinforced by the reunification of China by the Song in 960.

Wang Kŏn's new state was far from a strong centralized bureaucratic state, however, but was rather an alliance of warlords. Much of the work in creating a strong, centralized kingdom was left to his successors during the next two centuries. It was a slow process of building effective state institutions and creating an elite class that owed its prime allegiance to the dynasty. The result was largely successful in that Wang and his successors created a kingdom that lasted for a nearly half a millennium and that was inherited largely intact by the Yi dynasty that ruled for another five centuries. Together the two dynasties ruled a state that forged its inhabitants into one of the most homogeneous peoples in the world, a people with a strong sense of cultural identity and historical consciousness.

Wang Kŏn's base was in the Kaesŏng area, meaning the Imjin and Yesŏng basin area and the adjacent coastal area. There is some doubt about his real name since Wang Kŏn simply means "kingly founder," but it is believed that he was from a prominent local family with military and merchant connections. His grandfather reportedly was a merchant and his father a military naval commander. The name Koryŏ suggests that the new dynasty saw itself as a successor to the old Koguryŏ. Certainly the name still symbolized power and greatness in Northeast Asia at that time. Wang Kŏn established his capital at Kaesŏng, a more centrally located city to the north of the Han River. Soon after establishing his capital at Kaesŏng he made P'yŏngyang his secondary capital, naming it Sŏgyŏng (Western Capital), further suggesting the link between the once formidable state and the new kingdom. Perhaps he also sought to draw upon the geomantic power of the ancient city as well. But Koryŏ was strictly a peninsular state, possessing none of the Manchurian lands of its earlier namesake.

Major changes in government and society took place that marked Koryŏ as more than simply a change of ruling houses, yet there was also a great deal of continuity. The dynastic founder Wang Kŏn sought to underline this continuity and establish himself as the legitimate successor to Silla. He did this by marrying into the Kyŏngju Kim family of Silla and by incorporating many elite families of Silla into the power structure of Koryŏ. Indeed it would be more accurate to consider Koryŏ as a reformulation of the Silla state rather than a radical break in Korean history. Wang Kŏn took great care to establish his state as the legitimate successor to Silla, pensioning off the last king, appointing members of the Silla aristocracy to positions in the new state, and taking two members of the Silla royal family as consorts. Later Korean historians would largely accept this claim that Koryŏ was the successor to Silla, and that the "Mandate of Heaven" had simply been passed on to a new dynasty.

One of the dynastic founder's primary tasks was to consolidate power over a land where local families had their own powerful armies. In fact, the early Koryŏ was as much a confederation of powerful warlords and aristocratic families as a centralized state.[1] To establish his authority Wang claimed the Mandate of Heaven, the Chinese practice in which authority was legitimized by asserting that the ruler governed with Heaven's blessing. His invocation of Heaven's authority is reflected in the reign name he chose, Ch'ŏnsu (Heaven-Given). To further establish his authority he formed alliances with powerful warlords and prominent members of the old Silla aristocracy, including the Silla royal family, acquiring twenty-nine wives in total. His death in 943 consequently created succession problems due to the vast number of in-laws jockeying for power. Wang Kŏn's philosophy of government is summed up in his Ten Injunctions, which sought to promote Buddhism as a protective cult and warned against appointment of people from Paekche (see below). He sought the protection of the spirits of the land and was concerned that Buddhism be supported. His injunctions made it clear that while China was to be looked to as a model, Korea had its own customs and should not imitate the Chinese unnecessarily. In contrast to China, the seminomadic tribal peoples of the north, the injunctions state, were barbarians and their customs should never be copied at all.

The Wang court initially held little direct power over the countryside, where control was in the hands of local lords with their private armies and their walled towns. In realistic recognition of the entrenched power of these lords, the central government appointed them as officials in their home areas. Gradually the Koryŏ developed a *kun-hyŏn* (prefecture-county) system of local administration. Under this system the more powerful aristocrats headed *yŏng* (control prefectures) and control counties, occupied the local offices in administrative units, and also collected taxes from the less powerful families that held offices in the *sok* (subordinate prefectures) and counties. It was an odd arrangement that had no Chinese precedent. Most likely the system reflected the hierarchical order of local aristocrats who actually governed the countryside. The bone-rank system was replaced by the *pon'gwan* (clan-seat) system. Under this system aristocratic clans were identified by their place of origin. This clan-seat system closely linked aristocrats with a particular area where they generally held the key local offices.

The fragility of the new state was evident by the succession struggle after Wang's death. He named his eldest son, Mu, as his heir in 921. By the time of Wang Kŏn's death his son, who reigned as King Hyejong (r. 943–945), had long prepared for the assumption of his father's position. Yet he had to defend his throne against Wang Kyu, one of the powerful warlords whom Wang Kŏn had sought alliances with through marriage. Wang Kyu had married two daughters to Wang Kŏn and supported a grandson by one of these marriages for the throne. Hyejong died after only two years on the throne and his brother Chŏngjong (r. 945–949) defeated Wang Kyu and ended the rebellion.[2] But the private armies threatened the stability of the state. To counter the private armies of great aristocrats Chŏngjong created the Kwang-gun (Resplendent Army), an important step in consolidating royal power.

The fourth Koryŏ king, Kwangjong (r. 949–975), took further measures to consolidate monarchical power. He created a large military force from the provinces loyal to him, declared himself *hwangje* (emperor), and renamed Kaesŏng the Imperial Capital (Hwangdo). This was an unusual step since Koreans generally accepted the idea that there was only one emperor, the Chinese emperor. Not until 1897 would a Korean king again claim the imperial title. The pretension was abandoned when the Song dynasty was able to reassert Chinese authority in the region. In 956, Kwangjong issued a Slave Investigation Act aimed at determining those who had been illegally or unfairly enslaved during the Later Three Kingdoms period. During that time many peasants had been captured as prisoners of war, while others had fallen into debt, and in both cases they had become slaves. The king sought to reduce the power of the great lords by limiting the number of their slaves and returning the freed peasants to the tax rolls. Kwangjong also carried out bloody purges among the high aristocracy. In 960, he launched a purge of powerful aristocrats who held posts as Meritorious Subjects. Under Wang Kŏn and his immediate successors many individuals who had aided or allied with the monarchs as they established the new state or who helped them secure their throne had been granted the post of Meritorious Subject as a reward. The purge was designed to reduce their number and influence.

The next king, Kyŏngjong (975–981), abandoned the imperial pretension but strengthened the central government by issuing the *chŏnsi-kwa* (Field and Woodland) system. This was a system by which officials were given fixed incomes from designated lands according to rank. By providing support for officials the Field and Woodland system helped to transform the government from an aristocratic confederation into a central bureaucracy of officials recruited by and loyal to the throne.[3] Another early step in consolidating state power was carried out by Sŏngjong (981–997), who created among other institutions a Finance Commission (*Samsa*) to handle financial affairs, the Hallim Academy to draft royal edicts, and an inspectorate, the *Ŏsadae*, to check on the conduct of officials.

After early experiments with different types of institutions Koryŏ adopted the Tang Three Chancelleries system. The *Samsŏng* (Three Chancel-lories) were the chief administrative organs of the Koryŏ state. The *Chung-sŏsŏng* (Secretariat) was responsible for drafting policy, the *Munhasŏng* (Chancellory) reviewed policy, and the *sangsŏsŏng* (Secretariat for State Affairs) was responsible for executing policies through the *Yukpu* (Six Min-istries). Following the Chinese practice the six ministries were war, rituals (that included foreign affairs), finance, personnel, punishments, and public works. Heads of the Secretariat of State Affairs were often concurrently heads of the six ministries, but their positions were less prestigious than those of the directors of the first two chancellories. The first two formed a *Chungsŏ Munhasŏng* (combined Secretariat-Chancellory) under a *Munhasijung* (supreme chancellor), the highest of all officials. Officials were divided Chinese-style into nine grades. At the top of this hierarchy were the eight first- and second-grade officials of the *Chungsŏ-Munhasŏng* who become known as the *chaesin* or *chaesang*. Another important organ was the *Ch'ungch'uwŏn* (Royal Secretariat, later called the *Ch'umirwŏn*), which was responsible for military affairs and for transmitting royal orders. The top-ranking officials of the *Ch'ungch'uwŏn* formed a lesser elite group known as the *ch'usin*.

This complex system of administration was closely modeled on the administration of Tang China. Indeed, Koryŏ adhered much closer to the Tang model of administration than Silla did. But in reality Koryŏ functioned quite differently. In practice, the distinctions between the various organs of government were less sharply defined than in China. Furthermore, unlike China where members of nonaristocratic families and eunuchs held key positions, the government of Koryŏ was dominated by the members of the great pedigreed families. In what was a common Korean pattern, effective decision making was carried out by these men in the form of councils of high-ranking officials. These were represented in the *chaesin* and *ch'usin* elite officialdom, who collectively became known as the *Chaech'u* or Privy Council that met at joint sessions. Later in the dynasty the top council was called the *Todang*. The Three Chancelleries were typical of the councilor organs that characterized policy making and administration in premodern Korea. The desire to achieve positions on the Three Chancelleries and to be able to participate in the key *Todang* policy making sessions led to intense competition among the major aristocratic families.

Another characteristic of this system was civilian dominance. Military officers were drawn from military lineages that had less prestige than civilian lineages. The top military post was the *ang changgun* (grand general), whose rank was only senior third-grade, lower than the second-grade rank of the *chaesin* and *ch'usin*. In times of crisis civilians were given military commands. The division of officialdom into civil and military lines resulted in tensions that emerged in the political upheavals of the twelfth century.

A significant innovation of the early Koryŏ was the introduction of the *kwagŏ* or civil service examinations in 958. Until its abolition in 1894 this was a key institution in Korea for recruiting and appointing officials. Although Silla experimented with civil service exams, they only became significant when they were reintroduced in the tenth century. The civil examination system was developed in China in the first centuries C.E. and became an important avenue for recruiting officials under the Tang dynasty. Its purpose was in part to free the Chinese emperors from reliance on powerful aristocrats for their officials by selecting talented men from the provinces. In theory the exams were open to all commoners, and in practice too members of nonelite families often rose to high positions. It was also based on the Confucian ideal that the state should be ruled by men of merit. Although not all officials in China were recruited through this method, it gradually came to undermine the power and status of the old aristocracy, replacing it with a merit-based service elite of scholar-officials. In Korea, the civil examinations were less a tool for the recruitment of officials than a means of training members of the aristocratic elite for government office. Thus they did not undermine the old landowning aristocratic class but helped to transform it into a service nobility that needed to validate its status by producing sons who scored well in the state examinations.

King Kwangjong established the civil examination system as part of his effort to consolidate monarchical control over the state. He was assisted by a Chinese advisor, Shuang Ji (Korean: Ssang Ki). Shuang Ji was an official of the Later Zhou dynasty that controlled northern China just prior to the reunification under the Song dynasty. He came to Korea in 956 as part of a Later Zhou embassy, fell ill, and stayed behind. Apparently impressed by his erudition and administrative knowledge, Kwangjong persuaded him to stay on in Korea as an advisor. With Shuang Ji's help the king organized the first civil service exams in 958.[4] Three men were chosen on the basis of their mastery of the Chinese classics and two chosen on their demonstration of literary skills, and two others passed an examination on geomancy. It was a modest beginning for an institution that would eventually transform the character of the aristocracy.

Koryŏ's civil service system was primarily modeled after that of Tang. There were three types of *kwagŏ*: the *chesul ŏp* (Composition Examination), the *myŏnggyŏngŏp* (Classics Examination), and the *chap ŏp* (Miscellaneous Examinations). In the Composition Examination the examinees were tested on their skill in various Chinese literary forms such as poetry, rhyme prose, and sacrificial odes, and in writing problem-solving essays. The Classics Examination tested the candidates' knowledge of Chinese classics. Less prestigious than the first two were the Miscellaneous Examinations that were used to find officials with knowledge in such areas as law, medicine, divination, and geomancy. Of the two prestige degrees the Composition Examination was by far the most popular. From its implementation in 958 to the end of the dynasty four centuries later 252 exams were given; over 6,000 received the composition degree and about 450 the classics degree.[5]

The *kwagŏ* never served as the sole or even primary method of recruiting officials during the Koryŏ; most still owed their position to family connections rather than success in examinations. Higher-ranking officials, for example, held the *ŭm* privilege by which their sons received automatic appointment to office. The exams did, however, establish the principle of rule by merit and provided an avenue for the rise in power and status for some aristocrats, including some from minor families. Furthermore, the exams were important in enhancing one's prestige; even men from powerful families often took the exam. One study shows that during the period from 1070 to 1146, twenty-four of fifty-seven men who held the supreme and associate chancellor posts were examination graduates, five were protection beneficiaries, and five were from military, clerical, or palace backgrounds. The rest were of unknown background. Ten had served as examiners or *tong chignong-go* (associate examiners).[6] Although some of humble background may have risen to high office through the exams, it most likely that they functioned as a way of selecting offices among competing members of elite families. The civil exams were in theory a method of selecting the ablest officials to serve the state; they also had the effect of establishing the loyalty of officials to the ruler and the bureaucracy that served him. They also promoted literacy among the elite. Many Koreans identified the civil examination system as a mark of their land's civilized attainment. They had successfully emulated China or even surpassed it in this respect. A famous writer and official of the thirteenth century and successful exam passer said, "The success achieved in recruiting men of merit [through the examination system] under our dynasty cannot be matched even by [that of golden age of] Yao and Shun."[7]

Throughout the Koryŏ period a concern for education grew as a means of preparing men for the examinations and of promoting Confucian learning and moral training. To aid in this task a national academy, the *Kukchagam*, was established in 982. More important was the role played by private schools. In 1055 Ch'oe Ch'ung, a distinguished official who held many top posts, retired at the age of seventy-four and established a school, the Nine Course Academy, that trained young men for the civil exams and government service. Ch'oe became known as the "Confucius of Korea," and his school produced many of the kingdom's leading officials and scholars. Following his example other high-ranking officials established schools until there were twelve, which became known as the *Sibi to* (Twelve Assemblies). The bureaucracy became dominated by their students. To further ensure a supply of educated officials and to provide an alternative to these schools, King Injong in 1127 ordered that each *chu* (large districts) and *hyŏn* (district) establish a school, but schooling remained largely a private affair for sons of the elite.

Local administration was in the effective hands of local aristocratic families. Koryŏ rulers made attempts to create a Chinese-style regional administration, but had great difficulty in penetrating their governance to the local level. An early attempt to adopt the Tang system of dividing the country into *dao* (administrative circuits) under appointed officials was abandoned. Another attempt at orderly local administration was made by creating eight regions headed by an appointed official called the *moksa*. By the early twelfth century the eight original circuits were recreated, each administered by an *anch'alsa* (appointed governor). These formed the basis of the eight provinces of Korea today. Real power was at the local level, following the Chinese practice of dividing the countryside into prefectures and counties. But in practice the local county and prefecture officials were simply the local aristocratic lords. Gradually, however, the state gained more control over the countryside. By 1170, the central government appointed perhaps half the prefectural and county heads.[8] The slow process of appointing royal officials to local posts, along with the system of control and subordinate counties, meant that the countryside was ruled in a hierarchical fashion, with weaker regional lords under the control of greater ones. The latter in turn had their power recognized by the king with the appointment of official title such as prefectural head. *Sŏri* (central clerk) positions were often filled by sons of local officials, and this became a route to the ranks of the regular bureaucracy. Increasingly men were drawn from the countryside to the capital as the offices of the central government grew in prestige and in real power.

The state supported itself primarily by the Field and Woodland system. Under this system land was divided into *kongjŏn* (public land), whose tax receipts went to the central government, and *sajŏn*, which referred to land assigned to various classes of persons who provided services to the state. *Sajŏn* is sometimes referred to as "private land," but it was probably state-owned land for which people were allowed to collect rents. In theory at least these lands reverted to the state upon the death of an official. In practice, they were passed down in families over generations, becoming in effect private. Some smaller plots of land were made hereditary to families of deceased officials. Officials also received salaries paid in rice. Since there was a big difference between the theory of central and local bureaucratic power and the reality of aristocratic rule and authority, the Field and Woodland system was in practice different from its formal structure. It was probably little more than a legal confirmation of private land holdings of the elite or de facto tax exemptions on lands owned by the elite. Koryŏ also continued the Silla practice of assigning certain locales known as *so* to produce items of special economic importance such as gold, silver, paper, and porcelain. Other agricultural lands were assigned for the support of various government agencies, military camps, and schools

The Koryŏ state modeled many of its formal institutions and nomenclature on Tang rather than on the contemporary Song state. China experienced a great cultural resurgence under the Song (960–1279), which modified many of the institutions of government; and it evolved into a very different society, less aristocratic, with greater social mobility. The Song state also made far less use of Buddhism to legitimize itself and saw a great revitalization of Confucianism. Koryŏ did not follow this pattern. Partly this was due to the fact that Korea's contact with Song was more sporadic than it had been with Tang. This in turn was a result of Song's military weakness, that left Korea's immediate frontier in the hands of powerful seminomadic Khitan and Jurchen (or Ruzhen) peoples. Furthermore, the Tang impacted the society of Korea when it was at an earlier, more formative stage of political and social development. Korea's own native worship, patterns of marriage and kinship, and cultural traditions may also have coincided more with those of China in Tang times. Of course Song culture and its diplomacy did exercise considerable influence on Korea. Yet the Koryŏ dynasty with its attachment to Buddhism, its rule by great aristocratic families, and its adherence to Tang political institutions remained quite distinct from Song China.

KORYŎ IN EAST ASIA

Koryŏ's great external challenge was dealing with its northern frontier. The tenth-century upheaval resulted in a great influx of peoples from Manchuria to the Yalu and Tumen Rivers. Some of them entered the peninsula. The most troublesome of the new peoples along the frontier were the Khitan. The Khitan helped bring about the collapse of Parhae in 926, then laid claim to its land. They also claimed to be the heirs of Koguryŏ. For Wang Kŏn and his successors these tribal peoples posed a threat to their efforts to consolidate Koryŏ's position on the frontier. Wang Kŏn made his hostility to the Khitans clear when in 942 they sent envoys with fifty camels as gifts. He banished the envoys to an island and let the camels starve. His successor, King Chŏngjong, planned to move the capital to P'yŏngyang and created the armed force called the Kwanggun (Resplendent Army) to prepare against Khitan invasions. As part of the effort to expand northward, the Koreans from 949 to 975 established garrison forts beyond Ch'ŏngch'ŏn River.

The Khitan meanwhile created the state of Liao on the northern borders of China that ruled much of Manchuria. The Liao ruler Shenzong (983–1031) led a series of campaigns against the Song that ended with the Treaty of Shanyuan in 1005. Under this treaty the Chinese emperor recognized the frontier state as an equal. At the same time they were fighting the Chinese, the Khitans began to tighten their pressure on Koryŏ. In 993, the Khitan ruler Xiao Sunning led an invasion force. This invasion resulted in negotiations with the Koreans and a brief period of nonhostile relations began. The Koreans built six garrisons on the Yalu River, establishing it as their northern boundary for the first time. But the Khitan demanded that Koryŏ turn over the six garrisons to them. When Koryŏ refused, the Khitan emperor, Shenzong, launched another invasion in 1010. Initially Koryŏ under Yang Hyu was victorious, but an overconfident general Kang Cho was defeated and the invaders burnt Kaesŏng. King Hyŏnjong fled south and then agreed to pay homage in person at the Khitan court. Koryŏ did not fulfill this promise, which led to the invasion of 1018 under the Khitan leader Xiao Paiya. The Koreans defeated this force at Kuju fortress under the military command of Kang Kam-ch'an. According to the Korean chroniclers only a few thousand of the one hundred thousand Khitan invaders survived. Whatever the true scale of victory, it was not enough for Koryŏ to avoid submitting to the powerful invaders from the north. Korea kept its independence but was forced to pay tribute to the Khitan state of Liao.

After 1022, Koryŏ raised a corvée of three hundred thousand to reconstruct the destroyed capital and finished it seven years later. Between 1033 and 1044 the Koreans constructed a long wall and fortifications against the Khitans and another northeastern Asian tribal group, the Jurchens (or Ruzhen). Meanwhile, despite its resistance, Korea was forced to not only pay tribute to the powerful Liao state but in 994 to adopt the Liao calendar. Thus in effect the kingdom became a tributary state of Liao as it had in the past been a tributary of Tang. These were simply concessions to reality; the Koreans continued to regard the Khitan as barbarians. After 1054 the Liao yoke over Korea lightened and there appears to have been no tribute after that date.

The Khitan cut Korea off from the militarily weak but prosperous and culturally dynamic Song. Because of the existence of the powerful and hostile Liao state between them, there was little direct contact between Korea and China for a century. Taking advantage of a lessening of Liao militancy, China opened relations with Koryŏ in 1062. For a while, considerable trade flourished between China and Korea, enabling Koreans to participate in some of the intellectual and cultural activities in China. China sought to bring Korea into its tributary system, but relations between the two were not especially close. Partly this was because Korean-Chinese relations were complicated by the fact that Korea was a tributary of the Liao. Fearing close relations with China that might arouse Khitan hostility, the Koreans appear to have been cautious and selective in their relations with their great continental neighbor. There was a suspicion of Korea among the Chinese officials as well, some of whom saw the country as a potential ally of the Khitans and Jurchens. Some Song officials complained that vital information given to Korean embassies could find their way to the Khitan; consequently they restricted the Koreans' access to books.

Koryŏ was part of the network of trade that linked northeast Asia. The government established regulated markets in the northwest with Liao and in the northeast with Jurchen tribes. On its northern border Koryŏ supplied grain, iron, agricultural implements, and weapons to the Khitans and Jurchen peoples in exchange for horses. Koreans also carried out an active trade with Japan, importing folding fans and swords. After the reopening of relations with Song, trade with China greatly overtook that with Japan and the Manchurian-Siberian frontier in volume. Korean merchants sailed to the Song ports of Gwangzhou, Quanzhou, Hongzhou, and Mingzhou. Quanzhou merchants took the initiative in reestablishing trade. In 1078, Song sent two "divine ships," which were given a tumultuous welcome in Korea.[9] Most merchants traveled on Chinese vessels, although some trade was conducted on Koryŏ ships, mostly to the north China port of Dengzhou. The voyage from Mingzhou to the Hŭksan Islands off the northwestern coast of Korea took three weeks; from there it took several days along the Korean coast to reach Yesŏng. The voyage was dangerous and frequently resulted in wrecks.[10] Yet it could be highly profitable. Koreans imported Chinese teas, lacquerware, books, medicines, ceremonial robes, and a variety of luxury goods. Korea's most important import was probably porcelain. Merchants from Fujian in southern China sailed to Korea in large ships loaded with the highly prized products from their kilns. Even Arab merchants arrived in Korea from China to trade in 1024 and 1025. Koryŏ exports were copper, gold, silver, utensils, ginseng, pine nuts, silks, ramie cloth, paper, furs, and even horses. The balance of trade seemed to favor China, but this is not certain.[11] This foreign trade was a stimulus to commercial development. Major towns had permanent marketplaces, and in the thirteenth century Kaesŏng is reported to have had over one thousand shops and stalls. A government bureau regulated weights and measures.

The era of active foreign trade and contact came to an end with the rise of a new seminomadic power on the northern frontier, the Jurchens. The Jurchens created the state of Jin, conquered the Khitan in 1126, and then conquered northern China in 1127. Interestingly, the Jurchens claimed Koguryŏ ancestry. This testified to the reputation of Koguryŏ, but it also suggested that Jurchen ambitions included the peninsula. In response to this new threat Korea in the early twelfth century created a special military force, the *Pyŏlmuban,* to deal with the Jurchen challenge. After an internal debate the Koreans established a tributary relationship with the Jurchen state of Jin and broke off relations with China. The period that followed was a peaceful one on the northern frontier, allowing the Koreans to concentrate on their own domestic developments. Not surprisingly, during this period of relative isolation and external calm, Korean political and cultural institutions moved somewhat further away from the Chinese model. Another important result of this peaceful period was that it led to a further downgrading of the military and the ascendancy of civil officials. The decline of the military's prestige led to the 1170 coup that can be seen as a delayed reaction to these events (see next chapter).

INTERNAL POLITICS 935–1170

Politics in Koryŏ centered on competition between powerful clans for high offices in government. Studies indicate that a small number of clans held a large percentage of high offices in the period from 981 to 1146. Some of these clans were of Silla true-bone origin such as the Kyŏngju Kim, Kangnŭng Kim, and P'yŏngsan Pak. These were among the greatest producers of high officials. But leading clans came from all parts of the kingdom, indicating that the early Koryŏ state sought to win support from the aristocracy throughout the country. It also showed that the elite was being integrated into a common society, helping to establish a common social order and common culture.

One of the themes of Koryŏ history during the first two centuries was the attempts by the dynastic government in the capital to gain greater control over the countryside. Another was the intrigue among powerful clans. The problem of containing the power of great clans was compounded by the practice begun by Wang Kŏn of marrying members of the royal family into these clans to cement alliances with them. The result was powerful in-law families that could threaten the dynasty. In the early eleventh century, the Ansan Kim clan achieved a degree of dominance when an aristocrat, Kim Ŭn-bu, married three of his daughters to King Hyŏnjong (r. 1009–1031). After dominating the court for half a century the power of the Ansan Kim clan was eclipsed by that of the Kyŏngwŏn Yi. In the middle of the eleventh century, a member of that clan, Yi Cha-yŏn, emerged as the dominant figure in the government. He bound the royal family to his by marrying three daughters to King Munjong (r. 1046–1083). The Kyŏngwŏn Yi thereafter produced by far the most officials and continued to marry into the royal family. The clan grew in power until it posed a threat to the throne. In 1095, the clan leader Yi Cha-ŭi attempted to dethrone the king and replace him with a son of King Sŏnjong by Yi's sister, but he failed and was removed from power. Again in 1127, another leader of the clan, Yi Cha-gyŏm, purged many opponents and tried to depose the teenage King Injong (r. 1123–1146), who was both his son-in-law and grandson. His plan was to place himself on the throne with the aid of less illustrious clans, including new arrivals from the countryside. Rivals defeated Yi Cha-gyŏm and his clan fell from power.[12]

As happened so often in Korean history, factional rivalry during the Koryŏ was aggravated by external threats and tensions. Yi Cha-gyŏm attempted to align the dynasty with the rising Jurchen state of Jin in Manchuria and Northern China. Accordingly he sent an envoy to the Jin in 1126 following the Jin conquest of Liao. His opponents wanted to maintain good relations with Song rather than submit to yet another northern barbarian state. Yi was eventually overthrown but his realistic policy of acknowledging the power of the Manchuria-based empire that was gaining control over the northern half of China prevailed. The fall of the Kyŏngwŏn Yi shifted power to a number of northwestern-based clans that aimed at moving the capital near the northern frontier at P'yŏngyang. This group remained hostile to

Jin. They were led by the monk Myoch'ŏng, who used *fengshui* (Korean: *p'ungsu*) theory to argue that the geomantic forces around the captital of Kaesŏng had waned but that those of P'yŏngyang were strong. Myoch'ŏng urged the king to move there, declare himself emperor, and launch an attack on the Jin. When his effort failed he and his supporters attempted to establish a new state called Taewi in 1135, but this revolt was destroyed by forces loyal to the dynasty that included the Confucian scholar and historian Kim Pu-sik. Koryŏ then refrained from military adventurism.

To deal with the growing number of competing clans the number of top officials was increased, and the councils of aristocrats such as the privy council swelled in number, the latter eventually having seventy *Chaech'u* officials. Competition was aggravated by men from the *hyangni*, the local hereditary elite, seeking central government offices. Meanwhile there was growing domestic tension between the dominant lineages that supplied civil officials and the lineages that supplied the less prestigious and less influential military officials that resulted in a military uprising in 1170 (see next chapter). While all this gives an impression of constant political tension, it is important to note that politics was a struggle among great aristocratic families for power and privilege; it had little to do with most ordinary nonaristocratic peoples. As for the common people we hear little of them in the historical records except for an occasional peasant uprising.

KORYŎ CULTURE

The introduction of the civil exams in 958 did much to foster the spread of Confucianism in Korea. Exam questions included some from the *Analects* and the *Classic of Filial Piety*. Eventually scholars established twelve private academies known as the Twelve Assemblies to spread Confucian teaching as well as to educate the aristocratic youth. Some Confucian scholars became famous in the early Koryŏ. Among them was the eleventh-century teacher Ch'oe Ch'ung, who became known as "the Confucius of Korea." Confucianism, with its stress on order, hierarchy, and the importance of good government led by an enlightened monarch, was appealing to the state and was promoted by it.

While Confucianism was important in shaping ideas of government and morality, Koryŏ was very much a Buddhist kingdom in the sense that Buddhist ceremonies and rituals were at the center of social and cultural life. The state sought to utilize the power of the Buddha and bodhisattvas (Buddhist saints) to protect it from invasions and natural calamities. Most monks protected the kingdom through prayers and rituals, but there were also warrior monks who fought for it. Some of the most effective fighters against the Mongols in the thirteenth century and against the Japanese in the sixteenth century were monks. Accordingly, the court generously patronized Buddhist temples. Buddhist holidays punctuated the year as times of national celebration. Well supported by the state, a vigorous Buddhist intellectual life flourished. Buddhist thought and practice was roughly divided into Kyo (Textual) and Sŏn (Contemplative) schools. Each school had a hierarchy of Buddhist officials and its own set of examinations modeled on the state civil exams. The highest ranks among Buddhist officials were Royal Preceptor and National Preceptor. Both held enormous prestige.

Korean Buddhism was characterized by greater concern for unity than was found in Chinese or Japanese Buddhism. When Buddhism arrived in Korea from China, it was part of an established tradition divided into many different doctrinal traditions and practices. The diversity of Buddhism in China reflected both the richness and the diversity of Indian and Central Asian Buddhism, and the diversity and vitality of Chinese civilization. But Korea was a much smaller country, more homogeneous and conscious of its comparable smallness and its vulnerability to invasion. Partly for this reason, Koreans frequently sought unity in intellectual thought. A tendency toward syncretism appeared as early as Silla with Wŏnhyo. In the early half of the Koryŏ period the most important effort at bringing the schools of Buddhism together was undertaken by Ŭich'ŏn (1055–1101), fourth son of King Munjong (r. 1046–1083), known posthumously as Master Taegak. Ŭich'ŏn sought to compile as complete a set of Buddhist sacred works as possible in order to create a vast library of all known Buddhist wisdom. Against the wishes of his father he surreptitiously traveled to Song China in 1085, where he collected more than three thousand treatises and commentaries. He dispatched agents to China, Japan, and Khitan Liao to gather more Buddhist texts. He eventually had woodblocks carved for 1,010 Buddhist texts that were intended to supplement the *Tripitaka Koreana* (the complete Buddhist canon) that was also published. Unfortunately this vast collection of texts, along with the first edition of the *Tripitaka Koreana,* was destroyed in the 1231–1232 Mongol invasion. As he gathered his great collection he also attempted to merge the Sŏn schools of meditative Buddhism and the five Kyo textual or scholastic sects into Ch'ŏnt'ae (Chinese: Tiantai; Japanese: Tendai). Ch'ŏnt'ae was not a new Buddhist teaching. It was known in Silla times, and in 960 the monk Ch'egwan went to China where he became one of its masters. But it had not been an independent sect before Ŭich'ŏn. Despite royal patronage and the enormous respect he had acquired as a pious and learned man, Ŭich'ŏn's efforts to unify Korean Buddhism failed. Instead his activities resulted in still another flourishing sect.[13]

Buddhist ecclesiastical organizations were wealthy. Temples owned extensive holdings in land and slaves. Exempted from taxation these temples, which were also monasteries since monks and nuns lived year round in them, grew to become wealthy and play a major role in economic life. Temples

engaged in trade, wine making, and grain and money lending. The problem
of monasteries possessing a considerable amount of land and many slaves, all
exempt from taxes, came to worry state officials. Later in the dynasty it
would contribute to anti-Buddhist sentiment. Aristocratic families used temples as a means of extending their power by sending off sons to them. These
were often younger sons not needed to supervise the family estates. As
monks they advised the officials, served at court, and carried considerable
influence. Kings and officials also complained that too many peasants were
taking up orders, thereby depriving the state of military conscripts and productive farmers. To avoid some of these abuses the state promulgated laws
restricting the number of peasants who could become monks, barring children of monks who had married before they had taken vows from sitting for
the monk exams, and prohibiting monks from staying overnight outside of
the monasteries.[14]

In addition to Buddhism, Koreans believed in the hidden spiritual power
of prominent features of nature such as rivers, rocks, and especially mountains. From at least the thirteenth century the most sacred mountain was
Paektusan on the Korean-Manchurian border. Other mountains, such as
Chirisan in the southern part of the country, were also venerated. This worship of nature was blended with geomantic ideas imported from China. In
the twelfth century the Chinese visitor Xu Jing stated of the Koreans that "it
is their habit to make excessive sacrifices to spirits."[15] Shamanism was also
widely practiced. However, Koryŏ elites were often critical of shamanism,
accusing it of sponsoring vulgar and indecent rituals. Thus while Buddhism
ceased to be an elite religion and instead was practiced by every sector of
Korean society, a new religious boundary emerged during Koryŏ between
the elite and commoners. The common people sought the solace of shamans
as well as of Buddhist monks while the educated aristocrats turned away
from them, at least publically. To this day shamanism has been treated with
disdain, and more recently as an embarrassing part of their cultural heritage,
by middle- and upper-class Koreans while it has continued to maintain a
strong hold on many of the less educated and poor.

The aristocracy read and memorized Chinese poetry and wrote verse in
Chinese, the literary language of the elite. Tang and Song poets were
immensely popular. Koreans wrote poems in their style. Koryŏ aristocrats
sometimes left collections of their literary writings that often included both
prose essays and large numbers of poems. Noted writer and scholar Yi Kyu-
bo (1168–1241), for example, left 1,500 poems. Poems in the vernacular were
popular but were mostly sung or recited orally. Derived from folk songs,
they were often bawdy and satirical. Only a few were written down after the
invention of the phonetic alphabet in the fifteenth century, and even some
of these may have been edited to conform to the more prudish taste of later

times. Among the best known are *Ch'ŏngsan pyŏlgok (Song of Green Moun-tain)* and *Ssanghwa chŏm (The Dumpling Shop)*.

As in Silla Buddhism remained a major inspiration for art. A rich tradition of Buddhist paintings in the form of wall paintings, hanging scrolls, and illustrated manuscripts developed. Although few wall paintings have sur-vived, in recent years a number of Koryŏ period Buddhist scolls and illus-trated manuscripts have been discovered in Korea, in Japan, and in Western collections. These paintings can be distinguished from Chinese Buddhist art by the less extensive use of gold paste and by a preference for duller shades of red and green than their Chinese counterparts. The use of less bright col-ors would remain characteristic of the aristocratic art tradition in Korea. These paintings are an important source of information on the costumes of the time.[16] Secular painting and calligraphy in Chinese styles flourished. Among the most famous were the twelfth-century painters Yi Yŏng and his son Yi Kwang'p'il. Famous also were three Koryŏ calligraphers, Yu Sin (d. 1104), the monk T'anyŏn (1070–1159), and Ch'oe U (d. 1249). They became known, along with the Silla calligrapher Kim Saeng, as the "Four Worthies of Divine Calligraphy." Unfortunately, virtually all the secular paintings and calligraphy of the Koryŏ have been lost. The Silla traditions in sculpture continued in early Koryŏ. Later Koryŏ sculpture showed the influence of Lamaistic Buddhism from the Mongol court. The high standards of metal-lurgical craftsmanship continued with fine bronze and silverware. Koryŏ did not, however, produce the great bronze bells of the Silla. Since buildings were made of wood, it is not surprising that none survive from the early Koryŏ. The oldest extant wooden temple buildings are the Pongjong in Andong and the Hall of Eternal Life (Muryangsu-jŏn) at Pusok temple in Yongju, both from the thirteenth century. The latter with its tapered col-umns, three-tiered roof supports, dual roof edge, and its interior without a ceiling provides a sense of both refinement and grandeur.[17]

Perhaps the greatest of the art forms of the period was ceramics. The most famous of the ceramics of this period is a porcelaneous stoneware with a fine bluish-green glaze known by the French term celadon. Koryŏ celadon was developed early in the dynasty by potters who had imported the technique from Song China. It was produced throughout the Koryŏ period, although the quality declined from the thirteenth century. The center of celadon pro-duction was in Chŏlla in the southwest part of the peninsula. Korean potters derived a distinctive style by turning the straight lines of Song pottery into curves and the cold blue of Song into a soft greenish tone. In the twelfth century the style reached a peak of perfection when potters developed a vari-ety of innovative techniques such as painting in brown and red under the glaze and in gold over the celadon glaze. Today Koryŏ celadon is regarded as among the greatest ceramic masterpieces ever created. It is highly prized by connoisseurs in Asia and throughout the world. Korean potters also created innovative vessels in the shapes of animals and vegetables, as well as white wares, black wares, and unglazed stonewares.

KORYŎ SOCIETY

The spread of literacy encouraged by the civil exams along with the study of a common curriculum, the establishment of private schools, the gradual penetration of the state into local government, and the attraction of the capital that drew members of the elite from around the country all contributed to the creation of a shared cultural identity among the upper class. Yet even as Korea during the Koryŏ period was being integrated into a single society it maintained a three-part division that remained characteristic to the end of the nineteenth century. At the top was a hereditary aristocracy that became known as the *yangban*. The name yangban, literally the "two sides," referred to the two divisions of officials: *muban* (military officials) and the *munban* (civil officials). The term eventually was used to refer to the aristocracy from which the bureaucracy was derived. This class dominated politics, the economy, and culture. Next were commoners: some were probably small free farmers, and others were tenants working the fields of the aristocracy. A much smaller number of commoners served as merchants and skilled craftsmen. At the bottom of society were the low born. The low born consisted mostly of slaves. These were divided into public slaves owned by government agencies and private slaves owned by the aristocracy. Slaves were, along with land, a measure of elite status. How many Koreans were slaves? This is not known and estimates vary widely. The number probably fluctuated; perhaps slaves accounted for up to one-third of the population. Most worked the land of the aristocracy, but not on large estates. Large landholdings consisted of scattered parcels of land, and most slaves lived away from any direct supervision. Their living conditions probably resembled that of poor tenant farmers.

Most of the information we have on Koryŏ society is about the elite families and even here there is much that is not clearly understood. Social status was based primarily on family ancestry. This became determined not only by family surname but by the *pon'gwan* (clan-seat) system. Each family became identified with its place of origin. For example, the surname Kim was a very common one, but there were many different Kim clans with different places of origin such as the Kyŏngju Kim and the Kangnŭng Kim. The concept of a clan-seat remained a permanent feature of Korean society, and to this day Korean clans are identified in this way. Some of the Koryŏ's great clans were descended from Silla true-bone ranks such as the Kyŏngju Kim, the Kangnŭng Kim, and the P'yŏngsan Pak. A few were originally from head-rank-six families. Most, however, were descended from local strongmen who were incorporated into the Koryŏ elite. Unlike China and Japan there were no official lists of great clans, so their number is not certain. But it is clear from the records of officeholders that a small number of great families dominated society. One study found that from the mid-tenth to the mid-twelfth centuries twenty-nine elite descent groups held two-fifths of high government posts.[18] Clans, which could be very large, were divided into different lineages or segments. Some of these segments became more prominent than others. Most clans had their base in the countryside, deriving income from their estates worked by tenants and slaves. Gradually, however, some identified their status with officeholding, lived entirely in the capital, and lost ties with their rural roots. They came to form a small upper stratum of capital-based aristocracy linked together by marriages. There is some controversy over whether one inherited social status from both parents or whether social status was primarily inherited from the male side of the family. It seems clear, however, that a good marriage was key to maintaining or enhancing the status of an aristocrat, especially a marriage to a member of the royal family. Under the influence of Tang and Song China greater importance was gradually placed on the direct male lineage. Koryŏ, however, especially in earlier times, gave much more weight to the female side of the family in determining status than in China. This in turn gave greater status to women.

Compared to later periods the social position or women in Koryŏ times was high. Women could inherit property, and an inheritance was divided equally among siblings regardless of gender. A woman's property was hers and could be passed on to her children. Some women inherited homes and estates. Ownership of property often gave upper-class women considerable independence. Korean women remained to a considerable extent members of their natal families, not those of their husbands. For example, if a woman died without children her property passed on to her siblings, not to her husband. Wives were not merely servants of their husbands. Their importance was reflected in the practice of conducting marriages in the house of the bride. There was no bride wealth or dowry, and men often resided in their wives' homes after marriage. The two sexes mingled freely. The twelfth-century Chinese traveler Xu Jing was surprised by the ease with which men and women socialized.

We do not yet have a clear picture of marriage in Koryŏ.[19] Evidence suggests that marriage rules were loose. Divorce was possible, but seems to have been uncommon; separation may have been more common. Koreans may have also practiced short-term or temporary marriages; however, the evidence of this is unclear. Remarriage of widows was an accepted practice. Marriage between close kin and within the village was also probably common. Later Korean society was characterized by extreme endogamy in which marriage between people of even the remotest relationship was prohibited, but this was not yet the case in Koryŏ times. Plural marriages may have been frequent among the aristocracy. Xu Jing in 1123 said that it was common for a man to have three or four wives. Concubinage existed but it is not known how customary it was. Evidence suggests that upper-class men married at about twenty and women at about seventeen. Men lived with their wives' families until about the age of thirty. Widows as well as widowers appear to have kept their children. All this is a sharp contrast with later Korean practices (see chapter 7).

The Koryŏ elite was not strictly patrilineal. Instead members of the elite traced their families along their matrilineal lines as well. This gave importance to the wife's family since her status helped to determine that of her children. Although high status and rights of women in Koryŏ was in contrast to later Korean practice, in many ways it was similar to Japan in the Heian period (794–1192). Much less is known about either Sillan or early Koryŏ society than about Heian Japan, but it is likely that the two societies shared a number of common practices relating to family, gender, and marriage. It is possible that these practices may, in fact, be related to the common origins of the two peoples. This is still a matter of speculation; further study needs to be made before the relationship between Korea and Japan is clearly understood. Some changes took place over the nearly five centuries of the Koryŏ period. The adoption of the civil examination system in the tenth century led to careful records of family relations. At the same time the strengthening of Chinese influences resulted in the gradual adoption of the Chinese practice of forbidding marriage among members of patrilineal kin. As Koreans began to place more importance on direct male descent and the Confucian ideas of the subordination of women to men became more accepted, the position of women declined. The state, for example, enacted laws prohibiting a wife from leaving her husband without his consent. Most major changes in family and gender relations, however, took place only after the Koryŏ period.

THE *SAMGUK SAGI*

A rich tradition of historical writing existed during the Koryŏ period. The most important historical work was the *Samguk sagi* (*History of the Three Kingdoms*). The oldest extant Korean history, it was written in 1145 by Kim Pu-sik, a high court official. The *Samguk sagi* set out to give the history of the three kingdoms—Koguryŏ, Paekche, and Silla—from their founding to the end of Silla and the establishment of the Koryŏ state. An orthodox, Confucian history, the *Samguk sagi* is the most important single source for early Korean history. Much of the material is based on earlier, now lost sources, although the author seldom directly cites them. The work is an official history written in the Chinese *kijŏn* (Chinese, *jizhuan*) format, meaning it contains annals, that is, a chronological year-by-year history; treatises on various topics; and then a section of biographies. Kim with ten assistants compiled this history after collecting many sources. One hundred and twenty-three Chinese and sixty-nine Korean titles are given as sources; the most important is the *Ku samguk sa* (*Old Three Kingdoms History*), a work now lost. Adhering to the "praise and blame" concept of history, Kim Pu-sik added his personal comments on historical issues.

Following a tradition of history writing that began in China with Sima Qian's *Shiji* written over twelve centuries earlier, Kim Pu-sik viewed history as a guide to correct government and personal behavior. This East Asian tradition of history held that one can learn from the past, not just practical lessons of statecraft, but more importantly lessons on moral and ethical conduct. Modern scholars have sometimes criticized Kim's work for repressing the nativist traditions in favor of a Sinocentric Confucian view of history. It has also been criticized for excluding Parhae from Korean history and therefore placing Manchuria outside the definition of Korean history. The *Samguk sagi*, however, was not a slavishly pro-Chinese work. The author states that the work was intended to create a more accurate record of early Korean history that had not received the attention or accuracy it deserved in Chinese histories. The history also reflects the author's desire to affirm the Koryŏ dynasty as the legitimate and logical successor to the Silla state. The work also reflects the southern orientation of Kim Pu-sik, a man of Sillan descent, who led armies against Myoch'ŏng. Kim set Korean history firmly in the peninsula, with the northern Korean/southern Manchurian region of Koguryŏ and its successor Parhae marginalized. This is an important development in the evolution of a Korean ethnic identity since the *Samguk sagi* was influential in shaping Korean views of themselves and their history.

The *Samguk sagi* represents the high historical standards of the time. If translated into English (which it has not been) it would be several thick volumes long. It is an invaluable historical source for Korean history during the Three Kingdoms and Silla period. Our modern knowledge of that period, especially from the fourth to tenth centuries when the history becomes more reliable, is heavily dependent on this single source. It also reminds us how much of Korean history has been lost to us. Sadly, none of the sixty-nine Korean historical sources cited by the author exists today.

The *Samguk sagi* is also a rich source of stories, given as historical accounts not as literature, but serving as both. Especially useful is the *yŏlchŏn* (biographical) section, although there are also many good stories in the annals section. Some of these stories, especially those set in earlier times, appear to be imaginative legends, some with magical elements. For example, in one well-known story, Prince Hodong, a handsome son of the king of Koguryŏ, was offered the virgin daughter of the Chinese governor of Nangnang, but the prince refused to accept her unless she destroyed a mysterious drum-and-horn that sounded by itself at the approach of the enemy. The daughter surreptitiously destroyed the drum-and-horn and had word of her deed sent to Prince Hodong. He then had his father, the Koguryŏ king, attack the Nangnang (Lelang) capital. The governor put his daughter to death and then surrendered. In another episode, Hodong, who was the son of a secondary consort, aroused the jealousy of the queen, who feared the king would make him, not her son, the heir. She falsely accused him of making sexual advances on her. Rather than clearing his name by disgracing his father's wife and causing the king further grief he commited suicide. The commentary praises his filial piety.[20] The story represents the mixture of ancient tales whose meanings are somewhat obscure and the later Confucian gloss given them. The stories also suggest the strong warrior code of early Korea, a code that still made sense in Kim Pu-sik's time. Another example of this warrior code is the story of Wŏnsul who after a distinguished career lost a battle against the army of Tang China and returned home in disgrace. Kim Yu-sin recommended that he be beheaded for dishonoring the kingdom and his family. The king, however, pardoned him. Yet his parents refused to forgive him or even see him even after he restored his honor on the battlefield.

Wang Kŏn: Ten Injunctions[21]

I have heard that when great Shun was cultivating at Li-stan he inherited the throne from Yao. Emperor Kao-tsu of China rose from humble origins and founded the Han. I too have risen from humble origins and received undeserved support for the throne. In summer I did not shun the heat and in winter did not avoid the cold. After toiling, body and mind, for nineteen years I united the Three Han [Later Three Kingdoms] and have held the throne for twenty-five years. Now I am old. I only fear that my successors will give away to their passions and greed and destroy the principle of government. That would be truly worrisome. I therefore wrote these injunctions to be passed on to later ages. They should be read morning and night and forever used as a mirror of reflection.

His injunctions were as follows:
1. The success of every great undertaking of our state depends upon the favor and protection of Buddha. Therefore, the temples of both the Meditation and Doctrinal schools should be built and monks should be sent out to those temples to minister to Buddha. Later on, if villainous courtiers attain power and come to be influenced by the entreaties of bonzes, the temples of various schools will quarrel and struggle among themselves for gain. This ought to be prevented.

2. Temples and monasteries were newly opened and built upon the sites chosen by the monk Tosŏn according to the principles of geomancy. He

said: "If temples and monasteries are indiscriminately built at locations not chosen by me, the terrestrial force and energy will be sapped and damaged, hastening the decline of the dynasty." I am greatly concerned that the royal family, the aristocracy, and the courtiers all may build many temples and monasteries in the future in order to seek Buddha's blessings. In the last days of Silla many temples were capriciously built. As a result, the terrestrial force and energy were wasted and diminished, caused its demise. Vigilantly guard against this.

3. In matters or royal succession, succession by the eldest legitimate royal issue should be the rule. But Yao of ancient China let Shun succeed him because his own was unworthy, that was indeed putting the interests of the state ahead of one's personal feelings. Therefore, if the eldest is not worthy of the crown, let the second eldest succeed to the throne. If the second eldest, too, is unworthy, choose the brother the people consider the best qualified for the throne.

4. In the past we have always had a deep attachment for the ways of China and all of our institutions have been modeled upon those of T'ang. But our country occupies a different geographical location and our people's character is different from that of the Chinese. Hence, there is no reason to strain ourselves unreasonably to copy the Chinese way. Khitan is a nation of savage beasts, and its language and customs are also different. Its dress and institutions should never be copied.

5. I achieved the great task of founding the dynasty with the help of the elements of mountain and river of our country. The Western Capital, P'yŏngyang, has the elements of water in its favor and is the source of the terrestrial force of our country. It is thus the veritable center of dynastic enterprises for ten thousand generations. Therefore, make a royal visit to the Western Capital four times a year—in the second, fifth, eighth, and eleventh months—and reside there a total of more than one hundred days. By this means secure peace and prosperity.

6. I deem the two festivals of Yŏndŭng and P'algwan of great spiritual value and importance. The first is to worship Buddha. The second is to worship the spirit of Heaven, the spirits of the five sacred and other major mountains and rivers, and the dragon god. At some future time, villainous courtiers may propose the abandonment or modification of these festivals. No change should be allowed.

7. It is very difficult for the king to win over the people. For this reason, give heed to sincere criticism and banish those with slanderous tongues. If sincere criticisms are accepted, there will be virtuous and sagacious kings. Though sweet as honey, slanderous words should not be believed;

then they will cease of their own accord. Make use of the people's labor with their convenience in mind; lighten the burden of corvee and taxation; learn the difficulties of agricultural production. Then it will be possible to win the hearts of the people and to bring peace and prosperity to the land. Men of yore said that under tempting bait a fish hangs; under a generous reward an able general wins a victory; under a drawn bow a bird dares not fly; and under a virtuous benevolent rule a loyal people serves faithfully. If you administer rewards and punishments moderately, the interplay of yin and yang will be harmonious.

8. The topographic features of the territory south of Kongju and beyond the Kongju river are all treacherous and disharmonious; its inhabitants are treacherous and disharmonious as well. For this reason, if they are allowed to participate in the affairs of state, to intermarry with the royal family, aristocracy, and royal relatives, and to take the power of the state, they might imperil the state and injure the royal safety—grudging the loss of their own state [which used to be the kingdom of Paekche] and being resentful of the unification.

Those who have been slaves or engaged in dishonorable trades will surrender to the powerful in order to evade prescribed services. And some of them will surely seek to offer their services to the noble families, to the palaces, or to the temples. They then will cause confusion and disorder in government and engage in treason through crafty words and treacherous machinations. They should never be allowed into government service, though they may no longer be slaves and outcasts.

9. The salaries and allowance for the aristocracy and the bureaucracy have been set according to the needs of the state. They should not be increased or diminished. The classics say the salaries and allowance should be determined by the merits of those who receive them and should not be wasted for private gain. If the public treasure is wasted upon those without merit or upon one's relatives or friends, not only will the people come to resent and criticize such abuses, but those who enjoy salaries undeservedly will also not be able to enjoy them for long. Since our country shares borders with savage nations, always beware of the danger of invasions. Treat the soldiers kindly and take good care of them; lighten their burden of forced labor; inspect them every autumn; give honors and promotions to the brave.

10. In preserving a household or a state, one should always be on guard to avert mistakes. Read widely in the classics and in history; take the past as a warning for the present. The Duke of Chou was a great sage, yet he sought to admonish his nephew, King Cheng, with *Against Luxurious Ease (Wu-i)*. Post the contents of *Against Luxurious Ease* on the wall and reflect upon them when entering and leaving the room.

NOTES

1. John Duncan, *The Origins of the Chosŏn Dynasty* (Seattle: University of Washington Press, 2000), 16–19.
2. Hugh W. Kang, "The First Succession Struggle of Koryŏ, in 945: A Reinterpretation," *Journal of Asian Studies* 36, no. 3 (May 1977): 411–28.
3. Duncan, *Origins*, 40–44.
4. H. W. Kang, "Institutional Borrowing: The Case of the Chinese Civil Service Examination in Early Koryŏ," *Journal of Asian Studies* 34, no.1 (January 1974): 109–23.
5. Duncan, *Origins*, 79.
6. Duncan, *Origins*, 46–47.
7. Yong-ho Ch'oe, *The Civil Examinations and the Social Structure in Early Yi Dynasty Korea: 1392–1600* (Seoul: Korean Research Center, 1987), 3.
8. Duncan, *Origins*, 42–43.
9. Michael C. Rogers, "National Consciousness in Medieval Korea: The Impact of Liao and Chin on Koryŏ," in *China Among Equals: The Middle Kingdom and Its Neighbors, 10th–14th Centuries*, ed. Morris Rossabi (Berkeley: University of California Press, 1983), 151–72.
10. Keith L. Pratt, "Politics and Culture Within the Sinic Zone: Chinese Influences on Medieval Korea," *Korea Journal* 20, no. 6 (June 1980): 15–29.
11. William E. Henthorn, *A History of Korea* (New York: Free Press, 1971), 100.
12. Edward J. Shultz, "Twelfth Century Koryŏ Politics: The Rise of Han Anin and His Partisans," *The Journal of Korean Studies* 6 (1988–89): 3–38.
13. Robert E. Buswell, *The Korean Approach to Zen: Collected Works on Chinul* (Honolulu: University of Hawaii Press, 1983), 1–72.
14. Buswell, *Korean Approach to Zen*, 18.
15. Pratt, "Politics and Culture Within the Sinic Zone," 24.
16. Jane Portal, *Korea: Art and Archaeology* (London: British Museum, 2000), 91.
17. Portal, *Korea: Art and Archaeology*, 84.
18. Duncan, *Origins*, 56–57.
19. Much of this discussion of marriage and family is based on Martina Deuchler, *The Confucian Transformation of Korea: A Study of Society and Ideology* (Cambridge, MA: Harvard University Press, 1992).
20. Kim Kichung, *Classical Korean Literature* (Armonk, NY: M. E. Sharpe, 1996), 54–56.
21. Peter H. Lee and William Theodore De Bary, eds., *Sources of Korean Traditions*, vol. 1, *From Early Times Through the Sixteenth Century* (New York: Columbia University Press, 1997), 154–56.

5

Military Rulers and Mongol Invaders

Three developments shaped the latter part of the history of Koryŏ. In the twelfth century generals seized power and inaugurated a century of military rulers. In the thirteenth century the Mongols launched a highly destructive series of invasions and eventually reduced Korea to a vassal state of the vast Mongol Empire centered in northern China. During the century of Mongol domination a third major development occurred, less dramatic than the first two but more profound in its long-term impact on Korean society, the introduction of Neo-Confucianism. This school of thought, which had developed in China in the eleventh and twelfth century, provided the ideological basis of the establishment of a new Yi dynasty in the late fourteenth century.

MILITARY RULE

Koryŏ was a society dominated by a civil aristocracy (*munban*). Wealthy landed families held the key posts in the state, advised and intermarried with the Wang kings, controlled most of the land and economy, and supplied most of the leadership of Buddhist temples. It was from the ranks of the elite aristocratic civil officials that most of the kingdom's writers and scholars were drawn. There was, however, an inferior line of military officials (*muban*). Although they were aristocrats, they held less prestige and generally did not rise to the highest ranks in the bureaucracy. In general, their voices were seldom heard. Even Korea's military victories such as those against the Liao were usually attributed to the leadership of civil officials. It should be noted, however, that the civil officials wrote the official histories. Then in 1170, officers of the military aristocracy revolted and seized power.

Military-civil tension had existed long before the 1170 revolt.[1] For example, in 1014, the military revolted when civil officials tried to limit their salaries. Yet something changed in the twelfth century that gave the military leaders the desire and confidence to wrestle power from the civilian aristocracy. Perhaps when the military helped to defeat Yi Cha-gyŏm in 1126 and Myoch'ŏng in 1135 they realized their potential power. King Ŭijong (1146–1170), a patron of the arts, was not an effective king, and disputes between civil and military officials appeared to have gotten worse under his rule. The military grew more restless; as early as 1164 some military officials plotted to overthrow the state.

The leader of the 1170 coup was Chŏng Chung-bu. Chŏng belonged to the influential Haeju Chŏng clan but represented the less powerful and prestigious *muban* military lineages. Before coming to power Chŏng Chung-bu served as commander of the royal guards. According to tradition, Chŏng had been humiliated when Kim Ton-jung, son of historian Kim Pu-sik, set fire to his beard. Whatever its accuracy, the story symbolizes the growing tensions between the dominant civil aristocracy and the military aristocrats that led to the military revolt. The coup was carried out as King Ŭijong and his entourage of court officials visited a temple near the capital. Chŏng, along with two other generals, Yi Ŭi-bang and Yi Ko, massacred the entire court, sparing only the king, whom they exiled to Kŏje Island off the south coast, and the crown prince, whom they banished to Chindo, another island off the south coast. Ŭijŏng was later executed by drowning. Once in power, Chŏng Chung-bu carried out an extensive purge of civil officials and managed state affairs through the *Chungbang* (Supreme Military Council). He replaced King Ŭijong with his brother Myŏngjong, a more compliant king. But the new monarch had little real power. Power was now in the hands of military officers. The Wang line of Koryŏ kings continued to reign, and a civil government continued to carry out the formal functions of government. Actual authority, however, was wielded by generals who developed a parallel government administration based on military clan organs. Military leaders derived their support from their own clans based on *mun'gaek* (retainers) and *kadong* (house slaves).

The first quarter century of military rule was characterized by competition for power among rival military clans. Having seized control, the military rulers do not seem to have had a clear plan of how to rule the state. As a result the period from 1170 to 1196 was one of instability in which a number of generals plotted against each other. At first Chŏng ruled along with Yi Ŭi-bang and Yi Ko, two other military officers, but Yi Ŭi-bang killed Yi Ko, who in turn was assassinated by Chŏng's faction. Chŏng then ruled alone for several years until 1179 when the young military commander Kyŏng Tae-sŭng killed him. Eventually another general, Yi Ŭi-min, became paramount leader. Meanwhile, the countryside saw numerous rebellions. Peasants rose up against landowners and local officials, slaves revolted against masters, and even soldiers in the provinces revolted. The most famous of these revolts was that of the slave Manjŏk, a sort of Korean Spartacus. Manjŏk gathered an army of government and private slaves that met at North Mountain outside of the capital Kaesŏng in 1198 (see below). The leaders of this group were betrayed. Their revolt and that of others were eventually suppressed, but they reflect a general breakdown of authority that took place in the land during the first three decades of governance by military officials.

Stability came when in 1196, Ch'oe Ch'ung-hŏn seized power and established the rule of Korea by the Ch'oe family house that lasted fifty-eight years. Of the Ubang Ch'oe clan, Ch'oe Ch'ung-hŏn's father was an officer who had reached the top of the military hierarchy.[2] Ch'oe served as the *toryŏng* (military commander) and wrote a *Ten-Point Memorial* expressing dissatisfaction with the military rule under King Myŏngjong (1170–1197), its corruption, its inferior officials, and the interference of Buddhism in politics. He killed Yi Ŭi-min and became the new paramount military leader, thus the de facto ruler of Korea. Ch'oe restored order to the countryside that had been plagued by frequent peasant and slave revolts. He did this in part by offering some rebel leaders ranks and offices, and by freeing low-born inhabitants of special districts called *pugok* and *hyang* and merging them into the regular county system of local administration. He also broke the power of the Buddhist monasteries and temples that had ties to the courts and that had even threatened Ch'oe's authority with their armed monks. He crushed the armed monks and forced many of the clergy, especially the illegitimate princes who had become monks, to leave the capital. Ch'oe's twenty-two-year rule stands out in Korean history. Seldom did a single individual, who was not a king, manage to concentrate so much power in his hands.

Ch'oe created a stable rule by developing an innovative set of institutions. These institutions amounted to the establishment of two sets of government.[3] The monarchy, the court officials, and civil bureaucracy were maintained while he created a new parallel government based on house institutions that were under his direct control. The latter, in fact, became the real locus of power. The house institutions were staffed by his own retainers and slaves and by officials personally loyal to him. The most important of these was the *Kyojŏng Togam* (Office of Decree Enactment), which served as the effective center of political authority. The *Kyojŏng Togam* functioned as the highest administrative organ of his government. It had the power to collect taxes and investigate wrongdoing by officials. Having gathered effective power in his hands, Ch'oe preferred to create personal house organs that now had the actual civilian and military functions of government while preserving the older court-centered institutional structure that held only nominal power. Members of these organs were nominally appointed by the king, but were generally chosen by Ch'oe Ch'ung-hŏn. Ch'oe in effect created a sort of parallel dynasty to the Wang royal dynasty, passing his rulership to his son Ch'oe U, and his grandsons Ch'oe Hang and Ch'oe Ŭi.

Ch'oe Ch'ung-hŏn's son Ch'oe U, who governed Korea from 1218 to 1249, further elaborated on the structure of house organs. He created the *Chŏngbang* (Personnel Authority), an institution through which civil officials could enter government, the *Sŏbang* (Household Secretariat) that was formed from the men of letters among his retainers, and the *Sambyŏlch'o* (Three Elite Patrols) that served as a clan-controlled military force. The *Sambyŏlch'o* were elite military units that carried out police and combat duties. This military force originated in the two (left and right) Night Patrols Ch'oe U created as military units that would be outside the regular army command. A third unit, the *Sinŭigun* (Army of Transcendent Righteousness), was formed from fighters who escaped after being captured by Mongols. The Ch'oe rulers financed their house organs through *sigŭp*, extensive lands theoretically granted by the court, in which the Ch'oe family was allowed to directly collect taxes and tribute. In effect these lands provided an independent base of economic support for it.

Essential to the new government was the use of *mun'gaek*. *Mun'gaek* were private military retainers of great clans. The *mun'gaek* were important in the armies of the military clans that gained control of the Koryŏ government in 1170. After 1196 the clan of Ch'oe Ch'ung-hŏn was especially effective in promoting its *mun'gaek*. Under the Ch'oe military rulers many scholars became *mun'gaek* and served in the *Chŏngbang* (Personnel Authority) and other offices. The *mun'gaek* played an important role in the competition for power throughout the Koryŏ period. In addition to *mun'gaek* who were freedmen, *kadong*, male house slaves also served as armed retainers.

Ch'oe Ch'ung-hŏn asserted more direct control over local institutions. His task was an enormous one since under his military predecessors authority of all sorts had broken down in the provinces. Ch'oe had to deal with six peasant rebellions during his first twelve years. He utilized a variety of methods to reassert control over the countryside. The military ruler reinvigorated the power of the *hojang* (local headmen) and expanded the *kamugwan*, a central government office that oversaw rural jurisdictions. Ch'oe had officials called *anch'alsa* (appointed governors) meet directly with peasants and elevated or demoted a district's status as a reward or punishment.

The Ch'oe rulers sponsored a vigorous intellectual life through their encouragement of Confucianism as a means of legitimizing their rule. They carried out civil examinations with considerable frequency, and despite the disdain of civil officials (*munban*) toward military officials (*muban*), the Ch'oe succeeded in attracting a large proportion of the former to serve in their government as civil officials or personal retainers. The military rulers were also patrons of Sŏn Buddhism, and through their support Buddhism entered a period of intellectual vigor. At the same time the military rulers struggled to undermine the power of the capital area monasteries that were often headed by members of cadet branches of the royal family and by court-connected aristocratic families. These efforts led to a rebellion by armed monks in 1217 that Ch'oe Ch'ung-hŏn suppressed. Overall the Ch'oe rulers appeared to have stabilized the government and developed a set of effective institutions that secured their power. Hardly, however, had they accomplished this when they were faced with the Mongol invasions. The stubborn resistance of the Ch'oe rulers to the Mongols from 1231 to 1258, for the most part directed from the island fastness of Kanghwa, eventually contributed to their downfall when a faction suing for peace with the Mongols overthrew the last Ch'oe ruler, Ch'oe Ŭi.

SŎN BUDDHISM

Perhaps that most importance cultural legacy of this period was the promotion of Sŏn Buddhism under the Ch'oe. At this time Buddhism in Korea had become divided into Kyo or textual Buddhism, which emphasized the study of sutras and elaborate rituals, and Sŏn or meditative Buddhism. The civil aristocracy patronized Kyo and lavished great wealth on temples that supported a large number of monks. Kyo temples became major land and slave owners. The military rulers, while patronizing shamanist shrines, also sought to support Sŏn, which was more austere and centered in mountain temples far from the capital and its politics. By shifting patronage to Sŏn temples they also weakened the Kyo temples as a power base for the aristocrats that supported them. Partly as a result of this support meditative Buddhism flourished during the late twelfth and thirteenth centuries.

A key development in Korean Buddhism at this time was its revitalization under the monk Chinul, also known as Pojo Kuksa (National Preceptor Pojo) (1158–1210). Born in an aristocratic family, he took and passed the monk exams. But he quickly became disenchanted with the atmosphere of official Buddhism with its wealthy temples and politically ambitious monks. He sought to reestablish the spirit of Buddhism by working outside the official court-sponsored religious hierarchy. Trained in the Sŏn tradition, he spent most of his active years in remote mountain areas and founded Sŏng-wang-sa temple in Chŏlla Province, which became an important center for his teachings. Chinul was the first Korean Buddhist to practice *koans* (to use the Japanese term), the insoluble or nonsense problems that are designed to jolt one into sudden intuitive enlightenment. Derived from Chinese practice, the *koan* came to be practiced in Korea about the same time it was introduced to Japan. But for Chinul it was only a minor "supplementary" technique.[4] His aim was to bring together and reinvigorate the various Buddhist practices.

More successfully than the earlier effort by Ŭich'ŏn, Chinul established a Buddhist doctrine and practice that could embrace the many scholastic teachings with the antitextual Sŏn. This form of Sŏn became known as Chogye. He did so by developing an original synthesis combining the emphasis on sudden enlightenment of the Sŏn and the stress on careful study emphasized by the Kyo sects of Korean Buddhism. This synthesis was summed up in the terms *tan'o chomsu* (sudden enlightenment and gradual cultivation) and *chŏnghye ssangsu* (twofold training in quiescence [meditation] and activity). Chinul has been credited with unifying Korean Buddhism by creating a broad-based doctrine that was able to incorporate the major strands of Buddhism into a blended whole. Under his immediate successor Hyesim (Chin'gak Kuksa) Chogye received the patronage of the military rulers of Korea, beginning with Ch'oe U.

Under Chinul and his successors Korean Buddhism deviated somewhat from the path of development of Buddhism in China, evolving its own distinctive body of tradition and practices. One of the major features of Korean Buddhism became the tradition of syncretism. Kyo and Sŏn practices began to blend and sects were defined more by separate lines of transmission from a master than by sharp doctrinal differences. Within this syncretic tradition, Sŏn practices of meditation, austerity, and the disciplined seeking of enlightenment became central, and the influence of Chinul profound. To this day the majority of Korean Buddhists belong to the Chogye sect of Buddhism.

KOREA, JAPAN, AND FEUDAL EUROPE

Korea under the military governments developed institutions that in some ways resembled feudalism. Feudalism is usually defined as a decentralized political system in which a landowning or land-controlling warrior aristocracy supported by peasantry bound to the land is linked in a hierarchical scheme of political loyalty. It became a fully developed and dominant political-social system only in medieval Western Europe and in medieval Japan. Historians have long noted the similarities between Japanese feudalism and Western European feudalism. Less well appreciated is that many of the important transformations in Japanese society that took place in the twelfth century to establish the classic Japanese feudal society took place simultaneously in Korea. As one scholar has observed, "Civil aristocratic societies characterize both Korea and Japan at the start of the twelfth century."[5] In Japan as in Korea, the court and dynasty lost effective power to new military lineages, and in both after a period of struggle among military leaders a strong military leader emerged. In Japan this leader was Yoritomo, who in 1185 became paramount ruler of Japan, taking the title of Shogun in 1192; and in Korea Ch'oe Ch'ung-hŏn emerged as the effective ruler in 1196. In both countries the military hegemons established a parallel clan government with effective power while maintaining the dynastic organs of government. Both Ch'oe and Yoritomo made use of an elaborate system of personal retainers and military leaders who pledged to serve their military ruler through ties of loyalty, and who derived income from their extensive personal landholdings. Both recruited men of letters to serve in their private agencies and relied on these educated men to help them in administering the country. In both cases members of the old clans that had supplied the court with officials continued to serve as officials, although without the power and influence they previously had. Both patronized Zen (Sǒn) Buddhism, which became the religion of the warriors. In Japan, as well as in Korea, the late twelfth and thirteenth centuries became the great age of meditative Buddhism, which with the help of official support emerged as a major religious and cultural force. Military rulers in both Korea and Japan fiercely resisted the Mongol invasions.

But there were important differences. Yoritomo came out of a Heian order that witnessed the expansion of warrior and regional autonomy, while Ch'oe emerged from the Koryǒ system in which the military was closely tied to the dynasty. In Japan local autonomy and military culture grew stronger, while in Korea the Ch'oe, searching for appropriate forms of governance, restored many dynastic agencies, working closely with the king and his officials, thus reaffirming the importance of civil traditions in Korea. While in Japan the military traditions emerged as dominant, in Korea the civil traditions prevailed. Partly this was due to the use of the civil exams by the Ch'oe family to recruit men of learning for office, thus reinforcing the importance of scholarship. There was no civil exam system in Japan. In Japan, the emergence of military rule was a consolidation of trends that had been taking place for several centuries as power slipped away from the court and into the hands of local military elite. By contrast, in Korea, the emergence of military rule was a more dramatic break with tradition. Koryǒ monarchs were active in governing in the twelfth century, private armies had been effectively uprooted in the tenth century, the military was clearly subordinated to civil authority, and the central hierarchy was more clearly defined than in Japan.

Even under the Ch'oe the Korean government remained more centralized than was the case in either Europe or Japan. The military rulers of Koryǒ were based in the capital and maintained a orientation toward centralized rule. Yoritomo, by contrast, led a coalition of warriors rooted in the countryside. Furthermore, he had his own large provincial power base on the Kanto plain. Ch'oe had no such power base and was much more reliant on key court and military officials to support him.[6] Also the *mun'gaek* retainers were considerably smaller in number than those available to Yoritomo and the shoguns who succeeded him. More significantly, retainers in Korea could not own land, unlike the vassals who served their lords in Europe and in

Japan. An entire system of feudal law emerged in Japan and in Europe, but in Korea the Chinese-patterned legal system continued to function. So for all the parallels with developments in Japan, Korea never developed a truly feudal system. It is possible, of course, that with time Korea might have developed a more feudal-like system, but the tendency to recruit ever more civil officials during the Ch'oe clan's rule does not suggest this was going to happen. Perhaps Korea, unlike Western Europe and Japan, which were relatively free from outside invasions, simply could not function without a centralized state. Geography made Korea less secure. Unlike Europe or Japan, Korea had to deal with powerful and often aggressive neighbors from the Manchurian plains and grasslands of Inner Asia.

The final question is why such institutions appeared in Japan and Korea around the same time, in fact, at almost exactly the same time. The answer to this is not well understood, but the fact they did suggests that Korean and Japanese historical developments are more closely linked than most scholars have previously appreciated. Both were in contrast to China, where no similar trends occurred in the twelfth and thirteenth centuries. The power of the Chinese military aristocratic clans had declined sharply in the eighth to tenth centuries and saw no revival.

THE MONGOL INVASIONS

Would the Ch'oe family or another family have developed a dynastic system similar to the Japanese shogunate? We simply do not know, since Korea's period of rule by military warlords came to an end with the Mongol invasions. Emerging as a unified group in the thirteenth century under their leader Genghis Khan and his successors, the Mongols built a great empire based on the grasslands of Inner Asia and subjugated the greater part of Eurasia. Few countries suffered more from the ravages of the Mongols than Korea. From 1217 to 1258 Korea endured repeated invasions as a result of the rise of the Mongols. In 1217, Khitan tribes fleeing the Mongol invasions of North China crossed the Yalu and plundered northern Korea.[7] In 1218 the Mongols pursuing the Khitans aided Koryŏ forces in defeating them. The Mongols then demanded tribute from the Koreans: clothes, furs, and horses. They also demanded virgins, which the Koreans refused. For the Koreans the tribute demands were burdensome, especially horses in a country with little grazing land. In 1224, the Koryŏ stopped tribute payments and murdered the Mongol envoys. In retaliation the Mongols invaded in 1231.

The Mongols withdrew the following year after the Koryŏ government agreed to accept tributary status and to accept the placing of Mongol representatives, called *darughachi*, in Korea to oversee tribute collections. Later in 1232, Che Ch'oe house military rulers ordered the Koryŏ court to retreat to Kanghwa island and killed the *darughachi*. The military rulers then declared all-out resistance. From the protection of Kanghwa Island the Ch'oe rulers and their successors carried out a fierce and stubborn resistance that lasted four decades. The Ch'oe transferred the entire government to the small ten-by-seventeen-mile island, constructing palaces, temples, and administrative buildings where thousands of officials, soldiers, and monks carried out the functions of government. Some officials objected to abandoning the people; nonetheless, the small but easily defendable island proved to be an effective stronghold against the Mongols. The state was not, however, able to protect the countryside where the Mongol destruction was devastating. Much of the country's heritage, including the eighty thousand wood blocks for the *Tripataka*, was destroyed.

The 1232 invasion ended when the Mongol commander Sartaq was killed from an arrow shot by the monk Kim Yun-hu. In 1233, the Mongols launched a new series of invasions, led by Tanqut-batu and Prince Yeku, that dragged on for several years and eventually resulted in a six-year truce from 1241 to 1247. During this time distant members of the royal family were sent to the Mongol court as hostages under the pretense that they were crown princes. But the Koryŏ government continued to resist the Mongols, refusing to send tribute. As a result further invasions occurred in 1247–1248. The most destructive invasions were a series that began with the Mongol attack of 1254 led by Jalairtai. Small bands of Mongol warriors were sent to lay waste to the countryside in an attempt to wear down Korean resistance and cut off the grain supply to the court on Kanghwa. According to later Korean accounts the Mongols killed vast numbers of people and took away over two hundred thousand as prisoners. Historians recorded that "The fields were covered with the bones of the dead; the dead were so many that they could not be counted"; wherever the Mongol army passed, "the inhabitants were all burned out, so that not even dogs and chickens remained."[8] These tactics proved effective, and in 1258 the Ch'oe clan, still adamant in resisting the Mongols, was overthrown. A new leader, Kim Chun, attempted to seek an end to the invasions. Mongol military activity continued in Korea, however, when in 1269 the military leader Im Yŏn ousted the Mongol-supported king. The king was restored to power in 1270 with Mongol assistance, and resistance was limited to holdouts in the provinces. The *Sambyŏlch'o* forces, led by Pae Chung-son and by Kim T'ong-jŏng, continued to fight the Mongols until they were defeated respectively on Chindo Island in 1271 and Cheju Island in 1273.

From 1270 to 1356 Korea was under Mongol domination. While the court and bureaucracy continued to govern, Koryŏ was, in reality, an appanage of the Yuan or Mongol empire that moved its center from Mongolia to what is now Beijing. This period is sometimes called the *Pumaguk* (Son-in-law Nation), since King Wŏnjong (r. 1259–1274) married his son, later king

Ch'ungnyŏl (r. 1274–1308), to a daughter of the Yuan emperor Shizu (Kubilai Khan). He thus began a line of Koryŏ kings who had princesses of the Yuan imperial house as their primary consorts. The sons of these queens usually succeeded to the throne so that Koryŏ kings were sons-in-law of the Yuan emperors. During this period Koryŏ crown princes resided in Beijing as hostages until ascending to the throne. Even while reigning Koryŏ kings spent much of their time in Beijing rather than in Kaesŏng. Indicative of their subordinate status, Koryŏ monarchs did not take the exalted suffixes *cho* ("progenitor") and *chong* ("ancestor") as part of their posthumous temple names. Instead they took *ch'ung* ("loyal") as the first character of their name as an expression of their loyalty to the Yuan.

Kings under the Mongol hegemony saw their authority weaken. They were sometimes at the mercy of the Yuan emperors, who could depose them at will. Several were removed, sometimes with the support of members of the Koryŏ aristocracy. Yuan emperors appointed some monarchs as King of Shenyang, a region of southern Manchuria. Thus they created two courts among the members of the Wang royal family as a means of manipulating them by playing off royal relatives against each other. To reinforce Koryŏ's subordinate status, the organs of government were renamed to give them titles that carried less prestige or hint of sovereignty. For example, the *Samsŏng* (Three Chancelleries) were merged to form a single Council of State, and the *Chungchu'wŏn* (Royal Secretariat) was renamed the *Milchiksa*, which had the same meaning but was less exalted sounding.

As a vassal of the Yuan (Mongol) state Korea became a member of one of the world's most cosmopolitan societies. Korean court officials, scholars, and others seeking opportunities traveled and resided in Beijing where they encountered Chinese, Mongols, Vietnamese, Central Asians, and a handful of other peoples. For some it was a time of opportunity for social advancement. A number of Koreans, following the tradition of marrying into influential and wealthy families, formed marriage alliances with Mongols and Central Asians and rose to prominence in Beijing or back in Korea. Many Koreans adopted Mongol clothing and hairstyles. A number of foreigners also made their way to Korea and served as members of government. Often they filled the need for personnel fluent in Chinese and Mongol, or familiar with the complexities of the Yuan court. Foreigners in Korea numbered in the thousands. Several foreigners became members of the *Chaech'u* and others became military officers. Even after Korea broke with the Yuan court, three Mongols, In Hu, Hwang Sang, and Na Se, served as military commanders during Red Turban invasions in fourteenth century.[9]

Korea was also the base of two efforts to conquer Japan. Having subdued the last resistance to their rule in 1273, the Mongols drafted Korean shipbuilders and sailors to construct and pilot a large Mongol fleet that invaded Japan in 1274. The invasion, launched in typhoon season, was forced to retreat when a typhoon that the Japanese called the *kamikaze* (divine wind) came. A second invasion in 1281 also failed when another typhoon destroyed much of the fleet. For the Japanese this would remain until 1945 a sign that theirs was a special land of the gods protected from invasion, and it contributed to the myth of their uniqueness and invincibility. To the Koreans the two invasions and an aborted planned third invasion were a costly burden. Furthermore, along with the tribute of horses and women the Mongols extracted, the forced participation in the invasions of Japan was a humiliating reminder of their subordinate status. Yet, the Mongol rule was indirect, not direct. The court and bureaucracy in Kaeŏng continued to function. After the invasions of Japan there was little direct interference in Korean affairs. As a result Korea maintained itself as a separate kingdom with its own court and culture.

THE LEGACY OF THE MONGOL PERIOD

Historians differ in their evaluation of the importance of the Mongol invasions and their domination of Korea. Some emphasize the continuity in Korea. They argue that there was no change in dynasty, the bureaucracy underwent relatively minor changes in organization, and while some new powerful families emerged, the social structure remained essentially the same with most of the old elite lineages continuing to dominate society. Korea's vassalage to China was not a radical break with tradition. The Mongol rulers of China took on the role of Chinese emperors and assumed the big brother role that China often took toward Korea. When Korean kings paid homage to the Yuan rulers they were continuing a practice of seeking legitimacy by having their positions confirmed by the Celestial (Chinese) emperor.

Nevertheless, the destruction that resulted from the invasions was an enormous loss to Korea. To this day few structures before this period still exist. The scorched earth policy and the repeated and systematic invasions at least partially account for the fact that so few of Korea's pre-fourteenth-century literary and artistic works have survived. One has only to read the lists of compilations of poetry, the praise and descriptions of famous painters given in the fifteenth-century *Koryŏ sa* (*History of Koryŏ*), and the many works of history cited in the *Samguk sagi* to sense how much has been lost. The Mongol invasion may have contributed to a growing consciousness of Korean cultural identity. It was, for example, during the Mongol period that the legend of Tan'gun appeared in the written record in the *Samguk yusa* (see below) and in the long history in verse *Chewang un'gi* (*Song of Emperors and Kings*). During the Mongol period Korean monks also compiled the extant version of the *Tripitaka Koreana.*

The Mongol invasions may have made Koreans more cautious of outsiders.

Ming China, which drove out the Mongols, maintained a policy of greater isolation and wariness of outsiders than earlier dynasties. This is generally explained as a reaction to the Mongol invasion and rule. Similarly Korea maintained a policy of limiting foreign contact that would eventually earn it the sobriquet of "the hermit Kingdom." Most probably the experience and memory of the Mongols contributed to this idea that foreigners meant trouble. Korea's stubborn resistance and ability to maintain itself as a separate state even during this period may have also contributed to a sense of pride, and of being the inheritor of a distinctive cultural and historical tradition.

No less important was the fact that for a short time Korea was closely connected with the truly vast cosmopolitan Mongol Empire, the largest the world had ever seen. At its peak the Mongol Empire stretched from Russia and Persia to Korea. At this time Koreans at the Mongol court met peoples and ideas from all over Eurasia. Concepts about mathematics, astrology, and medicine reached some Koreans from as far away as the Middle East. But it was the relatively close contact the royal family members, courtiers, and others in Beijing had with their Chinese counterparts that made the greatest impact. This influenced painting, calligraphy, literature, and clothing fashions. Cotton and cotton cloth making became known to Koreans at this time. By tradition cotton was brought back from Yuan China in 1363 by Mun Ik-chŏm, who had gone there as part of a diplomatic mission. He gave the seeds to his father-in-law, who successfully planted them. Gunpowder too spread to Korea during this period. Credit for this introduction is given to Ch'oe Mu-sŏn, a minor official who learned the formula from the Chinese. In 1377 Koryŏ established an office for the manufacture of gunpowder and cannons, which were first used to fight Japanese pirates. The Mongol period was one of close contact between Korean scholars and officials and their Chinese counterparts whom they met at the Yuan court in Beijing. This contact resulted in what is perhaps the most significant legacy of the Mongol period, the introduction of Neo-Confucianism to Korea. (See below.)

LATE KORYŎ SOCIETY

For all the turbulence of the latter two centuries of Koryŏ the basic structure of the social and the political order remained largely intact. At the top of society was the dynastic family. The king reigned, if not always effectively ruled. Under him the upper strata of the aristocracy that was based in the capital dominated the organs of government. A lower stratum of rural-based aristocrats sometimes referred to as *hyangni* controlled much of the countryside and held local offices. Underneath them were commoners and the large number of slaves and certain outcaste groups. Military rule did little to change this, since most of the military rulers were quick to acquire *nongjang* (landed estates) and intermarried with the civil official-aristocracy in the capital. The Mongol period saw a number of new families emerge, but recent studies indicate that while some elite families fell in status and a few new ones appeared, the old aristocracy largely survived. The central aristocracy may have actually strengthened its dominance over society. Furthermore, new families adopted the style of the old.

There were some changes. The devastation brought about by the Mongol invasions destroyed much of the wealth of the *hyangni*. Because of this development and the gradual penetration of the central government into the countryside, the rural aristocracy probably declined in power. Significantly, while late Koryŏ was still an aristocratic society dominated by powerful families deriving much of their wealth from landed estates, increasingly, the dominant aristocracy, or *yangban* as it eventually became known, associated itself with service to the state. Korea involved into a bureaucratic polity with a ruling class that identified with the state and shared a common set of values.

The struggle of Koryŏ kings to gain some independence from the aristocracy continued. The situation of late Koryŏ kings was worsened by the loss of taxable lands. During the Mongol period a great deal of taxable public land (*kongjŏn*) slipped into private hands, and powerful families had consolidated their power in the capital. Furthermore, raids by Japanese pirates known as *wako* (*waegu* in Korean) devastated much of the coastal areas and countermeasures against them drained the public treasury. Late Koryŏ kings tried to check the power of the powerful families by appointing eunuchs, slaves, and other outsiders to office. Most notable of these efforts was King Kongmin's (r. 1351–1374) selection of a slave monk, Sin Ton, as his chief officer to carry out a redistribution of lands and slaves. This move was taken to undermine these powerful families and restore land and peasants to the tax rolls. Kongmin, however, was reported to have gradually lost interest in politics following the death of his Mongol wife in childbirth in 1365. According to the historical records he had a large shrine to his deceased wife constructed, hung a portrait of her that he painted himself, and spent hours in front of it grieving. Kongmin's efforts to reign in the power of the elite then failed. Sin Ton was exiled and killed and the king was assassinated at Hŭnggwang-sa temple in 1374 by a disgruntled aristocrat threatened by Kongmin's reforms.

THE END OF THE KORYŎ

The mid-fourteenth century was a time of upheaval in continental East Asia. Uprisings occurred in China against the Yuan dynasty, and a number of rebel bands emerged. One of these, led by former monk Zhu Yuanzhang, gained control over most of central and southern China. In 1356, Zhu set up a capital at Nanjing. Twelve years later, in 1368, Zhu's forces drove the Mongols out of Beijing and back to their Mongolian homeland. In that year Zhu proclaimed a new Ming dynasty. The Mongols formed a Northern Yuan rump state and carried on the struggle with Ming, but China was now unified and free from the Mongols.

Taking advantage of Yuan weakness, Kongmin in 1356 destroyed the pro-Mongol faction led by Ki Ch'ŏl, brother of Empress Ki, the second wife of Shun, the last Mongol Emperor. Korea was now independent of Mongol control. Kongmin then pursued a anti-Mongol, pro-Ming policy. He abolished the Eastern Expedition Field Headquarters, an institution through which the Mongols kept an eye on events in Korea, and his army annexed the Yuan commandery of Ssangsŏng based in what is now the northeastern province of Hamgyŏng. He also abolished the *Chŏngbang* (Personnel Authority), the organ of administration created under the military rule. In 1369, the Ming recognized Kongmin as king, and the Korean court adopted the Ming calendar. The old tributary relationship between Korea and the Chinese court was re-established.

Mongol domination had ended, but the last years of the Koryŏ were troubled ones. The collapsing Mongol power and the rise of the Ming dynasty in China created turmoil on the northern border, and Ming and Mongol forces fought each other in Manchuria. A product of this turmoil, a Chinese rebel/brigand army known as the Red Turbans plundered their way across Manchuria and twice invaded Korea, first, in 1359, with a force reported to have been forty thousand men, and two years later with a larger force of one hundred thousand, forcing the Korean court to flee to Andong in the southeastern part of the kingdom. Another threat came from the son of Ki Ch'ŏl, who led a group of Yuan refugees in Manchuria that menaced Koryŏ. Meanwhile along the southern coast Japanese pirates raided, plundered, and spread terror, even attacking Kanghwa Island and threatening the capital, Kaesŏng.

When Kongmin was assassinated his ten-year-old son came to the throne as King U. The real power, however, was in the hands of Yi In-im, head of an important clan. The Ming were suspicious of the new administration in Korea. Consequently, the Ming emperor refused to recognize King U. Yi In-im then abandoned the pro-Ming policies of Kongmin. But attempts to establish friendly relations with the Northern Yuan failed when the Mongols demanded the Koreans join them in attacking the Ming. Relations with the Ming were briefly restored but broke down when the new Chinese dynasty began to build a garrison at Iron Pass (Ch'ŏllyŏng) and create a commandery out of the former Mongol Ssangsŏng commandery in Hamgyŏng province. Domestically politics was torn between pro-Yuan factions, which included many families that had risen to prominence under the Yuan, and pro-Ming officials and aristocrats.

In 1388, the Yi In-im faction was driven out, led by a general, Ch'oe Yŏng, who became military commander. He appointed two of his supporters, generals Yi Sŏng-gye and Cho Min-su, as deputies. Ch'oe and King U then mobilized the country for an attack on the Ming and an expedition was launched under Ch'oe's leadership. Yi Sŏng-gye was given a command of some of the forces, but he opposed the launching of a military campaign against the Ming. At Wihwa Island in the mouth of the Yalu, Yi turned back, and with the support of general Cho Min-su ousted Ch'oe Yŏng. Yi and his supporters then deposed King U and replaced him with Ch'ang, his nine-year-old son. In the following year, 1389, he ousted the recently installed King Ch'ang on the grounds that he was really the son of Sin Ton and replaced him with Kongyang, a distant relative. Yi then removed Cho Min-su and made him a commoner. Yi's rise to power was relatively bloodless; a few high officials such as Yi Saek and Kwŏn Kŭn were banished, but otherwise he ruled with cooperation of the existing bureaucracy. With the aid of reform-minded scholar-officials he began to carry out sweeping changes. Yi supervised a new land survey, then in 1390, burned all registers in a big bonfire in the market. The next year he carried out a major land reform. With his supporters secure in high positions, he removed Kongyang in 1392. The deposed king was sent into exile and later murdered. Yi Sŏng-gye then proclaimed himself King T'aejo, the first of the new Yi dynasty, and renamed the state Chosŏn. The Wang dynasty and the Koryŏ state had come to an end.

LATE KORYŎ CULTURE

During the nearly five centuries of the Koryŏ the process of borrowing and adapting from China continued. With these adaptations a distinctive Korean cultural style and identity emerged. Among the most important cultural achievements in late Koryŏ were those dealing with papermaking and printing. Papermaking had been introduced from China in the Silla period. Under Koryŏ high quality paper made from the mulberry shrub was valued as an import by the Chinese. Woodblock printing, also borrowed from China, became highly developed, spurred by the demand for printed Buddhist sutras. Blocks were made from wood that was soaked and boiled in salt water then coated with lacquer. The greatest publishing project of the Koryŏ was the *Tripitaka Koreana*. This is the most complete extant edition of the *Tripitaka (The Three Baskets)* that contains the Buddhist canon anywhere in the world today.[10] The first copy was printed during the Liao invasions in the eleventh century and destroyed in the Mongol invasion of 1232. During the years 1235 to 1251, 81,137 woodblocks, enough to print 160,000 pages, were carved at Kanghwa and are now stored at Haein-sa temple in Mount Kaya.

This is one of the great cultural treasures of Korea and an invaluable resource for Buddhists.

In addition to the woodblock tradition, Koryŏ craftsmen, drawing upon their highly skilled metal-casting techniques, produced the world's first moveable metal type. Exactly when this happened is not known for certain. The first known use of moveable metal type was in 1234 to print twenty-eight copies of *Sangjŏng kogŭm yemun* (*Prescribed Ritual Texts of the Past and Present*). This was more than two centuries before Gutenberg. Indeed, some historians have speculated that knowledge of Korean moveable metal type may have reached Europe and inspired the development of printing there.[11] The Koreans, however, did not invent a printing press. In 1392, at the end of the dynasty, a National Office for Book Publication was established to cast type and print books. Using moveable type was useful since many different books could be published. Woodblocks were still used to print books, especially when a large number of copies of a single book were needed.

Late Koryŏ scholars produced a number of medical texts. The oldest existing Korean medical text, *Hyangyak kugŭp pang* (*Emergency Remedies of Folk Medicine*), was produced in the thirteenth century during the times of the Mongol invasions. Korea's medical tradition was derived from China but incorporated folk practices as well. A special problem for Koreans was that Chinese medical practice relied heavily on the use of medicinal herbs and had created a vast materia medica. But many of these plants were not available in Korea. Searches for indigenous medicines led to impressive compilations in the fourteenth century of native Korean *hyangyak isul* (prescriptions) using local materials. These efforts led to the eighty-five-volume *Hyangyak chip-songbang* (*Compilation of Native Korean Prescriptions*) published in the early fifteenth century.

The East Asian tradition of short prose essays, still popular in Korea, flourished in Koryŏ times. Koryŏ essays were classified as follows: admonition, disquisition, dirge, appreciation, proclamations, announcement, memorials, letters, and descriptions (or records). There were didactic and humorous stories written in Chinese and often set in ancient China. Authors of these essays and little stories were members of the elite, often leading officials. Among the most noted was Yi Kyu-bo, who passed the civil service exam in 1190 and rose to First Privy Councilor. Yi took the pen name "White Cloud" and styled himself as master of the lute, poetry, and wine. Yi Che-hyŏn (1287–1367), another highly regarded writer, placed first in the state exam in 1301 and had a distinguished public career.[12] Other prose writers of note were Yi Il-lo (1152–1220) and Ch'ae Cha (1188–1260). History and biographies modeled on the Chinese works, especially Sima Qian's *Shiji*, were popular as well.

With the Mongol threat and the relative isolation of Korea from China during the period of military rule, there appeared to be an interest in ancient history and legends. In the early thirteenth century Yi Kyu-bo wrote *Tong-myŏng wang p'yŏn (The Saga of King Tongmyŏng)*. This was a narrative poem that dealt with the legendary founder of Koguryŏ. The purpose in writing this, Yi Kyu-bo states, was "simply to let the world know that our country always has been a land of hero-sages." Yi Sŭng-hyu (1224–1300) composed the *Chewang un'gi (Song of Emperors and Kings)*, a long poem recounting the rulers of Korea starting with Tan'gun. Scholars also wrote a number of other works on Korean history, now lost. All this suggests a growing sense, among the educated Koreans at least, that they were part of a society with its own history and traditions distinct from that of its neighbors.

The most important result of this interest was *Samguk yusa (Memorabilia of the Three Kingdoms)*. The *Samguk yusa* is a history of Korea from its mythical origins to the end of the Silla kingdom in the tenth century written in 1279 by the monk Iryŏn. Along with the *Samguk sagi*, the *Samguk yusa* remains one of the two major sources for early Korean history. The work contains a chronological table that is often more accurate than the *Samguk sagi* and which is an important source of historical information. This is followed by a long section, "Records of Marvels," that contains valuable material on ancient Korea, including the earliest recorded legend of Tan'gun, a story, incidentally, not recorded in the *Samguk sagi*. The *Samguk yusa* is based on many now lost sources, such as the *Karak kukki* written in 1076 of which a synopsis is given. It also preserves some of the *hyangga* poems, the earliest literature written phonetically in Korean. The *Samguk yusa*, although an invaluable historical source, is better thought of as a collection of tales and stories containing many folk traditions in contrast to the *Samguk sagi*, which is an official history. It was written at the aftermath of the Mongol invasions by a Buddhist monk and has been viewed as part of a heightened awareness of a Korean cultural identity that many must have felt at this time. As such, it has been praised by twentieth-century nationalist historians who find the *Sam'guk sagi* to be too Chinese, and who see the real spirit and sentiment of Korea in Iryŏn's work.[13]

The *Samguk yusa* contains an especially rich collection of Buddhist legends and tales. The themes of these stories reveal the importance of Buddhist morality in Korean thought and literature at this time. In some beggars, outcastes, servants, poor peasants, and children turn out to be bodhisattvas. In one story a poor girl servant keeps trying to attend a temple service but is constantly blocked by her mistress. She becomes airborne and flies directly to the Buddha land. In another tale the famed monk Silla Wŏnhyo meets another monk, Hyekong. They go fishing, eat their catch, and then defecate on a rock. Hyekong, pointing to the excrement, says "Your fish is my shit," the meaning being that all things are part of the eternal changing world.[14] In a famous story known as "Chosin's Dream" a monk falls in love with the daughter of a magistrate. He prays for assistance in his love but the daughter marries another man. He has a dream where she appears and tells him that she secretly loves him and decides to spend her life with him. They live together for fifty years, have five children, and struggle with poverty. A son dies of starvation; a daughter becomes a beggar. Realizing their love has led only to their suffering they decide to part. Waking from the dream Chosin visits the spot in his dream where he buried his son and finds a Buddha statue buried instead. He establishes a monastery at the spot and dedicates his life to good deeds.[15]

The Rise of Neo-Confucianism

Late Koryŏ saw both a period of military-dominated government, the Mongol invasions, and the Mongol domination of the state. As important as these developments may be, neither probably had as much impact on Korean society as did the rise of Neo-Confucianism. Neo-Confucianism is a modern term for the school of Confucian thought that emerged during the Song period in China, culminating in the interpretations of Zhu Xi (1130–1200). Confucianism has had an enormous influence on Korea since the time of the Three Kingdoms. It was an ethical philosophy that taught that each individual should strive to pursue a virtuous life. This involved carefully and sincerely carrying out one's social obligations and serving family and society. It was also a political philosophy that stressed the duty of rulers to act as moral exemplars and to attend to the needs of the people in order to create a harmonious society. Confucianism respected formal learning and accepted a hierarchical society, a patriarchal family structure, and an authoritarian state. It viewed human nature as basically good if properly led, and saw human affairs as connected with natural affairs. Sometimes Confucianism is called familism in that Confucian thinkers saw the family as the primary unit of society and the state as a kind of superfamily with the ruler playing the role of the patriarchal family head. The ruler should be stern and proper but possess a fatherly love and a concern for those he rules.

But Confucianism was vague about the big questions such as: What is the nature of reality? Who is the real me? How am I connected with reality? Buddhism and to some degree Daoism supplied answers to these questions along with impressive rituals, practices of meditation, and the Buddhist concept of enlightenment. In China during the eleventh and twelfth centuries, Confucian scholars began to borrow metaphysical concepts and meditative practices from the Buddhists, and to a lesser extent from the Daoists. They began to reinterpret the Confucian classics, and to derive meaning and inspiration from them. Under Song thinkers such as Cheng Yi and Cheng Hao in the eleventh century and Zhu Xi in the twelfth these new formulations of

Confucianism, called by modern scholars Neo-Confucianism, were carefully elaborated in a set of works that became canonical to later generations.

The Yuan emperors sponsored this school of thought. Whatever its metaphysical teachings, the Yuan rulers saw Neo-Confucianism as a secular ideology that would assist them in the administration of their hybrid Chinese-Mongol state. When they revived the Chinese civil service exams in 1313 they made Zhu Xi's interpretations of Chinese classics authoritative for the exams. The close relations between Korea and Beijing in the late thirteenth and fourteenth century meant that there were many opportunities for Korean scholars and court officials to come in contact with Chinese scholars and Chinese intellectual activity. In addition, the Yuan was a cosmopolitan empire in which Koreans, Vietnamese, Central Asians, and others mingled. Foreigners were allowed to sit for the Chinese civil exams. Some Koreans studied and passed them, immersing themselves in Neo-Confucian learning. Many of these Koreans brought back to their country these new exciting formulations of Confucian thought. The introduction of Neo-Confucian learning brought more than just some new lines of interpretation. It caused many educated Koreans to reexamine their government, their society, and their personal behavior. This in turn led to a revolution that transformed Korean society and formed the basis of cultural norms, ethical standards, and conceptions about state and society that still influence Koreans in the twenty-first century.

During the period of Mongol domination some Koreans tried to promote Neo-Confucian learning in their own country. Starting with An Yu (1243–1306), they encouraged the rebuilding of the *Kukhak* (National Academy) and the *Munmyo* (National Shrine to Confucius). Both were carried out during the reign of King Ch'ungnyŏl (r. 1274–1308). These were important steps in the revival of Confucianism that marked the fourteenth century. By the late fourteenth century a group of eager scholars saw in Neo-Confucianism a blueprint for perfecting Korean society. Their basic ideas were: educate the ruler to act as a good moral exemplar for society; select only the virtuous to serve the monarch and govern society; eliminate the influence of Buddhism and any other rival and false schools of thought; and remodel both government institutions and family practices such as marriage on the ideals of Confucianism, especially the Zhu Xi interpretation of them. Foremost among these zealous scholars were Chŏng Mong-ju (1337–1392) and his rival Chŏng To-jŏn. They were especially hostile to Buddhism, which was "foreign" (that is, not from China or Korea), selfish since it stressed individual enlightenment instead of serving family and society, and too otherworldly.

The last years of the Koryŏ saw a continuation of the movement by some members of the aristocracy to promote Neo-Confucianism. In 1367 the state established the *Sŏnggyun'gwan* (National Confucian Academy) under the leadership of Yi Saek and Chŏng Mong-ju. There Zhu Xi's commentaries on the Four Books formed a central part of its curriculum. The faculty included Chŏng To-jŏn, who later played a central role in establishing the Yi dynasty. Its curriculum was a departure from previous schools. Education at private schools that aristocratic sons attended before serving in government included Confucian texts among the Chinese classics, but the emphasis was on belles lettres and developing formal literary polish. The scholars at this new school trained their students to examine the Chinese classics in order to grasp the underlying moral principles that governed the individual, society, and the cosmos. Not surprisingly they were highly critical of the society around them. They saw in Confucian principles the learned rules for ordering society and government, and they eventually sought to use their knowledge of these principles to assist a willing king. By the late fourteenth century, Neo-Confucian scholars joined with elements among the elite and military disgruntled with the court to establish the new Yi dynasty. Under this new dynasty Korea would undergo a significant cultural transformation.

Manjŏk's Slave Rebellion[16]

In King Sinjong's first year [1198], the private slave Manjŏk and six others, while collecting firewood on a northern mountain, gathered public and private slaves and plotted, saying, "Since the coup in the year *kyŏngin* [1170] and the countercoup in the *kyesa* [1173], the country has witnessed many high officials rising from slave status. How could these generals and ministers be different from us in origins? If one has an opportunity, anybody can make it. Why should we still till and suffer under the whip?"

The slaves all agreed with this, they cut several thousand pieces of yellow paper and on each put the graph *chŏng* [adult man] as their symbol. They pledged: "We will start from the hallways of Hŭngguk Monastery and go to the polo grounds. Once all are assembled and start to beat drums and yell, the eunuchs in the palace will certainly respond. The public slaves will take control of the palace by force, and we will stage an uprising inside the capital, first killing Ch'oe Ch'unghŏn and others. If each slave will kill his master and burn the slave registers, there will be no people of humble status in the country, and we can all become nobles, generals, and ministers."

On the date set to meet, their numbers did not exceed several hundred, so they feared they would not succeed and changed their plans, promising to meet at Poje Temple this time. All were ordered: "If the affair is not kept secret, then we will not succeed. Be careful not to reveal it." Sunjŏng, the slave of Doctor of Legal Studies Han Ch'ungyu, reported this incident to his master. Ch'ungyu told Ch'oe Ch'unghŏn, who seized Manjŏk and more than one hundred others and threw them in the river. Ch'ungyu was promoted to the warder in the Royal Archives, and Sunjŏng was granted eighty *yang* of white gold and manumitted to commoner status. Since the remaining gang could not all be executed, the king decreed that the matter be dropped.

—From *Koryŏ sa* 129:12–13a

NOTES

1. The major study of this topic is Edward J. Shultz, *Generals and Scholars: Military Rule in Medieval Korea* (Honolulu: University of Hawaii Press, 2000).

2. Edward J. Shultz. "Ch'oe Ch'unghon: His Rise to Power," *Korean Studies* 8 (1984): 58–82.

3. Shultz, *Generals and Scholars*, 54–109.

4. Robert E. Buswell, *The Korean Approach to Zen: Collected Works on Chinul* (Honolulu: University of Hawaii Press, 1983), 1–2.

5. Edward J. Shultz, "Ch'oe Chunghon and Minamoto Yoritomo," *Japan Review* 11 (1999): 31–53. Much of the comparison between Koryŏ and medieval Japan is drawn from this article.

6. See Jeffrey Mass, *Warrior Government in Early Medieval Japan* (New Haven, CT: Yale University Press, 1974).

7. William Henthorn, *Korea: The Mongol Invasions* (Leiden: Brill, 1963); William Henthorn, "Some Notes on Koryo Military Units," *Transactions of the Korea Branch of The Royal Asiatic Society* 35 (1959): 66–75; Gari Ledyard, "The Mongol Campaigns in Korea and the Dating of the *The Secret History of the Mongols*," *Central Asiatic Journal* 9 (1964): 1–22.

8. Kim Kichung, *Classical Korean Literature* (Armonk, NY: M. E. Sharpe, 1996), 62.

9. Peter Yun, "Foreigners in Korea during the Period of Mongol Interference," in *Proceedings of the 1st World Congress of Korean Studies: Embracing the Other: The Interaction of Korean and Foreign Cultures,* The Korean Academy of Korean Studies (Seoul: July 2002), 1221–28.

10. Paik Nak Choon, "Tripitika Koreana," *Transactions of the Korea Branch of the Royal Asiatic Society* 32 (Seoul: 1951): 62–78.

11. J. R. McNeill and William H. McNeill, *The Human Web* (New York: W. W. Norton & Company, 2003), 180.

12. Peter H. Lee, *Anthology of Korean Literature: From Early Times to the Nineteenth Century* (Honolulu: University of Hawaii Press, 1981), 51.

13. Choe Yong-ho, "An Outline History of Korean Historiography," *Korean Studies* 4 (1980): 1–27.

14. Kim, *Classical Korean Literature*, 66–67.

15. Kim, *Classical Korean Literature*, 69–71.

16. Peter H. Lee and William Theodore De Bary, eds., *Sources of Korean Tradition*, vol. 1, *From Early Times through the Sixteenth Century* (New York: Columbia University Press, 1997), 200.

6

The Neo-Confucian Revolution and the Chosŏn State

ESTABLISHING THE YI DYNASTY

Few events in Korea's premodern history are more important than the establishment of the Chosŏn state under the Yi dynasty. It was more than a change of dynasties; it was a long-term attempt to create a society in conformity to Confucian values and beliefs. The effort, while involving close study of Chinese models, contributed to the further evolution of a distinctive Korean cultural and political entity. Today when Koreans talk of "traditional society" they generally are referring the culture and society that emerged during this period.

The dynastic founder Yi Sŏng-gye, after deposing the last Koryŏ monarch, made himself king. He was posthumously designated King T'aejo, the first of the Yi dynasty that was to rule Korea to 1910. Yi Sŏng-gye placed his supporters, who he named "Dynastic Foundation Merit Subjects," in key positions, and these men dominated Korea for the next few decades. They established the institutions of the new state and promoted the ideals of Neo-Confucianism. The new government officially named the state Chosŏn so that the period of Korean history from 1392 to 1910 is referred to as either the Chosŏn or the Yi dynasty period. To mark a new start for his new dynasty Yi Sŏng-gye and his supporters in 1394, believing the geomantic force of Kaesŏng was exhausted, established a new capital at Hanyang (today called Seoul). Careful consideration based on geomantic principles went into the selection. The city was protected on the north by mountains, and on the south by the Han River. It was also a practical location since it was in the agriculturally rich and centrally located Kyŏnggi region. The location on the Han River, one of the major rivers of Korea, assisted in communicating with the interior. The actual construction of the city was largely left to Yi Sŏng-gye's successor T'aejong (r. 1400–1418), who in 1404 and again in 1412, summoned more than one hundred thousand corvée laborers to build the palaces, government buildings, city walls, and gates. The city was modeled on Chinese imperial capitals, albeit on a smaller scale, with the main streets laid on a north-south, east-west grid. Seoul soon came to be the great city of Korea, the center of government, learning, the arts, and commerce—a place it has occupied ever since.

Yi Sŏng-gye justified the new dynasty with the concept of the Mandate of Heaven (Chinese: *keming*; Korean: *hyŏngmyŏng*). According to Yi and his supporters the last years of the Koryŏ saw rule by immoral men who ruled through puppet kings. Confucian belief was that the ruler must be a person of integrity and virtue who sets a moral example or else the harmony between Heaven and Earth can not be maintained, there will be calamities, and the people will become restless. This, according to Yi, had happened in the years after Kongmin when self-serving, evil officials ruled through weak monarchs. To further justify his assumption of power the dynastic founders argued that the legitimate line of Wang kings had died out with Kongmin. In such a situation there was no recourse but to assume the throne. "The ancestral altar must surely be returned to the man of virtue and the great throne should not be left vacant too long. With merit and virtue, the public mind can be won. The ranks and offices [of government] should be correctly reestablished to pacify the people's discontent. I, lacking virtue, decline [the offer of the throne] repeatedly for fear that I may not be competent to carry the burden. Everyone is saying, however, that the Heavenly mandate has already been manifested in the popular will. No one should resist the public will. Nor should he go against Heaven. Holding this [principle] firmly, I have decided, with humility, to follow the public will and to accept the throne."[1]

The new dynasty carried out important reforms, most notably land reform. Prior to his assumption of the throne Yi Sŏng-gye carried out a comprehensive land survey, destroying old registrars of public and private land. The court created a new set of land registrars with the intention of making sure that less land escaped taxation. The king confiscated the huge holdings of the Buddhist temples, a move that weakened institutional Buddhism and that was enthusiastically embraced by the anti-Buddhists among his followers. The former temple holdings were redistributed to his supporters and added to the tax base.

The new dynasty was largely the creation of an alliance of military men such as Yi and a group of scholar-officials eager to reform society by creating a new state based on Neo-Confucian principles. The most important of these officials was Chŏng To-jŏn. Chŏng was from Ch'ungch'ŏng Province in southern Korea. His father was a government official from the lesser aristocracy. Most of his lineage had served as *hyangni* (local government officials). A student of Neo-Confucian scholar Yi Saek (1328–1396), he was appointed to the National Confucian Academy faculty when Yi Saek became its head. Chŏng To-jŏn was driven into exile for pro-Ming sentiments by Yi In-im in 1375. After living in poverty in a small village he went to Yi Sŏng-gye's remote frontier camp and became his chief political adviser. When Yi came to power Chŏng used his influence to secure key positions. As a civilian head of the armed forces command he worked toward abolishing private armies and creating a new central army under civilian control. His most important contribution was drawing up the *Statutes for the Governance of Chosŏn*, an outline for the new government.[2] Many of the institutions of the new dynasty were based on this outline.

A central part of Chŏng To-jŏn's program was land reform. In late Koryŏ most land was in the hands of large landholders. Most peasants worked as tenants paying a customary one-half their crops in rent. Based on the Confucian ideal that the ruler governed in the interests of the welfare of his people, as well as the practical need to bring more land under government taxation, he called for converting all land into public land. This would then be distributed equally among all the peasants, who would then pay a small portion in taxes. Chŏng To-jŏn cited the idealistic picture of Zhou China in the *Rites of Zhou*, which had become part of the Confucian canon, to justify this proposal. While too radical for adoption, it illustrates the idealistic zeal of Chŏng and many of his colleagues.

Chŏng and others wanted to end the relationship between Buddhism and the state. Late Koryŏ Neo-Confucianists such as Yi Saek had been critical of Buddhism. They chided monks for their moral laxity and their involvement in politics. The example of Sin Ton, who served as King Kongmin's chief advisor, was a case in point. Neo-Confucianist reformers were also critical of the expense of supporting temples and of elaborate rituals. Temples, they felt, owned too much land, reducing the tax base. Some officials of the new dynasty such as Chŏng To-jŏn regarded Buddhism as an undesirable alien faith. Buddhism, in their opinion, did not respect the social relations that held society together. Its tradition of celibacy was a threat to family and lineage, and its concept of abstract universal love was inimical to the graded love of Confucianism that gave primacy to family, then to friends, and then to neighbors. It encouraged withdrawal from society, not active participation in it. This harsh antipathy was not shared by Yi Sŏng-gye or by many of the members of court. It was a minority view at the start of the dynasty; however, it gradually prevailed. Consequently, Buddhism retreated from playing an active role in state affairs. There was some backsliding. King Sejo (r. 1455–1468), for example, was a vigorous patron of Buddhism, but the connection with Buddhism and the state was eventually broken.

Yi Sŏng-gye, nonetheless, emphasized continuity, not radical change. At the onset of his reign he ordered that all the rites of the Koryŏ be observed.

Most Koryŏ officials were kept. Only a small number of those were purged, such as the distinguished scholar Chŏng Mong-ju, who while supporting the movement for reform remained loyal to the old dynasty. In general, the change of dynasty was relatively smooth and bloodless. One of the major issues in Korean history has been whether the establishment of the Yi dynasty marked a revolution or simply a change of dynasties. The answer may be, while it was more than a simple change of dynasties it was not quite a revolution. The new dynasty brought a number of new individuals and clans into the seats of power, and restructured or newly created the institutions of government. Most of all, the promotion of Neo-Confucianism gave the new Chosŏn state a more rigid ideological orientation than had been the case in Koryŏ or Silla.

Many, if not most, of the great families that dominated late Koryŏ society survived into the new dynasty. Rather than a replacement of one dominant social group by another, a number of new people joined the ruling aristocracy of landed officials and scholars. Indeed, most of the Neo-Confucian reformers came from aristocratic families. Kwŏn Kŭn (1352–1409), one of the leading members of the new government, came from the Andong Kwŏn clan, one of the most illustrous families under the old dynasty.[3] Yi Sŏng-gye himself represented one of the small number of new number of men, mostly of a military background, who joined the old elite. Although Yi later claimed to be of a long distinguished family from Chŏnju in southern Korea, his family actually came from the northern frontier. Yi's family may have been of northeast Asian tribal origin. His father, Yi Cha-ch'un, rose to prominence during the Mongol period as a military commander and cooperated with Kongmin to retake the northeast region occupied by the Mongols. Yi Sŏng-gye, his second son, distinguished himself in campaigns against the Red Turbans, the Japanese pirates, and the Mongols. So while the dynastic family and some of its supporters were new members of the elite, most of officialdom came from the old aristocratic familes.

Furthermore, the change of dynasty did not mean a sharp ideological change. Neo-Confucianism had already begun to gain adherents in late Koryŏ. Nor was Neo-Confucianism itself an entirely new way of thinking. To a large extent it was a revitalization of Confucian values and ideas of government and society that had long influenced Korean culture. One major change was the anti-Buddhism of the new dynasty. But as mentioned above most Yi officials did not completely reject Buddhism, and it continued to have some hold on society; even many members of the royal family supported temples and consulted monks.

If the establishment of the Yi dynasty did not mark an immediate radical change, it nonetheless helped to set in motion a significant transformation in Korean society. Although Neo-Confucianism grew out of the long tradition of Confucian thought, it was revolutionary in its insistence that the state and society be structured according to the moral principles that governed the universe. While the initial changes were not revolutionary, eventually under the influence of Neo-Confucianism Korean society and culture went through profound changes. As a result of Neo-Confucianism, Korea under the new dynasty did see major changes in the family, the role of women, the conduct of the yangban, and art and literature. In the long run then, what took place in Korea is sometimes called a Neo-Confucian Revolution. These changes, however, took place gradually over several centuries. Only by the eighteenth century did Korea become the model Confucian society that most modern Koreans see as "traditional." Therefore, the dynasty inaugurated profound change, but in a more evolutionary fashion. Indeed, one could argue that the continuity between early Chosŏn Korea and the Korea of Silla and Koryŏ is just as striking as the changes.

THE CHOSŎN STATE

At the apex of the Chosŏn state was the king. Under him was a complex set of bureaucratic institutions to carry out his rule. The highest organ of government was the *Ŭijŏngbu* (State Council).[4] It was similar to the Privy Council of Koryŏ except that it had fewer members, only seven. Members reviewed important matters then gave their opinion to the king. After receiving his decision the State Council then transmitted it down the bureaucracy. The State Council had general powers of surveillance over all government offices and affairs, which were known as *sŏsa*, general supervisory authority. The three highest-ranking members, the High State Councilors, were especially important. The king frequently referred to them, and they often carried out public policy independently of the other members. No other position held as much prestige as being a High Councilor, and they tended to hold their positions for long periods of time. The four junior members tended to have little influence and held positions for shorter periods. In the early days Merit Subjects, people appointed to high office by the king in return for aiding him in some way, dominated High State Councilor positions. Most State Council members, however, came up through the civil examination system. Gradually during the long Yi dynasty the State Council declined in importance.

The day-to-day administration was carried out by the *Yukcho* (Six Ministries): Personnel, Taxation, Rites, Military Affairs, Punishments, and Public Works. Personnel was in charge of nominations for office, certification of appointments, ranks, titles, evaluation of the performance of officeholders, and conducting special procedures for recruiting personnel. Taxation carried out censuses, maintained population registers, made land surveys and land registers, collected taxes, distributed funds, and maintained warehouses.

Rites handled foreign relations, supervised the schools and examinations, licensed monks, and supervised state ceremonies. War included the supervision of post roads, beacon fire communication systems, fortifications, and weapons production. Punishments was the judicial branch of government in charge of both civil and criminal cases. Works dealt with construction and repair of public buildings, bridges, roads, state mining and lumbering operations, and the production of articles for state use by the corps of state artisans. Each ministry was headed by a board consisting of three or four ministers. Their direct access to the king made the ministers important.

Another important institution was the *Sǔngjǒngwǒn* (Royal Secretariat), an organ that transmitted documents to and from the king. At times it acted on its own without regard to other government bodies. There were six members, each in charge of dealing with one of the Six Ministries. Two recorders in the Royal Secretariat kept diaries of daily activities; their careful recordings were one of the sources for the *Sillok*, the official record of the reign (see below). These institutions were modeled on those of China, but fit the Korean pattern of rule by councils or committees of aristocrats.

There were eight provinces, which are still the provinces of Korea today: Kyǒnggi, Ch'ungch'ǒng, Kyǒngsang, Chǒlla, Hwanghae, Kangwǒn, Hamgil (today called Hamgyǒng), and P'yǒngan. Each had a centrally appointed governor and six government departments based on those of the central government. The provinces were divided into counties of which there were several types. The number of counties varied somewhat, but were around three hundred. Each was headed by a centrally appointed county magistrate. The county magistrate was an important figure who represented the state at the local level. Each county also had a *Hyangch'ǒng* (Local Agency) organized by yangban residents, which wielded considerable influence. The Local Agency was directed by a *chwasu* (overseer) and his assistants and undertook responsibilities for assisting the magistrate, rectifying public mores, and scrutinizing the conduct of the county's petty functionaries, called *hyangni*. The Local Agency served as a power base for the local yangban. To counter the power of the local elite a *Kyǒngjaeso* (Capital Liaison Office) in Seoul for each county, headed by central government officials from that county, existed to see that the Local Agency served the central state's, not local, interests.

The Yi rulers maintained the basic classification of officials into the *yangban* (two sides) consisting of *munban* (civil officials) and the less prestigious *muban* (military officials). The tradition of discrimination against military officials resumed and became more pronounced in the later years of the dynasty. Officials as in Koryǒ were graded into nine ranks, a practice developed in China a millennium earlier. Each rank was subdivided into senior and junior ranks such as senior first rank and junior first rank to make a total of eighteen grades of officials. The most elite of the officials were those of senior third rank and above, known as the *tangsanggwan*. Strict protocol and sumptuary laws governed the behavior and respect given to each rank.

THE CENSORATE AND THE *KYŎNGYŎN* (CLASSICS MAT)

One of the important institutions of Korea was the censorate, an institution with no exact counterpart in Western institutional history. Although borrowed from China, the censorate in Korea had far more power. The censorate existed in the Koryŏ period when it was known as the Ŏsadae. It played a greater role during the Yi dynasty. Under the Yi the censorate was known as the *Samsa* or three institutions. The two chief institutions that made up the censorate were: the *Sahŏnbu* (Office of Inspector-General) with six members, that dealt with political issues, official conduct and public morals, and the *Saganwŏn* (Censor-General), which scrutinized and criticized the conduct of the king. A third institution, the *Hongmun'gwan* (Office of Special Advisors), was created in 1478. Its members maintained books in the royal library, composed royal epitaphs and eulogies, and compiled state-sponsored texts. It also served as a panel of advisors to the king on policy and principle, and gave lessons on history and the orthodox Chinese writers. The *Hongmun'gwan* had seventeen members, mostly younger officials.

The censoring organs were the moral guardians or moral police of the state. They had the unique right to investigate the backgrounds of all those who were appointed to office to find out if they were morally fit to serve or if they had the proper aristocratic background. They also saw to it that no one with dishonorable or disloyal ancestors would serve the state. They reviewed the actions of officials and of the king himself, and issued moral condemnations for improper conduct. Since good Confucians made no distinction between private and public conduct, the censors carefully scrutinized the private as well as public lives of officials. They also reviewed the behavior of the general public and issued ethical guidelines. Most officials served as censors for only short periods, yet while in office censors, often quite young, frequently carried out their responsibilities with persistency and zeal. At times the censorate was used as a base for power by ambitious individuals and factions. Since most censors were well schooled in the tenets of Neo-Confucianism and were firm adherents of them, the organs acted as one of the institutional bases for the great undertaking of making Korea a model Confucian society.

Another base for Neo-Confucian reformist zeal was the *Kyŏngyŏn* (Classics Mat) (*Kyŏngyŏn*). Modeled on the Song China *jingyan* advocated by the Neo-Confucianist thinkers Cheng Yi (1033–1108) and Zhu Xi, the Classics Mat was instituted as a lecture program that in 1392 was organized with a staff of twenty-one. Although the first three Yi kings seldom attended, the fifteenth-century king Sejong attended daily. Later in the fifteenth century it met three times a day. Censors, historians, and a royal secretary attended. Since members of the censorate often supplied and conducted the lessons, the Classics Mat contributed to an increase in the power of censorial organs. At these sessions the reader would read and lead a discussion of the Confucian classics and commentaries on the classics by such luminaries as Zhu Xi. To further edify the monarch, historical works were included in addition to the Neo-Confucian texts. Readers could digress from texts to discuss implications for current affairs. The Classics Mat was designed to guide the monarch; it served as an agency for promoting Neo-Confucian concepts at court.

HISTORIANS

Another feature of the Yi dynasty was the significant role of the state historians. They too promoted Neo-Confucian ideals. The monarchs and officials of the Yi dynasty took history seriously as a guide to statecraft. Three High State Councillors supervised the *Ch'unch'ugwan* (Bureau of State Records), the official government archives. Daily records were kept by officials from the *Yemun'gwan* (Office of Royal Decrees). Low-ranking posts were usually held by young bureaucrats who held great prestige despite their age. Due to their importance, a careful and elaborate procedure took place for selecting them. They were to be free of vested interests and it was thought that their youthful idealism would keep "their brushes straight."[5] Careful daily records of all proceedings at court were kept. Historians followed the king and recorded both his conversations with officials and his facial expressions as well. No official business could be transacted without their presence. The records were not made available to the king. In contrast to Ming China where the first Ming emperor insisted on seeing what had been recorded, similar requests from Yi monarchs were denied. At the end of each reign the *Sillok Veritable Records* was compiled. This was a multivolume, detailed account of each reign.

Chosŏn-era Koreans regarded history and the role of the historian as matters of great importance. As good Confucian scholars they viewed history as an indispensable source of guidance for those that governed and as a source of moral tales providing examples of virtue and vice that would instruct all who read it. Since history was valuable for instruction for both governance and morality, historical works were included in the Classics Mat. Through their writing of history, Yi dynasty historians promoted the ideals and principles of Neo-Confucianism. Because of history's vital role in governance, great efforts were made to preserve the historical records. Four copies of the daily record of proceedings at court were kept, one in Seoul, and one each in the provincial cities of Sŏngju, Ch'ungju, and Chŏnju. This precaution served the dynasty well when the Japanese invasions destroyed all but the Chŏnju archives. The government then had all records copied and established new archives at remote islands and mountains.

To understand the past in order to guide them in their endeavor to create a moral society, scholars at the beginning of the dynasty began the work of compiling an official history of the Koryŏ. The *Koryŏ sa* (*History of Koryŏ*), after going through several versions, was completed in 1451. It reflected the Confucian commitments of its authors, who neglected to give any special attention to Buddhism. Furthermore it justified the establishment of the new dynasty by painting the later years of the Koryŏ as a time of decline when the dynasty had lost its mandate from heaven. Today it is the primary source for the Koryŏ period. In 1452, the *Koryŏ sa chŏryo* (*Abridged Essence of the Three Kingdoms*), a shorter official history in the *p'yŏnnyŏn* (annalistic format), was independently compiled. It contains information not found in the *Koryŏ sa*. Several other officially sponsored histories were compiled during the early Yi. One of the most significant is the *Tongguk t'onggam* (*Comprehensive Mirror of the Eastern Kingdom*), compiled by Sŏ Kŏ-jŏng in 1485. This covered all of Korean history from Tan'gun to the fall of the Koryŏ, and was possibly the most widely read history in the Chosŏn dynasty period. Another important work was Han Paek-kyŏm's (1552–1615) *Tongguk chiri chi* (*Treatise on Historical Geography*). Han's history influenced later historiography with his theories on the origins of the Three Kingdoms and the location of the three Han tribes.

THE EXAMINATION SYSTEM

Most officials in Chosŏn Korea were selected through the examination system. Since serving in office was the most prestigious occupation as well as a vital way to protect a family's interest it became the goal of most ambitious families to have a son who passed the exams. In a society where no other culturally sanctioned avenue to power and prestige existed, the exam system was of enormous importance. While education was recognized as an end in itself, in practice, it was also understood to be a means of social mobility and status selection. Potential office seekers had to go through a series of highly competitive examinations. These civil examinations were divided into the lower-level *sokwa* or *sama* exams where a student could choose to take either the *saengwŏn* (classics) or the *chinsa* (literary) exam. The passage of these exams did not secure an official post, but it did bring certain privileges, such as eligibility for government office and exemption from military duties. Most importantly it qualified its successful passers for the higher civil exam called the *taekwa* or *munkwa,* which was the real vehicle to high government office.

The lower-level *sama* or *sokwa* exams began at the provincial level. First, hopefuls took the *ch'osi* or preliminary exam at their province's capital. Those who succeeded in these provincial exams could take the metropolitan exam in Seoul. To insure representation from all parts of the country a quota was established for the number of candidates from each province and from Seoul. Those selecting the classics exam wrote two essays. In the first they explicated the meaning of a short passage that was given from one of the Five Classics of ancient China: *The Classic of Changes, The Classic of History, The Classic of Songs, The Spring and Autumn Annals,* and the *Classic of Rituals.* For the second essay they wrote on the issues involved in several passages given from the Four Books, the most revered works of Confucianism: The *Analects* of Confucius, *The Book of Mencius, The Great Learning* and *The Doctrine of the Mean.* Those who chose the literary exam were required to compose one *pu* (rhyme-prose) and one old-style poem, each based on a topic and rhyme given at the examination. A candidate could sit for both exams. Passing both brought great honor. Successful examinees received a white diploma presented by the king. This degree enabled the recipient to enroll in the National Academy in Seoul and to sit for the higher-level civil examinations. It generally did not result in an appointment for office. Since the Yi dynasty, holding a degree was important to confirm social status; for many this was enough and they returned home to play prominent roles in their local communities.

The higher level exam, the *taekwa* or *munkwa* was the real gateway to public office holding. Passing the higher civil examination was not easy and most lower exam passers never succeeded. There was no limit to how often one could take the exam, and some persistent candidates took it many times, well into old age. There were three stages to this exam. The first was a preliminary provincial-level exam. In taking the classics exam one had to write an essay on the Five Classics and the Four Books and another essay on an assigned topic. For the literary exam candidates had to compose a formal memorial or report and a dissertation on an assigned topic. The second stage was the metropolitan exam in Seoul. The third stage was the *chŏnsi* (palace exam) taken under the supervision of the king. The top thirty-three examinees received the coveted *munkwa.* All exams were triennial and were held throughout the dynasty until they were abolished in 1894, with the exception of 1594 and 1597 during the Japanese invasions and 1636 during the Manchu invasions. In addition to the triennial exams special exams were held from time to time. This practice of holding special exams became more common during the late Yi period.

Although a few men of commoner status may have been allowed to take the exams in the early years of the dynasty, they served chiefly to allocate official positions among members of the *yangban* aristocratic elite. The examination system acted as the main selection device for the limited number of government posts. Formal education was largely organized around preparation for the exams. Another feature of education and the examination system during this period is the incongruity between the ideal of meritocracy implied by the system and the reality of a society that emphasized bloodlines and kinship. For while in many ways Korea became the Confucian society par excellence, it was dominated by a hereditary aristocratic elite. The Neo-Confucianism that developed in Song China and that became the reigning orthodoxy in Korea in the fourteenth century had a strong egalitarian streak that emphasized the perfectibility of all men. It assumed that each individual was capable of benefiting from education and of achieving moral enlightenment. Neo-Confucianism emphasized the need for society to be governed by men of talent and virtue, which could best be demonstrated by mastery of the classics, self-discipline, and personal conduct. In conformity with this ideology, the schools and the civil examinations were opened to all except outcaste groups (see chapter 7), but in reality a number of practices arose that limited access to both state schools and the exams. In addition, preparation for the examinations required many years of study. Those parents who could afford to finance lengthy studies and hire tutors had an enormous advantage. And as studies have shown, Korean society was one where family lines, along with rank and hierarchy, were of vital importance. In reality, therefore, the examination system and the schools associated with it primarily served as a means of allocating power, privilege, and status, all closely associated with officeholding, among members of the *yangban* aristocracy.

Unlike in China there were no exam halls in Korea. All exams were conducted in the open. A fence would be put up around an area and candidates would have to take the exams with no protection from the elements. Many complained of enduring rain and snow. In the eighteenth century some examinees began to set up tents. Cheating was always a problem. Common forms of cheating were having someone take the exam for a candidate and collusion between the examinees. Bribery and nepotism were also a problem. Others cheated by smuggling notes written on thin paper and stuffing them up their nostrils, which led to the slang term "wisdom storage" for nostrils.[6]

The degree holders formed an important elite. Because of the law of avoidance, another Chinese practice, officials could not serve in their home localities. This meant that the local country magistrates and other local officials were usually not familiar with the area they administered. Degree holders living in the community were able to advise the official on local conditions. Degree holders also formed organizations such as *samaso* that acted as both social organizations and local pressure groups. Since taking the exams was such an intense experience, those who took and passed the same examinations often formed *tongnyŏnhoe* (classmate organizations) whose members met at regular reunions.[7]

Not all officials were recruited through civil examinations. Some came to office through the *ch'ŏn'gŏ* (recommendation system). Senior civil and military officials of the third rank and above submitted lists of three worthy men every third year to the Ministry of Personnel. If the ministry approved, the men could be appointed to office. Appointment was not automatic, and the candidate would be tested on one book of the candidate's choice from the Four Books and the Five Classics. Provincial governors, too, would sometimes recommend local men for submission to the Ministry of Personnel as candidates to be examined. The total number of officials appointed this way was not large, and it never rivaled the use of civil examinations as a way of recruiting the men who administered the state. Nonetheless, the recommendation system had its supporters among the elite. The recommendation system appointees were called *yuil* (people of merit and integrity). The practice went back as early as Han China and was used during the Koryŏ. It was based on the same Confucian principle of government by men of merit as the civil examinations. Many scholars and officials regarded the examinations as an inadequate or incomplete method of selecting worthy individuals. Recommendations were seen as a way to find such worthies who had been overlooked by the exams. Some scholars, such as Cho Kwang-jo in the sixteenth century, wanted to abolish the examination system and rely exclusively on recommendations.[8] Despite its champions, the recommendation system was strictly of secondary importance as a method of recruiting officials. In general *yuil* possessed less prestige than the exam passers and held only low-ranking posts. Another method of securing an office was through purchase. This practice, called *napsok pogwan* (appointment through grain contributions), was usually done during emergencies. This was a method of the state to raise money; often it meant only that a prestigious degree was purchased, not an actual appointment to office. Many degrees were sold this way during the Japanese invasions of the late sixteenth century, but at most times it was not common.

EDUCATION

Education in traditional Korea was valued as a means of personal self-cultivation and as a way of achieving status and power. An individual could become virtuous through the study of ethically oriented Confucian classics. He could go on to play an informal role as a moral exemplar and as a teacher and advisor to others, thus enhancing his status and influence in society. As in other East Asian societies, Koreans highly esteemed the written word and the prodigious efforts needed to master the accumulated body of literary and scholarly works. Furthermore, the examination system reinforced the importance of learning.

In order to have a supply of educated men from which to select officials, the early Yi dynasty leadership established a fairly comprehensive network of schools. These schools were seen as a means of establishing loyalty, maintaining orthodoxy, and recruiting officials. Basic education was provided for by village schools known as *sŏjae* or *sŏdang* and by private tutoring. The *sŏdang* remained the most common institution of formal education in Korea until well into the twentieth century. At a more advance level, a system of *hyanggyo* (state-sponsored local schools) existed to prepare students for the civil examinations. These included the *sahak*, four schools organized in four of the five districts of Seoul, and schools established in each of the provinces. The *sahak* in Seoul accepted one hundred and sixty and later just one hundred students in each of its schools. There were over three hundred *hyanggyo* (the figure varied somewhat over time) throughout the countryside. The state fixed the number of students assigned to each of these schools in the fifteenth century, ranging from thirty to ninety. Students entered at around the age of sixteen and at about the age of eighteen or nineteen were allowed to sit for the lower-level civil exams. Admittance to a *hyanggyo* brought with it the coveted status of *yuhak* that included exemption from military duty and eligibility for taking the civil service exams. At the pinnacle of Chosŏn education were those who passed the *sama* (lower-level examinations) and entered the *Sŏnggyun'gwan* (National Confucian Academy). These students were generally eighteen or nineteen years old when admitted. Sometime between the ages of twenty and twenty-three they would compete for the *munkwa*, the higher civil service examination.

The basic structure of Chosŏn schooling was set up in the early fifteenth century; however, there were significant changes during subsequent centuries. The official schools experienced a gradual decline. Although they continued to function until the end of the nineteenth century, their role as agents of advanced schooling was challenged by the *sŏwŏn* or private academies that emerged in the middle of the sixteenth century. Unlike the *hyanggyo*, which were usually located in administrative centers, the *sŏwŏn* sprang up in the countryside. They functioned as rural retreats for the literati, and as shrines to honor scholars and officials, as well as centers of learning. About 680 *sŏwŏn* were founded by the end of the eighteenth century, and they served as important bases for political factions until most of them were closed in the decade after 1864.

Education trained the cultivated generalist. There was disdain for the specialist and for technical training that prevailed into recent times. Although *chapkwa*, specialized technical exams, existed for certifying doctors, astronomers, interpreters, and other needed professionals, they remained far less prestigious; education was basically of a nonspecialized, literary nature that

has remained the preference of most Koreans. The people who took the specialized exams were largely from the *chungin* class, not the *yangban* aristocracy (see chapter 7).

Literacy in Korea among males was probably high by premodern standards, and most likely increased in the eighteenth and nineteenth centuries.
An indication of this is the growth in private academies that promoted education among the *yangban* class. But even commoner boys attended village
schools where an ability to read basic moral texts was considered essential
to being a good husband, father and neighbor. In addition, literacy no doubt
brought about advantages in legal disputes and enabled individuals to keep
informed of government regulations. Literacy among commoners was facilitated by the use of the Korean alphabet, *han'gŭl* (see below). There was also
a thriving popular literature of adventure stories and romances, an indicator
of high rates of literacy. For commoners schooling was confined to *sŏdang*
village schools. These consisted of a teacher and boys of different ages, often
quite young. The *sŏdang* became a feature of Korean village life. Literacy
among females was very low and largely confined to a small number of elite
women; some of these, however, were highly educated by private tutors.
Another exception was the *kisaeng*, the refined female entertainers (see chapter 7).

The scholar-teacher held an exalted position. Since organized religion was
peripheral to Chosŏn society, it was the school and the teacher, rather than
the temple and the priest, that served as the principal source of ethical coun-
sel. Consequently, the scholar obtained an almost sacred status. The learned
man was more than a scholar or teacher: he was the moral arbiter of society
and source of guidance at the village as well as the state level. Thus, the value
placed on learning and the position of the teacher in society were extremely
high. Teachers, scholars, and earnest students were vested with considerable
moral authority. This was the basis for the tradition of remonstrance, the
right to issue formal protests based on ethical principles. It was the duty of
the scholar to criticize the actions of the government, including the king;
since Confucianism perceived the universe as a moral order, improper behavior on the part of officials and rulers threatened that order. Scholars and
lower-ranked officials wrote memorials, and students at the *Sŏnggyun'gwan*
held protest demonstrations when they felt that those in positions of authority were not adhering to ethical standards or were improperly performing
rituals. Students in the Academy periodically withdrew from school in mass
protests, with nineteen such incidents recorded in the reign of King Sukchong (1674–1720) and twenty in the reign of King Sunjo (1800–1834).[9] This
tradition of equating education and scholarship with moral authority, hence
giving students and scholars the right and duty to criticize officialdom, has
been one of the most persistent features of Korean education. It is a tradition
still felt in Korea today.

AGRICULTURAL IMPROVEMENTS
AND THE STATE

The Chosŏn state was based on an agricultural society. The prosperity of the state was a result of the improvements in farming that eventually resulted in an increase in the population. Since the bulk of the population consisted of peasants and it was they who paid most of the taxes and provided most of the labor, the state was vitally concerned with agriculture. New farming methods developed during the Song period in the Yangzi River Valley and in southern China known as the "Jiangnan Farming Techniques." These involved improved strains of rice, intercropping, and the use of wet field rice production in which rice was planted and then transplanted in shallow flooded paddies. Wet field farming allowed for repeated cultivation of the same field. Korea's climate, colder and drier than the southern Chinese regions, hindered the spread of these techniques, but in the middle of the fourteenth century the new methods of transplanting rice were beginning to be practiced in Korea. It was not until the seventeenth century that this more intensive style of agriculture became dominant in the southern part of the country. However, it was already increasing the ability of the southern provinces Chŏlla and Kyŏngsang to increase production and support more dense populations in the early Chosŏn dyansty.

A number of other improvements in farming occurred. Farmers were beginning to make greater use of fertilizers; that meant less time letting the land remain in fallow. Under local government supervision hundreds of small reservoirs were constructed to minimize the impact of drought, and better strains of seed came into use. Interest in agricultural improvements by the elite is reflected in the appearance of agricultural manuals. Koreans had long been familiar with Chinese agricultural manuals; now they produced their own, adapted to local conditions. The first known agricultural manual, *Nongsa chiksŏl (Straight Talk on Farming)*, was compiled in 1430. It was followed by other published works on farming. New land was brought under cultivation. According to the national land-tax records the amount of arable land, which totaled about 930,000 *kyŏl* at the beginning of the fifteenth century, had reached 1,700,000 *kyŏl* by the middle of the sixteenth.[10] These records are notoriously unreliable and much of the land went unreported to evade taxation, but they do suggest that a considerable expansion of agriculture occurred during the early Chosŏn dynasty.

MILITARY AND FOREIGN AFFAIRS

With potentially dangerous tribal peoples to the north and Japanese raiders on the coast, the Yi rulers were aware of the need for a strong military.

Indeed, the dynasty was founded by a general. One of the first challenges of the early monarchs was to create an effective central army. With this in mind, T'aejo, the first Yi king, established the *Ŭihŭng Samgunbu* (Three Armies Headquarters) to provide central control over the military. In the early years of the dynasty members of the royal family maintained personal armed retainers. King T'aejong (1400–1418) abolished these private forces, bringing all soldiers under the authority of the Three Armies Headquarters. The era of private armies came to an end in Korea. Only the central state now had military forces. Sejo, in 1464, reorganized the army into the *Owi Toch'ongbu* (Five Military Commands Headquarters). The five commands were named after the regions of the country where they were stationed: Center, West, East, North, and South. The divisions were divided into five *pu* (brigades), which consisted of four *t'ong* (regiments), and these in turn were divided into *yŏ* (companies) and *tae* (platoons). Professional soldiers had to pass a series of tests, and these soldiers were supplemented by *chŏngbyŏng* (conscripts) in the capital garrisons. Beyond this were the provincial armies. Each province had an Army Command and Navy Command with control of provincial garrison forces called *chinsugun* stationed in *chin* (garrisons). Under this *chin'gwan* system district magistrates would assume defense of their own walled towns. Peasants were assigned as garrison forces serving on a rotation basis.

In the fifteenth century Korea maintained a policy of military vigor. But with the frontiers secured (see below), the army and navy went into a decline. The rise of Neo-Confucianism also contributed to this decline. Confucian officials tended to take less interest in military affairs and viewed military men with contempt. *Yangban* avoided the military while soldiers were recruited primarily from the peasantry and treated poorly. Since few volunteered, the state supplied the armed forces with men through the *popŏp* (Paired Provisioner) system. A team of two or three able-bodied men was supported while on active service by the provisioners, who supplied the conscripted soldiers with fixed amounts of cotton cloth. They were similarly supported when their turn to serve came up. This system was unpopular and ineffective. Conscripts under the Paired Provisioner system were poorly trained and had low morale. Peasants evaded service whenever they could. The decline in the military forces led to the disastrous defeats when the Japanese invaded in the late sixteenth century and the Manchus invaded in the early seventeenth.

Early Chosŏn foreign policy centered around securing its legitimacy, establishing correct relations with China, and securing its borders from the threats of its tribal neighbors on the Manchurian border and from Japanese pirates along the southern coasts. Establishing friendly relations with Ming China was a central component of the new political and social order established by the founders of the Chosŏn dynasty. Yet relations remained tense between the Ming and the Chosŏn courts during the first years of the Chosŏn. The Chinese looked at Korean attempts to establish their borders at the Yalu and Tumen Rivers with great suspicion. Memories of Koguryŏ and Parhae control over Manchuria mixed with fears of a Korean-Jurchen alliance. Several embassies were turned back on various excuses, such as that the horses sent as tribute were unfit. To mollify the Chinese, members of the royal family such as Prince Pangwŏn were sent to the Ming court at Nanjing as hostages. The Yi officials wanted good relations with China for ideological as well as practical reasons. China was the home of the sages, of Confucius, Zhu Xi, and of civilization. The Yi kings sought Chinese recognition as a way of legitimizing themselves as bearers of civilized values. Ming suspicions soon waned and relations improved in the early fifteenth century.

The Chosŏn court operated in a hierarchical world order. Its external relations were a matter of placing foreigners in that hierarchy and treating them accordingly. At the top of the hierarchy was Ming China, with which it maintained friendly relations in China's tributary system. The first Ming emperor limited Korean tribute missions to once every three years, but these later became annual and then three times a year. The court dispatched regular embassies to Beijing at New Year's, the emperor's birthday, the birthday of the crown prince, and the winter solstice. It also sent special embassies when an emperor died or when a new Korean king was enthroned. Technically these were tributary missions in which the Korean king offered tribute to the Chinese embassies, but in reality they were opportunities for both sides to engage in trade. Koreans traded horses, furs, cloth, and above all prized Korean ginseng and imported silk, medicines, books, and Chinese porcelains. These embassies also served as opportunities for Korean scholars to collect books, meet with their Chinese counterparts, and keep abreast of cultural trends in China by attaching themselves to the embassies. Korean kings claimed legitimacy by being enfeoffed by the Chinese emperors. The Chinese emperors, by confirming the right of Korean kings to rule, ensured peaceful relations with Korea and reinforced their own pretensions to being universal rulers. Koreans were generally well regarded in China for their scholarship and adherence to Confucian cultural norms, and Korean officials were usually seated closest to the Chinese officials at diplomatic functions, indicating the high rank of Korea in the Chinese world order.

This did not mean that relations were always free from problems. Ming officials were sometimes suspicious of Korea's attempts to establish friendly relations with the Jurchen tribes of Manchuria. Disputes arose over official Chinese histories. In one it was reported that Yi Sŏng-gye had murdered the last four Koryŏ monarchs, confusing him with Yi In-min. Korea sent an embassy to the Ming capital of Nanjing to ask that the correction be made. Yet the mistake continued to pop up in Chinese records. From time to time other incidents arose between Seoul and Beijing when the Koreans became offended at what they thought were erroneous and unflattering accounts of Yi kings in the Chinese records.

Early Chosŏn kings gave considerable attention to pacifying the nomads along their northern border. The principal threat came from the Manchurian Jurchen tribes. Yi Sŏng-gye, himself a skilled horseman and archer, had extensive experience fighting Manchuria-based warriors, including the Red Turbans who invaded in 1361. He began a policy that was pursued with some success by T'aejong (1400–1418) and Sejong (1418–1450) in using a threefold approach of launching vigorous military campaigns against the Jurchens, encouraging them to trade peacefully, and seeking to "civilize" them. The Koreans did this by opening trading posts where the tribal people could peacefully exchange their horses and furs for agricultural products and manufactured goods. Borrowing from an old Chinese practice, the Chosŏn court awarded tribal leaders with degrees and titles. One tribal leader, Yi Chi-ran, was awarded the highest honor of Merit Subject. Some Jurchen were enrolled in the Korean military, including the Royal Palace Guard. Tribal people living along the border were encouraged to marry Korean women and adopt Korean customs. Some of the tribal peoples did so and became assimilated into Korean society.

Nonetheless, tribal unrest still occurred. King Sejong launched more military campaigns, built six forts along the Tumen River, and carried out a resettlement policy. Sejong established the borders of Korea along the Yalu and Tumen rivers, approximately where they have remained to the present day. To make sure these new borderlands became a permanent part of Korea, he colonized them between 1431 and 1447 with thousands of Koreans, mostly from the heavily populated southern provinces. This action largely fixed the northern borders of the kingdom, and these areas have been an integral part of Korea ever since. Despite these efforts the rugged, mountainous northeastern region that made up Hamgyŏng Province remained for generations a frontier at the periphery of central government control. In 1453, the area's military commander, Yi Ching-ok, revolted against the government in Seoul with the support of some Jurchen tribes, declaring himself king of a new dynasty. The royal forces put down the revolt, but another sprang up in 1467 led by a local official, Yi Si-ae, who attempted to gain Jurchen support. This too was suppressed by dynastic forces.

Japanese pirates posed another problem. The increased frequency of *wako* raids in the fourteenth century contributed to the troubles of the last Koryŏ kings. Japanese pirate raids started becoming common in the thirteenth century; after 1350 they increased in frequency and scale. Some consisted of more than three hundred ships and penetrated deep inland where they looted and abducted thousands of Koreans to be sold as slaves. Koryŏ tried to negotiate with the government of the shogun in Kyoto, sending a mission as early as 1367. The weak central government of Japan, however, had little control over the western region of the country where local feudal lords found the raids highly lucrative. A successful military expedition against the pirate base of Tsushima in 1389 brought only temporarily relief.[11] The early Chosŏn rulers applied a policy of military raids against pirate bases coupled with attempts to persuade pirates to trade peacefully.

Particularly troublesome was the island of Tsushima across the Korea Straits, whose feudal lords were among the principal sponsors of pirate raids. In 1419, the Koreans launched a massive attack with 250 ships to destroy that base. Shortly afterwards the Japanese shogun Yoshimitsu offered to suppress pirates in exchange for a copy of the *Korean* Tripitaka. The Yi government then presented him the Buddhist collection in over six thousand volumes. But the central government of Japan maintained little control over the lords in the western part of the country. In 1443, Seoul established an agreement that allowed Japanese merchants to trade at several authorized ports along the southern coasts. This proved profitable enough for the rulers of western Japan that they no longer encouraged pirate raids. The ports were temporarily closed in 1510 when Japanese residents in the ports rioted and again in 1544 following a pirate raid.[12] Thus the Koreans eventually adopted an effective carrot-and-stick policy toward the Japanese similar to that used to control the Jurchens. This kept the coasts mostly peaceful until the end of the sixteenth century.

Besides the relations with China, Japan, and the northern tribal peoples, Korea maintained trade and contact with other Asian lands. Active trade and diplomacy existed with Okinawa (Ryukyu Islands), which until 1609 was an independent state. An embassy was sent to Thailand in 1393, and envoys from Java arrived in Korea in 1397.[13] There were some Korean merchants in Okinawa and in Southeast Asia. However, trade with Southeast Asia was generally carried out indirectly through Ryukyuan and Japanese merchants in the fifteenth and sixteenth centuries. Thus Korea participated in a wider Asian world of trade and contact beyond East Asia, but only peripherally. Korea had no direct contact with Europe before the seventeenth century. The first European known to visit Korea was a Jesuit priest, Gregorio de Cespedes, who arrived in 1597 in the company of Japanese invaders.

THE JAPANESE AND MANCHU INVASIONS

After a century and a half of peaceful relations with its neighbors Korea suffered from a destructive series of invasions. The first, and most devastating, came from the Japanese. In Japan, a bloody struggle for power among feudal lords temporarily ended when a powerful warlord, Hideyoshi, unified the country. Hideyoshi then launched an invasion of Korea with the intention of using the peninsula as a base to conquer China. It is unclear if he was motivated by megalomania or a desire to direct the energies of warriors harmlessly abroad. Or perhaps the invasion of Korea was merely a continuation of his drive to extend his power, the next step after he had brought the autonomous domains of western Japan under his control. Hideyoshi assembled a quarter of a million men for what was probably the largest overseas invasion in history before the twentieth century. Korean officials received rumors of preparations for an invasion by 1591, but debated among themselves over the reality of the threat and only made some inadequate efforts to strengthen their defenses. When the initial contingent of fifty-two thousand troops landed in Pusan on May 23, 1592, they overran the coastal fortifications that were defended to the death by the local commander. The Japanese forces then advanced quickly up the peninsula. Their foot soldiers were armed and well trained in musketry, which they used to great effect. One unit of Japanese would fire volleys of muskets into the Korean forces, overwhelming them with musket power, while other units would attack with swords on the right and left flanks, decapitating as many as they could. Korean troops, who would defend themselves by massing together, were then slaughtered in great numbers. So effective were Japanese tactics that three weeks after the start of the invasion the Japanese captured Seoul and then pushed north.

The Chosŏn court fled ahead of the enemy advance, abandoning the defense of the capital to slaves and commoners. Disgusted onlookers jeered and even threw stones at the royal entourage as it made its way to Ŭiju on the Chinese frontier. Slaves in Seoul took advantage of the chaos to burn palaces and offices and to destroy the registers that documented their status. After a pause for regrouping and supplying their forces, the Japanese under General Konishi captured P'yŏngyang on July 23. A second wing under General Kato Kiyomasa and General Nabeshima advanced northeast to the Yalu and Tumen rivers. The Korean army disintegrated under this massive and well-organized invasion. In desperation the Koreans appealed to China for help. The Chinese, fearful of this new threat from the east, responded with assistance. Led by General Li Rusong, himself of Korean descent, the Ming forces entered in January 1593 and defeated Konishi in battle at P'yŏngyang in February. The Chinese then advanced south, but did so too fast and were halted. Then the war began to stalemate in a way similar to the later Korean War.

Unlike the Korean War where Koreans fought on both sides, Koreans were united in their resistance to Japan, and after a poor initial showing they resisted more effectively. Peasants often fiercely fought to defend their villages from these strange, dangerous outsiders. Local yangban, monks, and others formed resistance bands called *ŭibyŏng* ("righteous armies"). Among the more effective groups were ones led by Cho Hŏn in Ch'ungch'ŏng province in south-central Korea, Kwak Chae-u in the southeastern province of

Kyŏngsang, and Kwŏn Yul in the southwestern province of Chŏlla. While most were defeated, they made the Japanese position difficult, and along with the pressure from the Chinese forces they forced Hideyoshi's troops to withdraw to the southern coastal areas. Especially successful was Admiral Yi Sun-sin (1545–1598), who waged a naval campaign that destroyed hundreds of Japanese ships and made supplying and reenforcing Japanese troops costly. Yi came from a family of officials but chose to take the military rather than the civil examinations. He served as an officer along the northern frontier and later in Chŏlla. Alarmed by the reports of a possible invasion, he launched a last-minute shipbuilding effort. Yi experimented with new weapons and tactics. His most ingenious innovation was the *kobuksŏn* ("turtle ship"), an ironclad ship designed to withstand Japanese cannon fire and to ram and sink its opponents' vessels. These were the world's first ironclad ships. The turtle ships proved to be highly effective. The first ship was completed just days before the Japanese landed. Yi with the help of his turtle ships led an effective naval campaign that prevented the Japanese from using the western coastal route to transport supplies and reinforcements to their army in the north of Korea, making resupplying their army in Korea from Japan hazardous.

With the war stalemated by 1594, the Chinese withdrew their forces to Manchuria and the Japanese to the southern coastal ports. A period of diplomacy began. Chinese diplomats came to Japan, but the negotiations revealed how little the Chinese and Japanese knew each other. The Chinese were willing to recognize Hideyoshi as the "king" of Japan and allow the Japanese to enter the Chinese tributary system. Hideyoshi in turn offered to form a marriage alliance with the Chinese emperor. Interestingly Hideyoshi offered to divide Korea, with the southern provinces coming under Japanese control and the northern parts under Chinese authority, thus roughly anticipating the division of Korea that the United States and the Soviet Union carried out three and half centuries later. Eventually negotiations broke down and the Japanese launched a second massive invasion in 1597. This time the Koreans and the Chinese under General Yang Hao were better prepared and limited the advance of the Japanese. Meanwhile, Yi Sun-sin, who had been removed from his post due to court intrigue, was given back his naval command. He scored a major victory at Myŏngnyang near Mokp'o. While chasing the retreating Japanese ship he was killed by a chance shot. Today he is remembered as a national hero and one of the world's great naval geniuses. Suffering defeats at sea and stalemate on land, the Japanese generals withdrew their forces to Japan to participate in the jockeying for power that followed Hideyoshi's death in late 1598.

The invasions, while a failure, were highly destructive since the Japanese, like the Mongols earlier, used a scorched earth policy to overcome resistance. As a result they left behind a ruined countryside and a legacy of bitterness and fearfulness of the Japanese among Koreans. The viciousness of the conflict was symbolized by the thirty-eight thousand ears of Chinese and Korean forces sent back to Japan by military commanders as proof of their military successes. These were pickled and buried in Kyoto in the Mimizuka (Mound of Ears). The conflict provided later generations of Koreans with heroes from the fighting monks and peasants to Admiral Yi. It also led to a temporary and partial breakdown in the social order as slaves took advantage of the war to seek freedom. A court in desperate need of money sold official titles to commoners and even outcastes. These titles, however, did not become hereditary. While the Ming only intervened when it became clear that the Japanese were a threat to Chinese security, the invaluable assistance of China reinforced Korea's tributary ties and its emotional connection with the Middle Kingdom. The conflict also brought Korean influence to Japan. Japanese forces brought back thousands of Korean captives. These included the scholar Kang Hang, who played a major role in introducing Neo-Confucian philosophy to that country, and potters whose rough-hewn Korean wares would influence Japanese ceramic traditions.

Hardly had Korea recovered from the Japanese invasions when it faced a new threat to the north with the rise of the Manchus. The Manchus were a Jurchen group who under their leader Nurhaci united the tribal peoples of what is now called Manchuria. In 1616, Nurhaci established the new state of Jin, a name derived from the Jurchen state of the twelfth century that conquered northern China. The Manchus then began attacking Chinese garrisons in the northeast. The Ming court called upon the Korean king for assistance. Realizing how vulnerable Korea was to a Manchu invasion, King Kwanghaegun sought to avoid becoming involved. When he sent forces to assist the Ming he secretly instructed his military commander to observe which way the battle was going, and when Manchu forces appeared to be emerging victorious the Koreans surrendered without fighting. Korea did not remain neutral for long. Kwanghaegun was overthrown in a power struggle led by some angered by his lack of support of the Ming, who had a generation earlier come to Chosŏn's rescue. The new group that placed Injo on the throne in 1619 pursued a pro-Ming, anti-Manchu policy.

Shortly afterward, Yi Kwal, a military officer who felt that his family had not been properly rewarded for his part in the coup, seized control of Seoul, forcing the court to flee. Yi Kwal was soon defeated. The new pro-Ming court then provoked a Manchu invasion of Korea in 1627. The court fled to its traditional refuge of Kanghwa Island while the Manchu forces looted P'yŏngyang. Bowing to reality the Koreans negotiated a tributary relationship with the Manchu recognizing them as elder brothers and accepting tribute payments of gold, cloth, and horses. The Korean court, however, still pro-Ming, broke off its tributary relations and allied itself again with Ming in 1636. Nurhaci's successor Abahai, who now styled himself emperor of the

Qing dynasty, invaded Korea to secure his southern flank as he struggled to conquer China. Crossing the frozen Yalu River in the winter of 1636–1637, Manchu cavalry forces advanced quickly and captured Seoul. Injo retreated to a fortress south of the capital while members of the royal family and their entourage fled to the safety of Kanghwa. Injo and his forces, after holding out against a Manchu siege for weeks, surrendered when news arrived that the Manchus, succeeding where the Mongols had failed, had captured Kanghwa and with it the royal family. Injo then pledged his loyalty to the Manchu rulers. Seven years later the Manchu captured Beijing and the Qing dynasty replaced the Ming.

For the next three and a half centuries Korea served as a tributary of the Qing dynasty. The Koreans, however, entered the relationship unwillingly, and hostility toward the Manchus remained strong. Some, such as the military commander Im Kyŏng-ŏp, sought to renew hostilities. A number of Koreans were held hostage, including two princes, Pohyŏn and Pongnim; the latter became King Hyojong (r. 1649–1659). Hyojong upon becoming king prepared to support Ming loyalists who were fighting the Qing in China and planned for an attack. The Qing, however, eventually put down the loyalists and Koreans came to accept the reality of Manchu rule. The Koreans thereafter maintained correct if not enthusiastic relations with the new dynasty (see chapter 8).

COMPETITION FOR POWER AMONG THE ELITE

Yi Sŏng-gye (reign name T'aejo) established the longest of Korea's dynasties, which lasted until 1910. In fact, the Yi, which ruled for over five centuries, was among the longest royal dynasties in world history. The succession to the throne, however, did not always go smoothly. Suffering from illness T'aejo abdicated in 1399, which led to a struggle among his sons, each backed by different powerful officials. One son reigned briefly as King Chŏngjong before being deposed and sent to exile in Kaesŏng by a younger brother, Prince Pangwŏn. The latter became King T'aejong (r. 1400–1418). T'aejong was an active and able monarch, trained in and committed to Neo-Confucianist principles. His reign saw the confiscation of Buddhist monasteries and the strengthening of the military. One of his moves to consolidate royal power was the establishment of the *hop'ae* identification system in 1413. Under this system high-ranking officials wore ivory identity tags, lower-ranking officials wore tags of deer horn, and yangban wore yellow poplar wood tags, while commoners wore small square wooden tags. Large square wooden tags were worn by outcastes and slaves. Tags of yangban and officials gave their titles, those of commoners their name, place, and date of birth.

Tags of slaves also provided information on the complexion and height of the tag holder. Each male from the age of fifteen was to make his own identity tag, which would then be stamped with a government seal by an official. Although only intermittently enforced, the *hop'ae* system provides an illustration of the attempt by the Yi rulers to establish an orderly, controlled society where everyone had a set place. It facilitated census taking, tax collection, and keeping track of migration and runaway slaves.

T'aejong, following the precedent of his father, abdicated in favor of his son, who became King Sejong (1418–1450). Today Sejong is regarded by Koreans as their greatest monarch and his reign is seen as a high point of Korean culture. Sejong successfully strengthened the northern frontier, establishing the present boundaries of Korea. He founded the *Chiphyŏnjŏn* (Hall of Worthies), a learned body that created the Korean alphabet, *han'gŭl* (see next chapter). Sejong was a patron of scholarship, the arts, and sciences, which all flourished during his reign. The monarch carefully attended the Classics Mat lectures, studied the classics diligently, and generally adhered to the role of the virtuous ruler who acts as a moral exemplar. Furthermore, he was an able administrator. Dutifully seeking to ensure an heir he fathered eighteen sons. Under his reign the throne reached a heightened prestige.

Nonetheless, Sejong was unable to ensure a smooth succession. Korean kings suffered from their involvement in court intrigue, and rather than an orderly father-to-eldest-son succession, a confused struggle for power often followed. Sejong was succeeded by a son and a grandson; the latter was deposed by his uncle who reigned as King Sejo (r. 1455–1468). Sejo's usurpation of the throne was accompanied by bloody purges of officials from rival factions in which hundreds were executed or banished into exile. These included six distinguished scholar-officials who became known as the *Sa yuksin* (Six Martyrs) and six high-ranking officials who resigned in protest. Since the latter were not executed they became known as the *Saeng yuksin* (Six Ministers Who Lived). Later, these ministers who supported the deposed king would be held as models of loyalty and virtue. Sejo tried to concentrate power in his own hands and limit that of the high-ranking officials. To that end he abolished the State Council and had the Six Ministries report directly to him. Despite his ruthlessness Sejo was an able as well as a strong-willed ruler. His attempt to bend the monarchical-aristocratic division of power in his favor, however, did not survive him. Shortly after his death Sŏngjong (r. 1469–1494) resumed rule through the high officials and presided over a prosperous state where the arts and scholarship flourished.

While most of the early Yi dynasty monarchs were strong and capable rulers, they were not always able to secure their throne from rival factions. Two conspicuous failures were Yŏnsan'gun (1492–1506) and Kwanghaegun (1608–1623), both of whom were deposed. Yŏnsan'gun has received a reputation for ruthlessness. The king attempted to strengthen royal authority by abolishing the Censor-General, the Office of Special Counselors, and the Office of Royal Lectures (Classics Mat). As tension arose between the king and much of officialdom a report appeared that his mother Lady Yun, who had died when he was only four, had been murdered as a result of court intrigue. The king responded with bloody purges of officials and other members of court. Many were killed; sometimes their corpses were dug up and mutilated. His officials deposed Yŏnsan'gun and demoted him from king to prince (hence his title "gun," meaning prince, instead of the usual honorific royal ending, *cho* [progenitor] or *chong* [ancestor]). Historians have depicted him as a depraved tyrant who wasted state revenues, ravished young women, defiled temples that he turned into pleasure palaces, confiscated land and slaves of officials, and seized the homes of thousands of commoners near the capital.

Yŏnsan'gun's alleged depravity and cruelty provided a negative example for later monarchs, and his removal from office an example of the limits of royal authority. The other Yi monarch demoted to "prince," Kwanghegun (r. 1608–1623), was by contrast an able monarch. He sponsored scholarship, rebuilt the historical archives that were destroyed by the Japanese, and conducted foreign policy with skill. But he fell victim to the struggles among two factions of officials—the Northerners who supported him and their rivals the Westerners (see below). The Westerners deposed him and placed their own royal candidate on the throne as King Injo (r. 1623–1649). The fates of Yŏnsan'gun and Kwanghaegun were in contrast to Ming or Qing China, where officials never deposed an emperor.

The political history of Chosŏn was in good measure the saga of intrigue among aristocratic factions in maneuvering for political advantage, as well as the story of the struggle of monarchs competing for authority with powerful aristocratic families. Factionalism often made political affairs tense and dangerous during this period. The fierce competition among aristocratic factions led to four "literati purges" that are famous in Korean history: the Purge of 1498, the Purge of 1504, the Purge of 1519, and the Purge of 1545.[14] These sometimes violent power struggles led to the death and exile of many high-ranking officials. Koreans have often considered factionalism as one of the curses of their politics. The term "faction" can be misleading, however, implying that these were merely struggles for power. Factions often represented lines of policy differences, which in turn often had an ideological basis, with factional leaders claiming to represent the correct path to virtue. Some of these differences dealt with foreign policy issues such as whether to support the Ming in its conflicts with the Manchus. Korean officials often faced difficult choices in dealing with dangerous neighbors, with dire consequences if their policies failed. Passionate disputes over these issues were understandable. Factional struggles were intensified by the nature of Neo-Confucian ideology and its interpretation. Since court ritual and behavior, and the personal morality of officials, were considered necessary for a harmonious society, every activity by the members of the court and by high officials was scrutinized. The censors had the right to review and rebuke improper conduct whenever they saw it. All this led to an often oppressive atmosphere in the capital in which the performance of seemingly minor rituals and/or minor breaches of conduct could led to demotion, exile, or occasionally execution. Exile could mean being sent for many years to live in remote places, such as on one of the many tiny islands that dot the west and south coasts.

In the late sixteenth century, these factions solidified into clearly identifiable groups. During the reign of King Sŏnjo (1567–1608) a dispute arose between factions of powerful officials, led by Kim Hyo-wŏn and Sim Ŭigyŏm, over appointments to influential posts in government. Since Kim lived in the eastern section of Seoul, his followers in the dispute became known as *Tongin* ("Easterners") and Sim's followers became known as *Sŏin* ("Westerners"). The rivalry between these two groups soon centered over a successor to King Sŏnjo. The king had no sons by his legal wives but had thirteen sons by his concubines. A dispute arose when the Westerners backed one of his sons by a concubine as crown prince and the Easterners opposed this. Then the Easterners divided into *Namin* ("Southerners"), those who were willing to accept this decision, and *Pugin* ("Northerners"), who took a hard-line opposition to having an illegitimate son as crown prince. Thus four major factions were formed. These factions later split further into subgroups such as "Great Northerners" and "Lesser Northerners." These factional struggles become entangled in foreign policy disputes, with the Northerners in the 1620s seeking to avoid involvement in the Manchu-Ming conflict and the Westerners pursuing a more pro-Ming policy. By the mid-seventeenth century the major factions were *Noron* (Old Doctrine), *Soron* (Young Doctrine), *Pugin* (Northerners) and *Namin* (Southerners). The first two were the result of a split among the Westerners. These groups, sometimes called the *sasaek* (four colors), remained the four major factions into the nineteenth century. Loyal disciples followed their masters so that the factions remained tied by family and political loyalty over generations.

Since the yangban had to a great extent become a service nobility and the number of high-ranking posts was limited, the factions centered around the competition for office, and the power and prestige that came with it. Ideology played a role as well, since faction members often took different sides on questions of interpretation of Confucian doctrine and its application to various situations. An example of factional rivalry over ideological disputes was the Mourning Rites controversy in the seventeenth century. This dispute arose over a disagreement on the proper mourning period for one of the wives of King Hyojong (see chapter 8). This led to a difference of opinion by the leaders of two rival factions. The dispute led to a purge of one faction and the coming of power in 1674 of another and to an eventual counterpurge in 1689.[15] Each dispute left a legacy of bitterness and resentment that was passed down over generations, making factionalism deeply rooted.

CHOSŎN POLITICS IN PERSPECTIVE

Although the voluminous historical records kept during the Yi dynasty read as a perpetual and vicious struggle for power, these conflicts and intrigues usually involved only a small number of elite officials and high-ranking aristocrats in the capital. That is, the factional conflicts were largely confined to a small upper stratum of society; they did not mean the country at large was in turmoil. Yi politics and the moral language it was couched in were convoluted, contentious, and occasionally violent. Yet, for the most part the institutions of the state worked well and functioned for nearly five centuries without breaking down. In fact, no ruling dynasty in China, Japan, Southeast Asia, or Europe (except, perhaps, the Ottomans) lasted so long without a major upheaval. The bureaucracy was staffed by well-educated people, who more often than not owed their positions as much to successful performance in the state-administered civil, and to a lesser degree military, examinations as they did to their family connections. Many took their duties and responsibilities seriously, trying to adhere to the ethical standards they had studied since childhood. In short, Korea under the Yi dynasty enjoyed centuries of stability. It was also a resilient state that survived the destructive Japanese and Manchu invasions without radical institutional or political change.

Yun Hoe: On the Harmfulness of Buddhism[16]

Yun Hoe [1380–1436], deputy Director of the Hall of Worthies, and others submitted the following memorial [in 1424]:
  We consider the harm of Buddhists to be prevalent still. Since the Han period the reverence for Buddha has been increasingly fervent, yet neither happiness nor profit has been gained. This is recorded in the historical books, which Your Majesty has certainly perused thoroughly. Must you therefore wait for your ministers to tell you?
  We think of all the heterodox teachings, Buddhism is the worst. The Buddhists live alone with their barbaric customs, apart from the common productive population; yet they cause the people to be destitute and to steal. What is worse than their crimes? Beasts and birds that damage grain are certainly chased away because they harm the people. Yet even though beasts and birds eat the people's food, they are nevertheless useful to the people. Buddhists, however, sit around and eat, and there has not yet been a visible profit.

—From the *Sejong sillok* 23:27a–b

Sin Ch'ŏjung: On the Deceitfulness of Buddhism[17]

Sin Ch'ŏjung, a licentiate at the Royal Confucian Academy, and one hundred and one others went to the palace and tendered the following memorial [in 1424].

Those Buddhists, what kind of people are they? As eldest sons they turn against their fathers; as husbands they oppose the Son of Heaven. They break off the relationship between father and son and destroy the obligation between ruler and subject. They regard the living together of man and woman as immoral and a man's plowing and a woman's weaving as useless.

If monks were forced to return to their home villages; if they were treated as men fit to join the military; if they were made to settle down in order to increase their households; if we burnt their books in order to destroy their roots and branches; if their fields were requisitioned in order to distribute them among the offices; if their bronze statues and bells were entrusted to the Office of Supply in order to mint copper cash; if the utensils they use were handed over to a ceremonial office in order to prepare them for official use; if within the capital the temples of each sect were divided up among the offices without buildings; if the temples outside the capital were all torn down in order to build postal stations and school buildings; if for funerals the *Family Rites* of Zhu Xi were exclusively relied upon, then, in a few years, the human mind would be corrected and the heavenly principles clear, the households would increase, and the number of soldiers would be complete.

—From *Sejong sillok* 23:30a–32b

NOTES

1. Ch'oe Yong-ho, *The Civil Examinations and the Social Structure in Early Yi Dynasty Korea: 1392–1600* (Seoul: Korean Research Center, 1987), 67.

2. Chai-sik Chung, "Chŏng Tojŏn: 'Architect' of Yi Dynasty Government and Ideology," in *The Rise of Neo-Confucianism in Korea*, ed. William Theodore De Bary and Jahyun Kim Haboush (New York: Columbia University Press, 1985), 59–88.

3. Michael C. Kalton, "The Writings of Kwon Kun: The Context and Shape of Early Yi Dynasty Neo-Confucianism," in *The Rise of Neo-Confucianism in Korea*, ed. William Theodore De Bary and Jahyun Kim Haboush (New York: Columbia University Press, 1985), 89–123.

4. This outline of institutions and translations follows Edward W. Wagner, *Literati Purges: Political Conflict in Early Yi Korea* (Cambridge, MA: East Asian Research Center, Harvard University, 1974).

5. Choe Yong-ho, "An Outline History of Korean Historiography," *Korean Studies* 4 (1980): 1–27.

6. Choe, *Civil Examinations*, 79–80.

7. Choe, *Civil Examinations*, 34.

8. Choe, *Civil Examinations*, 19.

9. Michael J. Seth, *Education Fever: Society, Politics and the Pursuit of Schooling in South Korea* (Honolulu: University of Hawaii, 2002), 8.

10. Yi Tae-jin, "The Influence of Neo-Confucianism in the 14th–16th centuries," *Korea Journal* 37, no. 4 (Summer 1997): 5–23. A *kyŏl* was actually a unit of crop yield that varied from two to nine acres depending on the fertility of the land. The figures do suggest an overall increase in acreage.

11. William E. Henthorn, *History of Korea* (New York: The Free Press, 1971), 132.

12. Kenneth Robinson, "From Raiders to Traders: Border Security and Border Control in Early Choson, 1392–1450," *Korean Studies* 16 (1992): 94–115.

13. Henthorn, *History of Korea*, 158.

14. Wagner, *Literati Purges*, 23–120.

15. Jahyun Kim Haboush, "Constructing the Center: The Ritual Controversy and the Search for a New Identity in Seventh-Century Korea," in *Culture and the State in Late Chosŏn Korea*, ed. Jahyun Kim Haboush and Martina Deuchler, 46–90 (Cambridge, MA: Harvard-Hollym, 1999).

16. Peter H. Lee and William Theodore De Bary, eds., *Sources of Korean Tradition*, vol. 1, *From Early Times through the Sixteenth Century* (New York: Columbia University Press, 1997), 312–13.

17. Lee and De Bary, *Sources of Korean Tradition*, vol. 1, 313.

7

Chosŏn Society

Korea during the Chosŏn (Yi dynasty) period became in many ways a model Confucian society. Confucian ideas shaped family and society in profound ways. Although China was the home of Neo-Confucian ideals and they were embraced by many in Japan and Vietnam, nowhere else was there such a conscientious and consistent attempt to remold society in conformity to them. The zeal and persistence by which Koreans strove to reshape their society in accordance to Neo-Confucian ideals helped to set them apart from their East Asian neighbors. These efforts initially began at the upper levels of society, but by the eighteenth and nineteenth centuries Neo-Confucian norms had prevailed, if to a lesser degree, among all social classes. As Neo-Confucian values penetrated throughout all levels of society, they helped bind the Korean people together as members of a single culture even while sharp class divisions remained. While it moved Korea closer to many Chinese cultural norms, Confucianization was also a creative process of adapting the ideals that originated in China to indigenous social practices. Indeed, it was during this period that many distinctive features of Korean culture, such as its unique writing system, emerged.

The basic ideals of Confucianism centered around proper social relationships. Three cardinal principles (*samgang*) guided these social relationships: loyalty (*ch'ung*) of subjects to their ruler, filial piety (*hyo*) toward one's parents, and maintaining distinction (*yŏl*) between men and women. Distinction meant that women had to display chastity, obedience, and faithfulness. Another Confucian formulation that defined the relationships that held society together was the five ethical norms (*oryun*): *ŭi* (righteousness and justice) that governed the conduct between ruler and ministers (subjects); *ch'in* (cordiality or closeness) between parents and children; *pyŏl* (distinction) between husbands and wives; *sŏ* (order) between elders and juniors; and *sin* (trust) between friends.[1] The ethical norms of Confucianism emphasized the importance of family relations, the hierarchical nature of society, the necessity for order and harmony, respect for elders and for authority, the importance of a clear distinction between men and women, and the subordinate status of women. Neo-Confucianists taught that each individual was to strive to cultivate his or her virtue. This was regarded as a lifelong task that involved sincere and persistent effort. Neo-Confucianists placed great importance on rituals and ceremonies, on honoring one's ancestors, on formality and correctness in relationships, on constant study of the classics as a guide to a virtuous life, and on the importance of public service. They valued frugality, thrift, hard work, and courteousness, along with refraining from indulgence in immoderate behavior. Neo-Confucianists could be prudes, disdainful of spontaneous or sensuous behavior.

It was a philosophy that emphasized rank and status; it was important for everyone to know his or her place and role in society. Concern about rank and hierarchy had always been a feature of Korean society, Neo-Confucian thought gave that concern ethical purpose. The Korean language reinforced rank consciousness. Lower-class people addressed upper-class persons with honorific forms that Koreans call *chondaeŏ* or *chondaemal*. As they addressed their superiors their sentences concluded with verbal endings that indicated levels of deference. The language contained many synomyms reserved for respectful usage. Superiors in age or social status spoke in turn to their inferiors in a speech style devoid of the elaborate honorific endings and special honorific terms, which came to be called *panmal*. This use of elaborate speech styles indicating levels of deference, intimacy, and formality is still part of the Korean language.

THE FAMILY

Family and lineage were fundamental to the Korean Confucian order. Lineage refers to those people who directly trace their origins to a common ancestor. In Korea these lineages were called *munjung*. Only those who were in the direct line traced through the eldest son or nearest male relative belonged to a lineage. To keep track of lineage Koreans began to keep *chokpo*, books where births, marriages, and deaths were recorded over the generations. This started to become a common practice in the fifteenth century and eventually became a universal custom, so that most Koreans, even today, can usually trace their ancestry back many generations. Families eventually began to keep *pulch'ŏnjiwi* (never removed tablets) with the names of their immediate ancestors at the home of the lineage heir, normally the eldest son. Many of the ceremonies and practices associated with lineage found their way into the law code, the *Kyŏngguk taejŏn,* compiled in 1469. Laws required all Koreans to perform the rites to their ancestors known as *chesa.*

In the *chesa* ancestral rites family members pay homage to *chosang* (ancestors). This emphasized that the ties of kinship extended to include the dead as well as the living. Ancestral rites became extremely important in establishing family ties. There were three basic types of *chesa*: *kije* or death anniversary commemorations, which were performed at midnight on the eve of the ancestor's death day; *ch'arye* or holiday commemorations, which were performed on certain holidays; and *myoje* or graveside commemorations performed on visits to a family member or to an ancestor's grave (*myo*).

At the *kije* and *ch'arye* rites the family members offered food and drink to the ancestral spirits. The rites came to symbolize the importance of maintaining order and properly adhering to rituals. Every aspect of the rituals followed a formal procedure. Food had to be arranged on an altar in a special order: fruit in the front row, then vegetables, soups, and meats, rice and thick soups, and spoons and chopsticks in the back. Red fruit was placed on the east and white on the west. Incense was placed in front of the food table, and a tray for wine was placed in front of the incense. Rites were performed by the eldest direct male relative, who began the ceremonies by kneeling and burning incense and then pouring three cups of wine. Others, generally according to rank, followed prostrating themselves with their heads touching the floor three times. Then the eldest male then took the cup of wine after rotating it three times in the incense smoke. When the wine offering was completed the family members left and allowed the ancestor to eat. The men returned and bowed and the food was then served to the family. These rituals came to be performed exclusively by men. *Chesa* rituals emphasized the importance of family, lineage, and maintaining a sense of order and propriety.

Marriage in Chosŏn Korea was characterized by extreme exogamy and a strong sense of status. Koreans generally married outside their communities and were prohibited from marrying anyone within the same lineage, even if that lineage contained up to hundreds of thousands of members as the largest ones did. Yet the concern for status meant that marriages remained confined within a social class. In early Koryŏ times marriages between close kin and within a village were probably common, but they became less so in subsequent centuries. The adoption of the civil examination system in the tenth century led to careful records of family relations and to the strengthening of Chinese influences forbidding marriage of patrilineal kin. However, in Koryŏ such marriages still took place. During the Chosŏn period the strict rules prohibiting kin marriages were enforced. Men and women married at younger ages than Western Europeans but not as early as in many Asian societies. In 1471, minimum ages of fifteen and fourteen were legislated for men and women respectively. Men generally married between sixteen and thirty years of age and women fourteen to twenty; the age gap between husband and wife was often considerable. Commoners often married at younger ages than yangban.

Weddings underwent changes in Korea during the Chosŏn period as the result of the impact of Neo-Confucianism. Zhu Xi's *Karye* (*Family Rituals* [Chinese: *Jiali*]) became the basis for rules governing marriage ceremonies and practices. Koreans did not always blindly adhere to them, and wedding practices were modified somewhat to conform to Korean customs. For example, Koreans had traditionally married at the bride's home. But Zhu Xi and other authors stated that it should be done at the groom's home. Scholars and officials debated whether to follow Chinese custom or *kuksok* (national practice). A compromise was worked out in which part of the ceremony was performed at the bride's home, after which the couple proceeded to the groom's family home to complete the wedding. To this day when marrying, Korean women say they are going to their groom's father's house (*sijip kanda*) and men say they are going to their wife's father's house (*changga kanda*). In Koryŏ times many if not most newlyweds resided at the wife's family residence. This custom, contrary to notions of patrilineal family structure, gradually died out and brides moved into their husband's home. In many cases, however, young couples lived with whomever's family was nearest or with whichever parents needed care or had land available to farm.

A variation of marriage custom was the *minmyŏnuri*, a girl bride who entered house as a child, often at the age of six and seven. Koreans never felt entirely comfortable with this custom, boasting that, unlike the Chinese at least, they did not take girls at infancy.[2] The girl bride would be ritually sent back to her home to reenter upon marriage, although this was not always practiced. The Yi government disapproved of the custom and set minimum marriage ages, but these were not enforced. Child marriages were practiced mainly by the poorer members of society who needed the child labor and who could not afford costly weddings. Often the family of the bride could not afford a dowry. One advantage of child marriages was that the girl would be trained to be an obedient daughter-in-law, but in general it was a source of shame and a sign of poverty. Many grooms who were too poor to obtain a bride found this to be their only option. It was not unusual for the groom to be a fully grown adult so that an age gap of as much as thirty years between husband and wife was possible. Korean tales talk of the abuse these child brides received from their mothers-in-law. No doubt for some life was miserable. For much the same economic reasons some families had *teril-sawi* or boy child grooms, although this was less common.

Great emphasis was placed on direct male descent, usually through the *chongja* (first son). While this was always important in Korea, it was reinforced by Neo-Confucian thought, especially the influence of Zhu Xi. So important was direct male descent that even the posthumous adoption of a male heir (usually a close male relative) was necessary if a man died before leaving a male offspring. Men also took secondary wives, not just to satisfy their lusts but to insure they had male offspring. Inheritance patterns in Korea differed from those of its neighbors. While in China land was divided equally among sons, and in Japan all rights went to a sole heir, in Korea the trend during the Yi was to exclude daughters from inheritance and to give the largest portion to the first son, although all sons had the right to some property. This meant that most of a family's property was kept intact and not divided, or at least kept in the lineage.

In short, Korean families during the Yi dynasty became increasingly patriarchical in that the authority of the males was enhanced. They became patrilineal in organization in that property was inherited through males, and that descent and the status that came with it was traced primarily through direct father-to-son or nearest male relative lines. The habit of residence in the groom's family home after marriage reinforced male dominance. Families and lineages were exclusive; nonmembers could not be adopted into families. Nor could they join lineages, although disgraced members such as traitors and criminals could be expelled from them. Family and lineage truly mattered in Korea, as evidenced by the huge number of printed genealogies produced, perhaps unmatched in volume per capita anywhere else in the world.

WOMEN DURING THE YI DYNASTY

The status of women declined during the Chosŏn period. This can be attributed at least in part, if not primarily, to the fact that Neo-Confucianists stressed direct male descent and the subordination of women to men. Women were urged to obey their fathers in youth, their husbands in marriage, and their sons in old age. Books written for women emphasized virtue, chastity, submission to one's husband, devotion to in-laws, frugality, and diligence. Moral literature, a great deal of which was published under the Yi, emphasized that women should be chaste, faithful, obedient to husbands, obedient to in-laws, frugal, and filial. Some of this literature was published by the state. To promote these values the state in 1434 awarded honors to women for virtue. Literacy was very low among women since the village and county schools admitted only men. Those small proportion who could write, perhaps amounting in the eighteenth and nineteenth century to only 3 or 4 percent at the most, generally did so in *han'gŭl* rather than in the more prestigious Chinese characters.

The decline in status was gradual. Households headed by women disappeared early in the Yi dynasty, but women still inherited property until the seventeenth century. Widows were no longer allowed to remarry since they were supposed to be loyal to their husbands even after their partner's death.

As the marriage customs shifted from earlier practices, brides usually left their families after marriage. A daughter was a *todŭngnyŏ* ("robber woman") since she carried away the family wealth when she married. A married daughter became a *ch'ulga oein* ("one who left the household and became a stranger").[3] This contributed to the practice of reducing or eliminating a daughter's share of her inheritance. Since the daughter was thought to leave her family there was less reason to bequeath a portion of the family estate to her. Women could not divorce men, but men could divorce women under the principle called *ch'ilgŏjiak* (seven evils), which legitimized the grounds for divorce. The seven grounds for divorce were disobedience to parents-in-law, failure to bear a son, adultery, jealousy, hereditary disease, talkativeness, and larceny. So associated were women with their families that they were generally referred to by their relationship to their male family members rather than by their name. It has been suggested that by late Chosŏn, women became "nameless entities," being referred to as "the wife of" or as the "mother of (son's name)." They had, in other words, not only lost their rights to divorce, to property, to participating in public life, they had also lost any identity of their own.

Women could no longer freely mix with men socially and their lives were restricted in many ways. The official legal code, the *Kyŏngguk Taejŏn*, forbade upper-class women from playing games and from partying outdoors with penalties of up to one hundred lashes. Horse riding, a common activity among upper-class Koryŏ women, was forbidden by law in 1402. Women had to seek the permission of husbands or family heads before participating in social activities. In later Chosŏn women in Seoul were allowed in the street only during men's curfew hours from nine p.m. to two a.m. At other times it became customary for women to wear veils when entering the street. The segregation and restriction of women became reflected in the architecture of the Korean home, which was divided between the *sarang ch'ae*, the outer section for men, and the *anch'ae*, the inner section of the house for women, also called the *anbang* (inner room). Even poor families often had three rooms: one for men, one for women, and the kitchen. Husbands and wives often lived virtually apart in their own home. Separation of religious functions occurred as well with the women in charge of *kosa*, offerings to household gods, and the men *chesa*, Confucian rites to the ancestors. Unlike in China, women were excluded from the rites to the ancestors. In Korea there was a clear gender division in ritual responsibilities.

Particularly tragic was the position of widows. Since a woman was not allowed to remarry, or head a household, once her husband died she became an inconvenience for her family. There were stories of widows being pressured to commit suicide, but this was probably rare. A widow was sometimes called a *mimangin* (a person who has not died yet). Among commoners and outcastes widows were sometimes married off to a poor man, sometimes to a widower who needed a wife but could not afford a marriage. The man would enter the house and carry out the woman, supposedly in a big sack, resulting in what was sometimes referred to as a "sack marriage." This might be arranged by the widow's family against her will.[4] Also difficult was the life of women in a household where a man took a concubine. This practice was an opportunity for a poor slave or commoner woman to enter an upper-class household. But her life could be made difficult by the jealous first wife and her children, and by the stain of illegitimacy given to her children (see below). First wives could also feel miserable by the entry of a new younger wife with whom they had to compete for their husband's attention.

The same Confucian demand on loyalty and chastity that made remarriage unacceptable resulted in the custom of presenting a woman with a *p'aedo*, a suicide knife. This custom, which began among the elite, became common to all social classes in the southern regions. There were reported cases of women using the knife to protect themselves from attackers. In one such case a government slave girl, Tŏkchi, used her *p'aedo* to kill a number of Japanese who had attempted to rape her during the sixteenth-century invasions. But the purpose of the knife was for a woman to protect her virtue by committing suicide. A particularly sharp knife was called a *chamal p'aedo* after another slave girl who after being embraced by her drunken master always kept her knife sharpened.[5] A woman had to not only protect her honor but, most importantly, protect her family from even the slightest hint of scandal. Sometimes even rumors of an indiscretion were enough for a woman to be pressured to commit suicide for the sake of her family's reputation.

The sign of a married woman was the *tchok*, long braided hair coiled at the nape and held together with a *pinyŏ*, a long pin. Single women wore their long hair unpinned. Ideally women were kept from public view, secluded in their women's quarters and venturing out only in screened sedan chairs or at night. In reality, only the upper class could afford this. Rural women worked in the fields, participating in all the tasks except plowing and threshing which were men's work. Women could not engage in business, but women's loan associations called *kye* were an important source of income for rural women. Commoner and low-caste women mixed with men at festivals. The separate existence of men and women was an ideal most honored at the upper reaches of society.

There were also some exceptions to the restricted roles of women. *Mudang* (women shamans) were an important part of life since at least Silla. During Chosŏn times the great majority of shamans were women, although their social status declined as a result of the official Confucian disdain of traditional religions. Some women became entertainers. These were generally from outcaste and slave families from whom attractive young girls were often purchased to be trained as entertainers known in Chosŏn times as *kisaeng*.

Women prevailed in some performing arts such as singers in the nineteenth-century dramatic form *p'ansori*.

Perhaps the most interesting exception to the restricted lives of women were the *kisaeng*. The *kisaeng* were carefully trained female entertainers similar to the Chinese singsong girls and the Japanese *geisha*. *Kisaeng* often came from the slaves. Attractive ones would be taught to read and write, appreciate poetry, and perform musical instruments so that they could entertain men, especially yangban. Since the lives of men and women were increasingly segregated the *kisaeng* offered men a chance to enjoy the company of women who were not only attractive but able to engage in learned conversation and witty banter. There were also common prostitutes; however, the *kisaeng* were considered more virtuous as well as highly educated, fitting companions for upper-class men. *Kisaeng* were able to engage in conversation with men and be intellectual as well as romantic companions to men in a way that good, virtuous Confucian wives could not. Some *kisaeng* were official *kisaeng*, recruited and employed by the state. These were carefully trained in government regulated houses. During the early dynasty about one hundred *kisaeng* were recruited every three years for the court while others were trained and sent to provincial capitals.

Most *kisaeng* were privately employed by the hundreds of *kisaeng* houses throughout the country. There were, however, also medical *kisaeng* who besides their duty entertaining men also served to treat upper-class women, since women of good families were unable to see male doctors who were not related to them. Others were also trained to sew royal garments. *Kisaeng*, although never entirely respectable, were often admired and loved by men. Some were celebrated for their wit and intellect as well as their beauty and charm. A few talented *kisaeng* won fame for their artistic and literary accomplishments, such as the sixteenth-century poet Huang Chin-i. (See below.) Another, Non'gae, according to legend, became a hero when she jumped in the Namgang River with a Japanese general during the Hideyoshi invasions. But these were exceptions; most *kisaeng* led humble lives in which the best they could hope for was to be some wealthy man's concubine.

SOCIAL STRUCTURE

Legally Korean society was divided into *yangmin* and *ch'ŏnmin* (base people). In practice, however Chosŏn society was divided into three basic classes: the yangban elite, commoners, and the "mean people," consisting of slaves and outcaste groups. Under Yi law this threefold distinction was often obscured. For example, all *yangin* (good people, that is, not slaves or outcastes) had the right to enter schools, take exams, and serve in office. In reality, however, the yangban could be distinguished from commoners. The key was family history; only those with prominent ancestors were yangban. The yangban were generally wealthier than commoners. The wealth of yangban was derived from owning land and slaves. While there were relatively few large estates, yangban families tended to hold more land than nonyangban, although these holdings might be in scattered parcels. Yangban differed from earlier aristocracy of Korea and from the *bushi* or samurai, Japan's warrior-aristocracy, in that they were not a military group; they derived and maintained their status and power through officeholding.

Yangban were also called *sadaebu*, derived from the Chinese term *shidafu* meaning scholar-official, but they differed from the scholar-bureaucrats of China in that there was a greater importance attached to heredity. Another way they differed from their Chinese counterparts was that ownership of slaves as well as landowning and officeholding was a basis of status, wealth, and power. While commoners did own slaves, most census figures from the seventeenth and eighteenth century indicate that yangban families almost always had more slaves than commoners.

Wealth was important as a distinction between yangban and commoner, but yangban status was determined primarily by ancestry, and demonstrated by a display of learning and virtue. In general, yangban families needed to produce officials in order to maintain their prestige if not legal status. This generally meant producing degree holders through the examinations. They also needed to display a knowledge of and regularly perform the Confucian rituals, as well as display skill in poetry and calligraphy and a mastery of the classics. While exams were usually a crucial factor in establishing or reaffirming power and status, some families of *hyangban* (rural yangban) were able to maintain high status even without producing higher exam passers for generations. Yet generally, the exams were a key to defining as well as securing yangban status. Legally commoners could take the civil exams, and a few did before 1600. As Chosŏn society became more rigid, family history and pedigree was the only basis for determining who could take the exam. The ancestors of the examinee were reviewed for three generations on his father's side and one on his mother's to make sure he came from a good family. Yangban status was also tied to tax privileges. Yangban were free from the household tax; they were also free from corvée and from military service.

Yangban totally dominated Chosŏn. They manned the bureaucracy and served as the moral and cultural leaders of society. From their ranks were drawn most of the nation's scholars and writers, and many of its leading artists. In the countryside the yangban served as the local elite. They advised local officials, gave public talks that served as sermons for the local people, and provided informal leadership in the community. The yangban were segregated from commoners, living in different neighborhoods, and yangban met and socialized at private academies and at *kisaeng* houses. Yangban were identified with their hometowns, with which they maintained ceremonial and political ties. During the Chosŏn period single-name villages where all were at least distant kin became common. Identification with a hometown or region may have become stronger during the later centuries. During the early Chosŏn yangban often relocated in far-off parts of the country seeking economic opportunities, but later they tended to stay near their home base, moving, if at all, only to neighboring counties.

The greatest goal of a yangban was to serve as a high official, and the most ambitious were drawn to the capital; but even officials in the capital tended to return to their home villages. They held exclusive membership in the *Hyangch'ŏng* (Local Agency) and later in Yi the local yangban associations called *hyangan*. Income from official posts was important for many, some tutored the youth of other yangban, but for yangban wealth mostly came from landowning. Not all yangban were big landowners and not all big landowners were yangban. Nonetheless, most major landowners were yangban, and generally yangban were the biggest landowners in their communities. Unlike the Silla or early Koryŏ aristocrats, most yangban of the Chosŏn did not have military backgrounds and were contemptuous of the skills of warriors. Some scholars see the military weakness of late Yi dynasty Korea, a nation that once fiercely resisted the Chinese and the Mongols, as due to the domination of society by people who failed to value military skills. Yangban were also forbidden to engage in the demeaning profession of commerce.

The term yangban meant the two orders of officials, the *munban* (civil officials) and the *muban* (military officials). But by the sixteenth century the term had come to mean the entire elite aristocratic class of Korea. Aristocratic status was linked to officeholding with the civil examinations being the most important route to office. Society was dominated by civil officials; however, the military examinations continued to be a secondary path despite the general disdain for warriors. The military exams included a test on the exposition of the classics and a test of martial skills such as archery, lance-wielding, polo, and field hockey. The exams were open to yangban and commoners. Many took the exam; between 150,000 and 170,000 passed it during the five centuries of the Yi dynasty, considerably more than passed the civil exams. By comparison, during the Chosŏn dynasty some 14,607 passed the highest *munkwa* exam, 47,000 passed the lower *sama* exam, and 12,000 passed the *chapkwa* (technical exams).[6] To prepare students for the military exams the state set up a number of *muhak* (military schools) throughout the country. Although the military exams were open to commoners, it was the provincial yangban who often turned to these exams as a secondary path to certify their status as a degree holder. By the eighteenth century if not earlier, yangban who were military degree holders belonged to different lineages or sublineages from the civil officials. While proud of their status, for the most part they held few offices of significance and had little power.

Commoners were the majority of the population. There may have been some social mobility at times, but in general a wall of privilege separated them from the yangban. Unlike the yangban they had no tax exemptions, were required to perform corvée duties and to serve in the military, and in practice were barred from the examinations. Most commoners were poor farmers, working small plots of their own land or working as tenant farmers. Sometimes they both owned some plots of land and farmed plots of yangban-owned land for a share of the crops. Many engaged in crafts such as cloth making to supplement their incomes. A few became wealthy farmers. Others engaged in commerce, an activity yangban were prohibited from engaging in (see next chapter). In theory the government ruled in a benevolent manner with concern about the welfare of the common people, but the tax on commoners could be very burdensome. Corvée labor could be burdensome as well; at times vast numbers of peasants were mobilized for labor on public works. They were also sometimes victimized by local officials or exploitative landlords. When conditions became intolerable they rebelled. Most of these rebellions were localized and easily contained, but they were a source of concern for the state.

SLAVES AND OUTCASTES

Although most commoners were poor, they at least enjoyed the legal protections of being *"yangmin."* Below commoners were *ch'ŏnmin* ("mean people"). The largest group of these "mean people" were slaves. Slavery was a major social institution in Korea from the Three Kingdoms period to its abolition in 1894. Various attempts have been made to analyze the scope and nature of Korean slavery; however, these have been hindered by the lack of records, difficulties in interpreting them, and the problem of defining different levels of servitude as slavery. In general, slaves appear to have constituted a larger percentage of the population of Korea than was the case in its East Asian neighbors. Perhaps the emphasis on inheritance of status contributed to this. Slaves were classified into *sanobi* (private slaves) and *kongnobi* (government slaves). The former were owned by members of the royal household, the officials, private citizens, and by Buddhist temples, while the latter were owned by central and local government agencies and by the royal family. Both private and government slaves were classified into *solgŏ nobi* (household slaves) and *oegŏ nobi* (out-resident slaves). Household slaves served on duty at palaces and government offices, as personal retainers of military and civil officials, and as domestic servants. Out-resident slaves often possessed their own property and paid rents to their owners, and were little different than tenant farmers or commoners.

In fact, the legal status of slaves was complex. For example, there was a system known as *chakkae* in which a slave was assigned two types of agricultural fields: one in which all produce he cultivated was turned over to his master and the other in which he kept all the produce for his own consumption or sale.[7] Some out-resident slaves paid their owners a personal tribute, sometimes as bolts of cloth, while others shared a portion of the crop much as did free tenant farmers. Slaves could purchase their freedom or win free status through military service or government favor. The number of slaves in Korea is difficult to determine but appears to have fluctuated. Some estimates place the number of slaves as high as 30 percent of the population both during Koryŏ and the early Yi period.[8]

Slavery was generally accepted in Korea, although some rulers and individuals were praised for their compassion in freeing some. For the government, too many private slaves were a problem since it meant there were fewer taxpaying free peasants and fewer commoners to serve in the armed forces. Slaves were exempted from compulsory military service. But government slaves were an important source of income and labor for the state. Yi Sŏng-gye, following his coup in 1388, converted eighty thousand slaves of Buddhist temples to government slaves. State slaves reached about three hundred fifty thousand in number by the late fifteenth century. While the origins of slavery are not clear, many slaves were descendants of prisoners in wars and rebellions and of criminals. Often commoners in debt wound up enslaved. Chosŏn regulations strongly reinforced the permanent hereditary nature of slavery, going as far as declaring that if the direct family line died out the nearest relative in the same lineage would inherit them. If there were no near relatives to the fourth cousin they would then became the property of the state. Marriage between slaves and commoners was prohibited under Koryŏ, and this prohibition was carried on during the Yi dynasty. Yet, despite the frequent reissuing of this rule it was widely ignored.

Slavery created concerns for the state. While no one is recorded as calling for the abolition of slavery, the moral problem of slavery was occasionally mentioned. An official in the Office of Remonstrance in 1392 said, "Even though slaves are base, they are still Heaven's people, [and yet] we usually talk of them as chattel goods and actively buy and sell them, exchanging them for oxen and horses."[9] Monarchs and officials expressed worry that too many slaves meant a loss of taxpaying, military-serving commoners. King T'aejong tried to limit the ownership of slaves to 150 for officials and 40 for commoners but abandoned this attempt after too many objections were raised.[10] Disputes over ownership of slaves created an enormous backlog, reaching thirteen thousand cases in the early fifteenth century. Yet slavery was important to the economy of Korea. It was one of the major bases for elite status along with land- and officeholding. Scholars such as Yu Hyŏng-wŏn in the seventeenth century argued that slavery brutalized both the slaves and their masters, claiming that it did not exist in the distant past, and that the ancient Chinese did not measure wealth in slaves as Koreans do. Still, even he did not call for its total abolition.[11]

Slavery did decline somewhat in late Yi dynastic times. From the eighteenth century the number of out-resident slaves appears to have shrunk despite an overall increase in population. Exactly why is not clear. Perhaps the growth of tenant farming blurred the distinctions between commoners and slaves and made slave ownership less important to the prosperity of the elite since they could make do just as well from rent collecting. It may also have been the result of the population increases in the seventeenth and eighteenth century and the resulting abundance of labor. Resident slavery did not disappear; even in the late nineteenth century most prosperous yangban families had at least one or two household slaves. The number of official slaves declined to less than one hundred thousand in the late eighteenth century. Official slavery with a few exceptions was abolished in 1801 and the records of sixty-six thousand slaves were destroyed. Hereditary slavery was not abolished until 1886. All forms of slavery were legally abolished in 1894, and it disappeared in practice too.

Besides slaves various categories of outcastes existed. These included innkeepers, ferrymen, prostitutes, entertainers, and people involved in unclean professions such as leather working and butchering. *Paekchŏng* or butchers are the best known of these outcaste groups, and the term *paekchŏng* has come to be applied to outcastes in general. Little is known of the origins of these outcaste groups except that they existed since at least Silla times. Some professions such as entertainers were assigned to these outcaste groups because the Confucian elite held them in low regard. The outcaste designation of others such as butchers and leather workers may have originally been influenced by the Buddhist aversion to the harming of animals. Outcastes lived apart from society and occupied a place similar to the untouchables in India. In fact, Korea can be said to have had a caste system that was not unlike that of India in practice, but without the religious sanctions and with less elaborate distinctions. It is still unclear if the social structure was as rigid in practice as it appears in the historical record. There was, no doubt, some social mobility. But in general, the life for those at the bottom of the social scale was hard, with little hope of major improvement.

Another small hereditary group in Korea, the *chungin*, did not fit into the threefold distinction of yangban, commoners, and "mean people." The *chungin* (middle men) was the term given to technical officials and hereditary clerks. This originally pejorative term came into use during middle Chosŏn period. The technical specialists were those who sat for the *chapkwa* (specialized exams) for scribes, accountants, legal professionals, astronomers, interpreters, and geomancers. The line between *chungin* and the officials became more sharply drawn as the dynasty progressed, reinforced by Confucian preference for generalists with lofty moral principles and the yangban disdain for technical knowledge and technicians.[12] The origins of the *chungin* are not clear, but some were descended from mixed yangban and nonelite marriages. In a society where bloodlines largely determined status these "middle men" were excluded from high government posts. They became a hereditary class that depended on the specialized exams to reconfirm their status and to gain access to government posts. Especially coveted were positions as interpreters and medical officers, since these brought with them the opportunity to join tribute missions where they could engage in profitable trade.

Another group that was like the *chungin* below the yangban but above commoners in status were hereditary local clerks known as *hyangni*, literally local officials, also known as *sŏri* or *ajŏn*. In Koryŏ times, *hyangni* were powerful local aristocrats who controlled much of the countryside, but their status declined by early Chosŏn. Despite their lower status they were indispensable to the operation of government. It was the *hyangni* who collected taxes, kept the local and provincial government records, supervised local granaries, served as census takers, did police work, and in some localities also managed the local militia.[13] Each of the approximately three hundred counties had some *hyangni* lineages. Since due to the law of avoidance magistrates could not serve in their home districts and their term of service was usually short, they were heavily dependent on the *hyangni* for information and advice. Yet they were strictly separated by status from the magistrates they served. The hereditary local clerks were prohibited by law from marrying yangban.

In later Chosŏn, the *chungin* groups—the technical specialists and the hereditary officials—formed a small subelite modeled somewhat on their yangban superiors. They formed their own kin organizations, lineages, and compiled genealogies. In the eighteenth and nineteenth centuries many contributed to literary works and anthologies. At the same time the *chungin* gained greater control over the local government and became indispensable to the functioning of the government. Since their salaries were often meager at best and they were not independently wealthy, they supported themselves by exacting fees on the commoners. As a result of this practice they were often the object of peasant discontent. Because some of the technical specialists were trained in foreign languages, and were generally less restrained by custom than the yangban, some were able to play an important role in introducing Western culture into Korea in the late nineteenth century.

The social structure of Chosŏn Korea is illustrated by the problem of illegitimate sons. It was common for upper-class men to take commoner or slave concubines. This wife was known as his *ch'ŏp*. It created a problem of the *sŏja* or children by these *ch'ŏp*. Early in the Yi dynasty if there were no sons by his legal wife a *sŏja* could be named heir. But this was not approved of and it became customary to name a nephew or other male relation as heir instead. *Sŏja* were generally prohibited from taking the civil exams and holding office. As a result they formed another hereditary group that became known as *sŏŭl*. The problem of *sŏja* and their discrimination in society was of great concern throughout the period. It seemed unjust to many scholars and to some Yi kings, who were also sometimes sons of concubines. But such was the growing strength of the patrilineal organization that the plight of the *sŏja* only became worse as it became harder, although not impossible, for a father to have a son by a secondary wife inherit all or some of his property. The problem illustrates the strength of the Confucian concept of family, and perhaps just as importantly, the aristocratic nature of Chosŏn society with its sharp division between the yangban elite and the rest of society. Allowing for a *sŏja* to take the civil examinations or inherit estates would blur this division. It also indicates that maternal lineage and inherited status in general were more important in Korea than in China, where such sons faced no comparable discrimination.

CRIME AND PUNISHMENT

Chosŏn law was based on Ming law. The major legal code was the *Kyŏngguk Taejŏn* promulgated in the fifteenth century, which followed the Ming Code *Da Ming lü*. During the Koryŏ period Koreans borrowed extensively from Chinese law. The Yi dynasty not only borrowed from Chinese legal practice, but it thoroughly followed the Ming Code. Chosŏn law, however, tended to vary from Chinese because case decisions, as well as various government pronouncements, supplemented this basic law code so that over time it became adapted to Korean circumstances and customs. The Ministry of Punishments was in charge of justice, but in Korea, as in China, there was not a separate judiciary. Instead administrative officials acted as investigators, prosecutors, and judges. Most criminal cases were handled by the county magistrates. Their assistants would make arrests and gather witnesses. The magistrate would then interrogate the defendants, plaintiffs, and witnesses, and pronounce sentence in accordance with the law code. More serious cases such as murder went before the provincial governor, who worked with a legal advisor from the Ministry of Punishments. The Ministry of Punishments also ran prisons, although the Board of War, the Office of the Censor-General, and the State Tribunal ran prisons as well. Difficult cases could be referred to the Ministry of Punishments in the capital. At the top of the judicial system was the *Ŭigŭmbu* (State Tribunal). This too was a Chinese-modeled institution; however, unlike in China it met irregularly only whenever the court was convened. It reviewed serious or difficult cases.

The legal process was based on the principle that the punishment should fit the crime. This meant that the intention of the criminal was taken into consideration. For example, courts had to determine whether the crime was one of passion, or whether it was planned, intentional, or accidental. The law served to enforce class distinction, not establish legal equality. "Mean people" were often punished for passing as commoners, commoners for insulting yangban or violating sumptuary laws. Yangban often carried out their own informal investigations and punishments for crimes, especially theft. Domestic violence was not generally a matter of judicial concern. If a husband beat his wife it was not considered a criminal matter unless he broke her bones. Even then it was up to the wife to report the crime, negotiating herself through the legal process. She was likely to receive severe punishments if she could not prove her charges. Discriminatory attitudes toward women are suggested by the fact that most wives charged with murdering their husbands were given the death penalty, while husbands charged with murdering their wives most often received a reduced sentence.[14]

Legally prescribed beatings were common. Light beatings were prescribed for minor punishments and were carried out by the local magistrate, while heavy beatings for more serious crimes would be carried out by the governor or the Board of Punishments. Murder and treason were often, but not always, punished by execution. Mitigating circumstances for a murder might result in imprisonment, enslavement, or severe beatings. Torture was routinely used during interrogation, not only of suspects but also of witnesses. A uniquely Korean custom was the use of *churi*, which involved tying a suspect's legs tightly together, placing levers between the shins, and twisting. Not only was this very painful, it sometimes resulted in the breaking of the legs and even the permanent crippling of the suspect.[15] Not only suspects and witnesses but those who brought complaints to the state as well as petitioners were also tortured in order to assess their sincerity. Not surprisingly most commoners and lower-class peoples avoided being entangled in the legal system. Instead, many crimes were settled informally between families or by prominent members of the community. Officials often complained about the problem of finding people with information on criminal cases to step forth. Fear of the legal system was exacerbated by corrupt underlings of officials who used the threat of legal actions to extort money out of villagers.

One exception to the general avoidance of the law was the practice of petitioning high officials and the court to redress miscarriages of justice. Petitioners ran considerable risk to themselves, for they could be held and questioned under torture, and punished if the grievances were found unjustified. Many lined up along the roads whenever the king and his entourage traveled. During the reign of King Chŏngjo (1776–1800) more than four thousand such petitions were recorded.[16] Others traveled to the capital to beat the petition drum outside the palace that was kept for this purpose. Most were illiterate peasants who no doubt desperately grabbed at any chance to save a loved one from execution or other punishment. For most quarrels villagers simply went to village elders or the local yangban to informally settle their disputes with in-laws or neighbors.

Many crimes and acts of violence were caused by drunkenness, a problem that was a matter of concern to many. King Sejong complained that wine undermined moral behavior: "How then can the little people of the villages be expected to avoid the suits and criminal cases which arise in such number from this?"[17] A large percentage of all the criminal cases at the village level were caused by alcohol-influenced brawls, beatings, and sometimes sexual assaults. Another problem was the huge amount of grain, especially rice that was used to make wine. To conserve food grains, the state issued prohibitions against making wine during periods of drought and famines, but these laws were widely ignored.

RELIGIOUS BELIEFS AND PRACTICES

Buddhism greatly declined during the Yi dynasty. Buddhist temples were banned from the capital and cut off from official patronage. Monasteries lost their tax exemptions and it was no longer proper for yangban to support temples. Yet despite the predominantly anti-Buddhist sentiment of the Neo-Confucian scholar-bureaucrats, the religion continued to play a role in the lives of many if not most Koreans. Several thousand temples and hermitages existed, mostly in the mountains and the countryside where they offered a retreat from the pressures and concerns of everyday life. Two basic sects of Buddhism, Kyo and Sŏn, continued their line of teachings, and a few significant Buddhist thinkers emerged. Foremost among them were Sŏsan (1520–1604), who achieved fame during the Hideyoshi invasions by organizing armed resistance by Korean monks, and his contemporary Puhyu. Many later Korean Buddhist teachers traced their line of transmission to Sŏsan, who was also an impressive intellectual figure, and to Puhyu. Individual members of the upper classes, including even some members of the royal family, privately supported Buddhism. Commoners continued to visit temples and Buddhist rituals remained part of popular culture. For example, in the eighteenth century the practice of *yŏmbul* (recitation of the name of Buddha) became popular among women. Still the religion declined, becoming more peripheral to Korean society. With much of its royal and upper-class patronage gone Korean Buddhism declined in intellectual vigor until its revival in the first half of the twentieth century.

In addition to Buddhism a variety of folk religions flourished. Neo-Confucian thought left little room for the supernatural. Everything it taught was part of the natural interplay between *li* (principle) and *ki* (material force). There were no gods, afterlife, or an eternal soul. In practice, however, most Koreans were concerned about the world of spirits. Most believed in a complex spiritual realm and in spiritual forces. Restless spirits of the dead were a source of deep worry since they could cause diseases and other woes. Spirits of the ancestors were central to popular religion and ritual. To some Confucian intellectuals this was symbolic, but probably to most Koreans *kwisin* (spirits) were real.

Many elements of the popular religion were of indigenous and ancient origin. These included worship of spirits that inhabited natural phenomena such as trees, rocks, and especially mountains. Shrines to *Sansin*, the Mountain Spirit, were so prevalent that they were incorporated into Buddhism where almost every temple had one. Other spirits, such as *Ch'ilsŏng* (Big Dipper), were and are still often found in temples. Women conducted pilgrimages to mountains to pray to the spirits for the health of children, a custom still practiced at the end of the twentieth century. Belief in the hidden spiritual power of prominent features of nature was blended with geomantic ideas imported from China. These centered on the importance of rivers and mountains. Mountains were especially venerated. Since at least the thirteenth century Paektu Mountain on the Korean-Manchurian border area was considered the most sacred mountain. A number of other mountains such as Chiri and Myohyang were also of great spiritual importance.

There was a host of household gods. *Sŏngju* (House Lord) inhabited the beams above the porch, *Samsin Halmŏn* (Birth Grandmother) the inner room, *Chowang* (Kitchen God) the kitchen, and *Pyŏso Kakssi* (Toilet Maiden) the toilet; *Chisin* (Earth God) dwelt in the foundation; *Sumun* (Door Guard) protected the main gate; and *Ponhyang Sansin* (Mountain God) and *Ch'ilsŏng* (Big Dipper) inhabited the storage jars. Behind the house lived the *T'ŏju Taegam* (Site Official).[18] *T'ŏju Taegam*, the Site Official, was particularly important and had to be appeased with ritual offerings of food. Even in modern Korea offerings to the Site Official are common when the construction of a building takes place. Each village also had a *Sŏnghwang*, a local guardian god, and shrines were constructed for them. There were additional deities that some families worshiped. Most of these household and location spirits were derived from China, although the rituals differed in Korea.

One of the distinctive features of Korean popular religions was the extent that ritual functions were segregated by gender. This was done to a degree not found among the Chinese and Japanese. While after the fifteenth century Confucian rites were carried out by men, women presided over the complex of household gods. Each of the household gods was given offerings at their place in the home. *Kosa*, the ritual offering to these gods, was exclusively performed by women, with the senior women generally in charge, especially of the rituals for the Kitchen God. In addition to the household gods, numerous beliefs were associated with fertility, especially having sons. Women venerated rocks shaped like genitals, rocks with vaginal-shaped holes, and two intertwined trees. Candlelight prayers by women at rocks and the hollows of trees was and is still practiced. Another object of veneration was the Marrying Tree, with a phallic-shaped rock in y-shaped branches.

Shamanism was also an important part of Korean spiritual life. Since ancient times shamans (*mudang* or *mansin*) acted as mediums between the world of the spirits and the human realm. The gods often descended into the *mudang* during the *kut*, the shamanist ceremony. These spirits included *chosang* or ancestral spirits who were sometimes restless and caused problems for the living. Shamanism lacks a cosmology or cosmogony, and is therefore not a systematic religious tradition; but it was important in Korean spiritual life. Shamans served as healers and as diviners, and both the Koryŏ and Chosŏn state patronized them as such. The state was ambivalent about shamanism, and most good Neo-Confucianists had disdain for them. Chosŏn officials, while tolerant of *p'ansu* (blind exorcists) and fortune-tellers, were intolerant of *mudang*. In part this was due to the fact that shamans, with their power to possess spirits, were a potential threat to the authority of the state and its officials. Yet shamans were useful as a channel of communication with the common people. The state registered all *mudang* and created an office to supervise them. Shamans were taxed, although some criticized this tax as it made the government dependent on them for income. In early Chosŏn shamans participated in state-sponsored rituals, and monarchs and their families often consulted them. There was even a royal *mudang*, but this position was abolished in the seventeenth century as official disapproval of shamanism increased. Yet local officials to the end of Yi dynasty often hired shamans to perform ceremonies at local tutelary (*todang*) shrines and to drive malevolent spirits from the local government office. Shamans also, often at the request of officials, performed *kut* to end droughts and to ward off storms. During the Yi dynasty shamanism increasingly became the domain of women. As men turned away from shamans women continued to seek them to help in problems such as child illness. Some shamans were men; most, at least in later times, were women. In late Chosŏn women shamans formed *mubu*, regional associations run by their husbands, who were able to handle the business and public aspects of their professions. They frequently performed music during their wives' ceremonies.[19]

Elite and nonelite Koreans practiced geomancy. Koreans took the proper location of graves and homes seriously to make sure they were in accord with geomantic principles. *Chisa,* wandering geomancers, assisted rural folk in selecting grave sites and gave other geomantic advice. So important was this that there are stories of people illegally digging up bodies from graves so that they could bury their own family members in an auspicious site. Even the layout of Seoul was based on geomancy. It was protected from malevolent northern forces by Puksan (North Mountain) and safeguarded in the south by the Han River.

PHILOSOPHY

Chosŏn Korea saw a great flowering of philosophical scholarship. Philosophy was not simply an intellectual pursuit by a few scholars but was central to the society. The entire Yi dynasty can be said to be based on a great philosophical enterprise, an endeavor to discern the Way and bring the political and social institutions in conformity to it. Determining the Way thus was a vital activity. Yangban men generally saw themselves as scholar-bureaucrats. From childhood they were trained for government service. Since government service meant mastering the Confucian classics in order to pass the civil exams, Confucian learning came early in life beginning with such primers as *Xiao Xue* (*Lesser Learning*), a collection of passages on ethics drawn from the classics by Zhu Xi's student Liu Zucheng.

Chosŏn scholarship focused more exclusively on the Cheng-Zhu school of Confucianism than was true in Ming and Qing China or Tokugawa Japan. A constant vigilance was maintained against heterodoxy. Pak Se-dang, a seventeenth-century scholar and official, for example, was attacked for criticism of Zhu Xi. Pak came from a distinguished line of bureaucrats and was himself an official in the Ministry of Rites. His *Sabyŏnmok* (*Thoughtful Elucidations*) contained critiques of Zhu Xi's interpretations and commentaries on the Daoist classics *Dao De Jing* and *Zhuangzi* in which he included sympathetic remarks. He also argued that Zhu Xi's amendments to the texts of the *Great Learning* and the *Doctrine of the Mean* had failed to restore the original form that had been lost during the Qin. He then provided his own corrections.[20] Also condemned for deviating from orthodoxy was Yun Hyu, a scholar and official who took a more critical look at Zhu Xi. While seeing himself as being in the Cheng-Zhu tradition, he suggested that civilization was continuing to develop so that it was not necessary to rigidly adhere to all Zhu's teachings. Since most of his contemporaries saw Zhu Xi's commentaries as representing the purest transmission of the Way, such remarks were dangerous. Consequently, he was denounced and purged.

Philosophic debates became so intense because defending orthodox philosophy was defending civilization against barbarism. Koreans saw philosophy as a tradition that came down from the ancient sages of China. It was their duty to carry on this line of transmission and see to it that it was applied to everyday life. That Korea carried on this line in its purest form was a source of enormous pride. It was also a matter of practical politics. It was the duty of the scholar-official to advise the rulers and see to it that they acted as a moral example for others. Even slight deviations from these standards could have disastrous effects for society. Governing meant maintaining a constant vigilance against the threats to civilization. Naturally officials often disagreed on how rulers should act and behave. These disagreements became the basis of political factions and power struggles. Thus, moral ideals, philosophical interpretations, and power politics became intertwined. An example of this was the Rites Controversy of 1659. In that year when King Hyojong died it became unclear from the manuals on rituals how long the queen dowager should mourn. Some officials in the State Council, such as Song Si-yŏl and Song Chun-gil, the leaders of the *Sŏin* (Westerners) faction, argued that she should observe a full one year of mourning, which was appropriate since she was the mother of one of the sons of her husband. Other scholars, including those such as Yun Hyu associated with the *Namin* (Southerners) faction, insisted that since Hyojong was a king she should observe three years of mourning, the maximum period according to the rituals. The debate was joined by nonofficials from the private academies who accused the officials of not fully respecting the royal family. Fifteen years later, the Ritual Controversy took place when Queen Insŏn, Hyojong's widow, died. Since a wife was mourned according to her husband's status, Queen Dowager Chaŭi's mourning was based on her daughter-in-law's husband's status. But Korean law stipulated a one-year period of mourning for the wife of an eldest son, nine months for others. The Ministry of Rites chose a nine-month period of mourning. King Hyŏnjong (1659–1674), outraged by this decision of the *Sŏin*-dominated bureaucracy, demanded one year of mourning and began punishing *Sŏin* bureaucrats, but his death shortly after brought the purge to an end.[21]

Yet within this narrow confine of orthodoxy an impressive outpouring of scholarship emerged. The sixteenth century in particular was a creative period. The century saw two of the most important Neo-Confucian thinkers of East Asia during this time: Yi Hwang (1501–1570), also known by his pen name T'oegye, and Yi I, also known by his pen name Yulgok (1536–1584). The main thrust of their thinking dealt with the relationship between matter and principle. The universe was viewed as a complex interaction between the two, but which came first? Which was more fundamental? Was the world made of primarily material stuff or were principles, vaguely analogous to the Western concept of ideals, more fundamental? What were the implications of these and how could such knowledge instruct people in their daily lives? These were some of the problems Korean philosophers dealt with. T'oegye placed more emphasis on the idea that *li* (*yi*), the patterning principle of the universe, was fundamental and Yulgok stressed the *ki* (Chinese: *qi*), the primal matter-energy. As abstract as these debates may seem, they occupied the attention of intellectuals for several centuries. T'oegye in particular was admired by scholars as far away as Japan and Vietnam, and he has been rediscovered by Western students of Eastern thought today, who have recognized him as a seminal thinker.

T'oegye also was involved in a debate with a young scholar-official, Ki Taesŭng (pen name Kobong, 1527–1572), on human nature, a debate known as the Four-Seven Debate. This also dealt with the problem of dualism. Human nature consisted of feelings, conventionally called the Seven Feelings: desire, hate, love, fear, grief, anger, and joy, a concept taken from a passage in the *Book of Rites.* Committed to the perfection of humanity, Neo-Confucian scholars worried that these feelings were not always good. But human nature was basically good, a natural goodness argued for by Mencius in his "Four Beginnings." This natural goodness, Mencius had argued, was seen in the disposition for compassion, shame and dislike, yielding and deference, and approving and disproving. The cultivation of these natural elements of goodness transformed them into the fundamental virtues of humanity, righteousness, propriety, and wisdom. T'oegye in his debates with Ki associated the Four Beginnings with *li*, and the Seven Feelings, that may or may not be good, with *ki*. Later Yulgok argued that the Four Beginnings and the Seven Feelings are generated by *ki* but that *li* directs them. The issue was whether one side of human nature is governed by goodness and another by feelings or passions that may not necessarily be good, or if human nature is one and good. This friendly debate was a search to establish a unity in humanity and in the universe.[22]

Although works outside of the Zhu-Cheng tradition were largely banned, many scholars discreetly read them. One heterodox school of Confucianism was the Wang Yangming school of thought. Chŏng Che-du (pen name Hagok, 1649–1736) was an outstanding proponent of Wang Yangming. After Chŏng a line of scholars continued to study the fifteenth-century Chinese writer. Buddhism still held intellectual interest for some scholars. Later in the Yi dynasty a truly heterodox teaching, Christianity, would also find a small number of adherents. Overall, there were few deep ideological divisions among Koreans, who increasingly came to share a common set of values.

ARTS, LITERATURE AND SCIENCE

One of the greatest cultural achievements of the early Chosŏn period was the creation of *han'gŭl*, the indigenous alphabet. The Korean language had been written using Chinese characters. A number of systems had been devised to write Korean phonetically with Chinese characters. But they were cumbersome and did not gain lasting use, in part because the complex sound system of Korean made using a phonetic script difficult. Under King Sejong a group of scholars were commissioned to create a simpler script to make the written language more accessible to the common people. Analyzing the sounds of the Korean language, the scholars established a system based on sophisticated linguistic principles. The twenty-eight-character alphabet was so scientific that even the shapes of some letters were partly based on the position of the mouth and tongue making them. The script took these phonetic symbols and then combined them into syllables, no doubt influenced by the Chinese writing system in which each character represented a syllable. The result was a unique, practical system of writing. The new script was proclaimed in 1446 and was called *hunmin chŏngŭm* (correct sounds to instruct the people) or *ŏnmun* (vernacular script). The term *han'gŭl* (Korean writing) came into use only during the twentieth century.

But it took a while for it to gain acceptance. This was because the prestige of Chinese characters was so great that scholars were reluctant to abandon them. Rather *han'gŭl* was used mostly by women and to write popular literature. Official publications, scholarship, and most of the literature written by yangban was in Chinese or in Korean using Chinese characters. Gradually it became the vehicle for popular literature and informal writing. Only in the twentieth century did *han'gŭl* become the principal system of writing, although Chinese characters are still sometimes used in a mixed script form. *Han'gŭl* is the only major system of writing in use today that does not have its origins in the ancient Middle East, India, or China. It has become an important component of Korea's identity as a culture, and a great source of national pride for contemporary Koreans.

The yangban of Chosŏn saw themselves as scholars, not as artists, and did not pursue the arts as a profession. But an aesthetic sensibility was part of the pride of cultivated gentlemen. Many dabbled in amateur painting, producing some outstanding literati painters such as Kang Hŭi-an (1419–1464). The ideal in Korea, as in China, was that of the talented amateur who combined scholarship and literary knowledge with mastery of the brush stroke. Landscapes remained the most popular form of yangban painting. Chinese styles were admired and emulated, although fashions differed. Early in the dynasty the Northern Song school with its monumental landscapes was imitated; later the softer landscapes of the Southern Song and various Ming schools were popular. The court-sponsored art and a *Tohwasŏ* (Bureau of Painting) was established in Seoul. It was attached to the Ministry of Rites because painting was important for recording ceremonies and rituals. Artists in this office, sometimes with the help of yangban amateurs, produced elaborate books of ceremonies and rituals, some recording actual events. These are not only beautiful works of art but provide an important visual record for modern historians. Court artists had to take a qualifying exam based on copying old masters. Artists were judged in four categories of descending importance: first, bamboo; second, landscape; third, people, animals, and birds; and fourth, flowers. These reflected the traditional Chinese order of importance.

Professional artists, who were mostly from the *chungin* class, held less prestige than the yangban literati amateurs. These professional artists, however,
appear to have been held in more respect than their Chinese counterparts;
some achieved fame as painters, such as An Kyŏn in the fifteenth century
and Yi Sang-jwa in the sixteenth. An Kyŏn was especially admired for his
Korean landscapes. The most famous is *Dream of Strolling in a Peach Garden (Mong yo towŏn to)*. This, the only surviving painting that can positively
be attributed to him, is regarded by Koreans as one of their great masterpieces. Buddhist paintings, reflecting the decline in aristocratic and royal
patronage, were of lesser importance. Still, many beautiful works were produced by anonymous artists. An interesting tradition was the *taenghwa* or
banners that became popular from the sixteenth century. Influenced perhaps
by Tibetan art, this tradition gained popularity in Korea as it was dying out
in China and Japan. Calligraphy continued to be a highly esteemed art; many
yangban dabbled in it.

Ceramics, as in the Koryŏ period, was also highly esteemed. In the fifteenth century an official government-controlled factory near Kwangju in
Kyŏnggi province (not to be confused with the city of Kwangju in the southwestern Cholla province) was established on the model of the great Chinese
official production center at Jingdezhen. Kwangju is still a center for traditional pottery production. The demand for the products of these official
kilns was so great that they had to be relocated every ten years when the
nearby forests were cut down. *Punch'ŏng* was the predominant ceramic ware
from the 1390s to the 1590s. It was made of the same gray clay used in celadon but was coarser in texture, with white slip decoration. Koreans did not
follow Qing in its use of bright colors in porcelains and enamels. Instead, Yi
dynasty pottery contains a simplicity and purity of design lacking the elaborate decorative embellishments of Ming and Qing ceramics. A number of
deliberately rough-hewn ceramics were produced. The simplicity of Chosŏn
pottery appealed to the Japanese and it was used in their tea ceremony.[23]
During his invasions of Korea the Japanese ruler Hideyoshi brought back
hundreds of Korean potters who established a number of kilns in Japan.
Korean potters in Japan with the rough simplicity of their stoneware and
porcelain established the basis for *raku* and other natural, deliberately
unpolished styles that later would greatly influence the pottery of the West.

Chosŏn architecture survives today in many temples, palaces, schools, and
private dwellings. It made no radical departures from established traditions.
Building styles continued to follow Chinese patterns. Almost all larger
structures were made of wood with characteristic curved overhanging roofs
with ceramic tiles. Koreans, however, preferred their own distinctive and
often less bright shades of red, blue, yellow, white, and greens. Producing
these colors developed into an art form known as *tanch'ŏng*. The city of
Seoul was laid out on the model of Chinese imperial cities. The royal palaces

as with their Chinese counterparts were symmetrical structures laid out behind each other facing south. The Kyŏngbok Palace best exemplifies this Chinese imperial style. Other palaces and public buildings tended to modify the rigid symmetry of Chinese official architecture. Palaces and wealthy homes often had gardens. Most famous of Chosŏn gardens is the Piwŏn (Secret Garden) in Seoul. It best illustrates the rough, natural, almost uncared-for style of Korean gardens that is quite different from the manicured gardens of China and Japan. Restricted in number in the cities, Buddhist temples took advantage of remote mountain locations so as to blend into their natural settings. Temples in Korea tended to adhere to pre-Song styles.

Poetry flourished in Chosŏn Korea. Every yangban was supposed to appreciate poetry, and many composed verses in Chinese and Korean. A major genre was *sijo* poetry. This was a short suggestive poem, similar to Chinese *jueju* and the Japanese *tanka* and *haiku*. The *sijo* emerged in the late fourteenth century and became the most beloved poetic form in Korea. It is still popular. The name *sijo* is a modern one; in the Chosŏn period it was usually referred simply as *tan'ga* (short song), a name that suggests its link with lyrical songs. *Sijo* has three lines each with fifteen syllables, although the last line varies somewhat in length. They total about forty-five syllables. Each line is divided into two parts divided by a pause in the middle. The first line presents the theme and the second line either reinforces or elaborates on it. The final line often introduces a "jolting twist or counter theme."[24] Unlike Chinese poetry, Korean poems rely on alliteration or on cadence, not rhyme. This beloved form was written by Koreans of all professions. Thousands of *sijo* from the Yi dynasty survive today. Some were simply moral precepts in poetry; others extolled the beauties of nature. A famous one is the "Song to Five Companions" by Yun Sŏn-do (1587–1671), who is regarded as among the greatest masters of *sijo*:

> How many friends have I, you ask?
> The streams and rocks, the pines and bamboo;
> Moon rising over eastern mountain
> You I welcome too.
> Enough. Beyond these five companions
> What need is there for more?[25]

Kisaeng also composed a number of *sijo*. Most famous is the Hwang Chin i (1506–1544), who was one of its great masters. Unlike most women, *kisaeng* were relatively free to express their emotions and they were often highly literate. One of the subjects of their poetry was the sadness associated with love. Their often intense passions for clients always had an impermanent quality about them, forcing them to explore the nature of love. This is illustrated in the following poems by an anonymous seventeenth-century *kisaeng*:

> An anchor lifts, a ship is leaving.
> He goes this time, when to return.
> Far over the sea's vast waverings
> one can see a going as return.
> But at the sound of that anchor
> lifting the night could feel her
> insides turn.[26]

Another poetic form was the *kasa*, a longer, open-ended type of poem. The *kasa*, which was mostly probably derived from lyric songs, began in the fifteenth century and was perfected by masters such as Chŏng Ch'ŏl (1537–1594) and Hŏ Nansŏrhŏn (1563–1585). A popular theme of this form of poetry was the beauty of nature. Kasa were written in *han'gŭl* and partly for this reason were popular among women as well as men.

Stories of the mysterious and bizarre, derived from the Chinese tradition of *quanqi* (tales of wonder), were popular in Chosŏn times. Among the best known was *Kŭmo sinhwa* (*New Stories from Golden Turtle Mountain*) by Kim Si-sŭp (1435–1493), an eccentric writer who lived part of his life as a wandering monk. Another popular work was the *P'aegwan chapki* (*The Storyteller's Miscellany*) by Ŏ Suk-kwŏn (fl. 1522–1544), a Chinese interpreter. The Yi period also saw the emergence of the Korean novel. Hundreds of Chosŏn novels survive, the majority by anonymous authors. Widely read, most were romantic tales of adventure and love. One of the first was *Hong Kil-tong* by Hŏ Kyun (1569–1618). This is the story of an illegitimate son of a high official who suffers the discrimination of being an illegitimate son. Hong studies martial arts, and then leads a bandit gang with other illegitimate sons and social outcasts called the "Save the Poor" Gang. In Robin Hood style they rob the unjust rich, including corrupt officials and greedy monks, but not the poor. The hero has magical powers that assist him. In general the novel is filled with fantastic elements and lacks the character development expected in modern Western novels. It has been called the first Korean novel, but it is rather short and it is perhaps better to call it a romantic prose tale. Very popular, it also has been viewed as a story of social protest, criticizing the Chosŏn society for valuing bloodlines over talent and virtue. The author, himself a legitimate son of a high-ranking yangban, appeared to identify with the society's outcasts, especially its illegitimate sons. Hŏ was executed in 1618 for allegedly plotting an uprising against the state.

Another great classic novel was *A Dream of Nine Clouds* (*Ku un mong*) by Kim Man-jung (1637–1692). It has been called the oldest major novel in *han'gŭl* but may have been originally written in *hanmun* (Chinese characters). As with so many Korean stories it was set in China, in this case during the Tang. In the novel a Buddhist monk dreams he is reborn as another person. In his new life he meets eight beautiful women in different settings; two become his wives and the others his concubines. Skilled in both martial and literary arts, he has many adventures and becomes an official in the imperial court. One day in retirement he wakes up to find it all a dream. While superficially a Buddhist tale of the transitory nature of existence, in reality it is a sexual and romantic fantasy.

TECHNOLOGY AND INVENTIONS

Koreans showed a lively inventive spirit. A number of water clocks were made. A water clock of 1398 had a bell that struck at sunrise and sunset. In the fifteenth century the inventor Chang Yŏng-sil earned fame for many mechanical devices, including a self-striking water clock. Under Sejong a royal observatory with an elaborate armillary sphere and a forty-foot bronze gnomon to measure the exact altitude of the sun was constructed. Skilled artisans manufactured numerous other astronomical clocks, water clocks, and sundials, including imitations of Western mechanical clocks in the seventeenth century. This concern with timekeeping was stimulated in part by the widespread use of wet field agriculture, which made keeping an accurate calendar ever more crucial. Consequently, Koreans made careful studies of astronomy and the weather. In 1442, a system of rain gauges (*ch'ugugi*) was placed throughout the kingdom to keep accurate records of rainfall. This system was discontinued in the late sixteenth century and resumed in 1770. Korea thus maintains the longest records of measured rainfall in the world. Worried by foreign invaders Koreans experimented with weapons such as a multibarreled cannon. The most famous invention was the "turtle ship," the world's first ironclad ship, built in the late sixteenth century.

The inventions, the outpouring of philosophical writings, and the literary and artistic achievements of Chosŏn Korea from the fifteenth through the seventeenth centuries all reflect a flourishing society. As Neo-Confucian values pervaded society and shaped its family and political life, they lent a unity and stability to Korean society. This along with improvements in agriculture made this period a prosperous and productive one in Korea's long history.

THE CREATION OF THE *HAN'GŬL* SCRIPT[27]

King Sejong: Preface to Correct Sounds to Instruct the People

The sounds of our language differ from those of Chinese and are not easily communicated by using Chinese graphs. Many among the ignorant, therefore, though they wish to express sentiments in writing, have been unable to communicate. Considering this situation with compassion, I have newly devised twenty-eight letters. I wish only that people will learn them easily and use them conveniently in their daily life.

—From *Hunmin chŏngŭm* 1a

CHŎNG INJI: POSTSCRIPT TO CORRECT SOUNDS TO INSTRUCT THE PEOPLE

In general, the languages of different countries have their own enunciations but lack their own letters, so they borrowed the Chinese graphs to communicate their needs. That is, however, like trying to fit a square handle into a round hole. How could it possibly achieve its objective satisfactorily? It is, therefore, important that each region should follow the practices that are convenient to its people and that no one should be compelled to follow one writing system alone.

In the winter of the year *kyehae* [1443], His Majesty, the king, created twenty-eight letters of the Correct Sounds and provided examples in outline demonstrating their meanings. His Majesty then named these letters *Hunmin chŏngŭm*. Resembling pictographs, these letters imitate the shapes of the old seal characters. Based on enunciation, their sounds correspond to the Seven Modes in music. These letters embrace the principles of heaven, earth, and men as well as the mysteries of yin and yang, and there is nothing they cannot express. With these twenty-eight letters, infinite turns and changes can be explained; they are simple and yet contain all the essence; they are refined and yet easily communicable. Therefore, a clever man can learn them in one morning, though a dull man may take ten days to study them. If we use these letters to explain books, it will be easier to comprehend their meanings. If we use the letters in administering litigations, it will be easier to ascertain the facts of the case. As for rhymes, one can easily distinguish voiced and voiceless consonants; as for music and songs, twelve semitones can be easily blended. They can be used whatever and wherever the occasion may be.

—From *Hunmin chŏngŭm* haerye 26b–29b

NOTES

1. Andrew Nahm, *Korea: Tradition & Transformation* (Elizabeth, NJ: Hollym International, 1988), 113.

2. Youngsook Kim Harvey, "Minmyŏnuri," in *Korean Women: View from the Inner Room*, ed. Laurel Kendall and Mark Peterson (New Haven, CT: East Rock Press, 1983), 46.

3. Mark A. Peterson, *Korean Adoption and Inheritance: Case Studies in the Creation of a Classic Confucian Society* (Ithaca, NY: Cornell University Press, 1998), 3.

4. Research Center for Asian Women, Sookmyung Women's University, *Women of the Yi Dynasty* (Seoul, Sookmyung University, 1986), 169.

5. Hyun-key Kim Hogarth, "The Widow's Suicide in Pre-Modern Korean Society," *Korea Journal* 36, no. 2 (Summer 1996): 33–48.

6. Eugene Y. Park, "Military Examinations in Late Chosŏn: Elite Substratification and Non-elite Accommodation," *Korean Studies* 25, no. 1 (2001): 1–49.

7. James B. Palais, *Views on Korean Social History* (Seoul: Institute for Modern Korean Studies, 1998), 39

8. James B. Palais, *Confucian Statecraft and Korean Institutions: Yu Hyŏngwŏn and the Late Chosŏn Dynasty* (Seattle: University of Washington Press, 1996), 4.

9. Palais, *Confucian Statecraft*, 218–19.

10. Palais, *Views on Korean Social History*, 33.

11. Palais, *Confucian Statecraft*, 235.

12. Palais, *Views on Korean Social History*, 33.

13. Kyung Moon Hwang, "Bureaucracy in the Transition to Korean Modernity: Secondary Status Groups and the Transformation of Government and Society, 1880–1930" (PhD diss., Harvard University, 1997), 381–417.

14. William Shaw, *Legal Norms in a Confucian State* (Berkeley, CA: Institute of East Asian Studies, University of California, Center for Korean Studies, 1981), 3.

15. Shaw, *Legal Norms*, 97.

16. Han Sang-kwon, "Social Problems and the Active Use of Petitions during the Reign of King Chongjo," *Korea Journal* 40, no. 4 (Winter 2000): 227–46.

17. Shaw, *Legal Norms*, 82–83.

18. Descriptions of these household spirits are given in Laurel Kendall, *Shamans, Housewives, and Other Restless Spirits: Women in Korean Ritual Life* (Honolulu: University of Hawaii Press, 1985).

19. Boudewijn Walraven, "Popular Religion in a Confucianized Society," in *Culture and the State in Late Chosŏn Korea*, ed. Jahyun Kim Haboush and Martina Deuchler (Cambridge, MA: Harvard-Hollym, 1999), 160–98.

20. See Mark Setton, *Chŏng Yagyong: Korea's Challenge to Orthodox Neo-Confucianism* (Albany, NY: State University of New York Press, 1997).

21. Jahyun Kim Haboush, "Constructing the Center: The ritual Controversy and the Search for a New Identify in Seventh-Century Korea," in *Culture and the State in Late Chosŏn Korea*, ed. Jahyun Kim Haboush and Martina Deuchler, 46–90 (Cambridge, MA: Harvard-Hollym, 1999).

22. See Michael Kalton, *The Four-Seven Debate: An Annotated Translation of the Most Famous Controversy in Korean Neo-Confucian Thought* (Albany, NY: SUNY Press, 1994).

23. Jane Portal, *Korea: Art and Archaeology* (London: British Museum, 2000), 137–41.

24. Kichung Kim, *Classical Korean Literature* (Armonk, NY: M. E. Sharpe, 1996), 78.

25. Ki-baek Lee, *A New History of Korea*, translated by Edward W. Wagner with Edward J. Shultz (Cambridge, MA: Harvard University Press, 1984), 220.

26. Constantine Contogenis and Wolhee Choe, *Songs of the Kisaeng* (Rochester, NY: Boa Editions Limited, 1997), 14.

27. Peter H. Lee and William Theodore De Bary, eds., *Sources of Korean Tradition*, vol. 1, *From Early Times through the Sixteenth* (New York: Columbia Press, 1997), 295.

8

Late Chosŏn

The period stretching from the late seventeenth to the early nineteenth century was one of peace, stability, and prosperity in Korea. In general this was true of East Asia as a whole. The Qing had consolidated their rule in China and presided over an era of demographic and commercial expansion. Japan under the Tokugawa entered a period of limited contact with the outside world, but it was also a time of economic growth and domestic order. The Qing had gained firm control over Manchuria, securing that region. Korea thus faced no major threats from its neighbors. Internally several centuries of efforts to promote Neo-Confucian values and institutions had resulted in a major transformation of society. Educated Koreans were proud of this transformation that made their society a center of civilized values. Yet there was still a wide discrepancy between the ideals of society held by Confucianists and the reality around them. Consequently, many Koreans called for various reforms that would solve the problems of poverty and social injustice and strengthen the state. A large body of literature critical of society emerged and a number of reforms were carried out, although seldom as vigorously as their adherents hoped.

The eighteenth century also saw a cultural efflorescence as Koreans produced many works of art and literature, including some new genres. Koreans wrote a number of histories and studies of their own culture during this period. Some historians today see in the eighteenth century a heightening of national consciousness and a growing awareness and appreciation by Koreans of the distinctiveness and uniqueness of their culture. Koreans also began to see their land as the truest bastion of the great Confucian tradition. More than China, it was Korea, they believed, that kept the line of transmission of civilization in its purest, most unbroken form. Yet for all the increasing pride and confidence literate Koreans felt in their society, many remained concerned about its problems.

THE POLITICS OF LATE CHOSŎN

The late seventeenth century saw Korea ridden with factional struggles centered in the capital. The *Namin* (Easterners) came to power in 1674. They were ousted by the *Sŏin* (Westerners) in 1689, who soon split into rival *Noron* and *Soron* (Old and Young Doctrine) factions. The Old Doctrine emerged as dominant. Then two very able monarchs came to power. The first, King Yŏngjo (r. 1724–1776), made a practice of appointing officials from all the major factions, a policy that brought a half century of political stability as he carefully balanced factions and exerted a strong personal influence on the court. During his exceptionally long reign he gained the experience and skill to dominate his officials. He was succeeded by his grandson Chŏngjo (r. 1776–1800), who also strove hard to provide orderly government. Factional disputes and court intrigue continued, but during their long rule the two exemplary monarchs were able to moderate the intrigue and attract many talented scholars and administrators to the central government.

In many ways Korea during the reigns of Chŏngjo and Yŏngjo came as close to being a model Neo-Confucian society as ever appeared in East Asia. As good Confucians the Yi monarchs employed the concept and rhetoric of the sage-king. However, kings not only used the rhetoric, but had also to submit to the rigors the ideal demanded. The king was the father-ruler. Koreans believed that humans through the power of reason could make society moral, orderly, and rational on the model of and in harmony with the larger universe. In order to establish such an order the Mandate of Heaven (Chinese: *tianming;* Korean: *ch'ŏnmyŏng)* was conferred upon a certain individual to become a ruler. This idea vested every action by the king and his court with enormous importance. It was also a heavy burden since every action had major moral and cosmic significance. The ruler was at once chief priest to his people, dynastic instrument to his forebears, promoter of civilization, upholder of the classics, and exemplar and father to his people.

A Korean monarch's role as a model of Confucian conduct restricted him. His every utterance was carefully scrutinized and he had to constantly display his virtue. His authority was also limited by the fact that the Chinese emperor, not he, was the center of the universe. The investiture ceremony of the Korean ruler by the Son of Heaven symbolized this peripheral and subservient position of Korean king. The monarch's power was further restricted by the fact that a relatively small number of powerful aristocratic families monopolized the greater portion of top posts and were power centers in themselves. In addition, Koreans took the moral authority of scholars seriously. Learned men serving as censors and private scholars issued memorials that criticized the actions of the king and his officials. Yŏngjo, in particular, availed himself of the rhetoric and ritual to fashion an image as a moral ruler. It was not an easy task, because the bureaucrats had their own claims to be wise and upright upholders of the moral order. The king had to continually and scrupulously adhere to the letter and spirit of Neo-Confucianism. Much of a king's time was spent in performing rituals, and Yŏngjo exerted his power in part by dutifully and carefully performing them. Adding to his prestige and influence, Yŏngjo created a new ritual of expressing sympathy with the people during times of famine or epidemics when he would meet with afflicted families and do what he could to ease their sufferings.[1] His grandson and successor Chŏngjo followed in his path.

But even these able monarchs could not free themselves from court intrigue. Yŏngjo's principal queen had no sons; two, however, were born from lesser wives, and one died young. The surviving son, Changhŏn, was made crown prince and assigned duties at court. The prince's behavior became increasingly erratic and bizarre as he manifested symptoms of mental illness. In 1762, the king ordered his son placed in a rice chest and smothered to death. This became a famous episode in Korean history. Two major new factions emerged over these events: the *si* that opposed them and the *pyŏk* that accepted them. Thus for all his skill as a king, Yŏngjo created still new factions. The next king, Chŏngjo, was Changhŏn's son. He had to contend with the struggle for power between the P'ungsan Hong clan and the Ch'ŏngp'ung Kim clans. Accounts of his reign, while fairly uneventful, nonetheless are full of tension for life at the royal court was often a perilous one. Every action by every member was subject to criticism. A mistake among even members of the royal family could lead to exile or death.

LATE CHOSŎN AND THE CONFUCIAN WORLD ORDER

Meanwhile, Korea maintained correct if not warm relations with China under the Qing (Manchu) dynasty. The Manchus had defeated Korea in 1636, forced the Koreans to pay indemnities, and held members of the royal family as hostages. Initially harsh, the tribute extracted by the Manchus, who after 1644 ruled China as the Qing dynasty, was considerably reduced in the seventeenth century. Still each year the Koreans supplied rolls of their prized paper, furs, and bolts of cotton and other cloth. This tribute continued until the mid-nineteenth century. In addition to the inconveniences of tribute, Koreans continued to view the Qing rulers as barbarian usurpers. King Hyojong (r. 1659–1674), who had spent eight years as a hostage, harbored a hatred of the new Chinese rulers. He plotted to organize a "northern expedition" to attack the Qing that never materialized. Anti-Qing forces were encouraged by the resistance of Ming loyalist groups within China, but with the defeat of the last Ming loyalist base in Taiwan in 1683 those hopes faded.

The Yi court then became reconciled with the reality of the Manchu rule of China.

Despite the contempt many Koreans felt for the new dynasty and for the way Chinese officials had compromised their integrity by serving it, relations gradually improved. Under the able emperors Kangxi (r. 1662–1722) and Qianlong (r. 1736–1796) China prospered, and Koreans came to admire the flourishing culture and economy of Qing. Trade along the border and during diplomatic exchanges prospered. Korean embassies continued to visit Beijing during New Year's, at the ascension of new emperors, and at various other occasions. Chosŏn monarchs still found the investiture ceremony by the Son of Heaven useful for legitimizing their authority. Furthermore, the diplomatic missions continued to be an important source of information and cultural exchange. Many of Korea's leading scholars and officials participated in these missions, where they had an opportunity to meet with Chinese officials and scholars and collect books. Korean officials visiting Beijing, especially in the eighteenth century, were impressed by the prosperity and by the high cultural attainment of Qing China. As in the past they were eager to follow the latest trends from what they regarded as the world center of culture.

Most Koreans, however, felt more loyalty to the old Ming dynasty and regarded the Manchu rulers as both usurpers and part barbarian. While outerly submitting to the Qing they continued to discreetly honor the memory of the Ming. In 1704, King Sukchong built an altar, the Taebodan, to the Ming emperors. Court officials built another altar in 1717 to the Ming emperor Wanli, who had sent troops to assist Korea during the Hideyoshi invasions. In a number of quiet but subtle ways the Chosŏn government hinted at its disdain for its powerful neighbor. Tribute missions to China that had been called *choch'ŏn* (Chinese *chaotian*, "going to court") were given the less exalted title of *yŏnhaeng* (mission to Beijing). Koreans continued to use a calendar that was dated from the last Ming emperor rather than adopt the calendar of the Qing. The Qing in turn remained somewhat suspicious of Chosŏn, and restricted trade and contact with them.

One line of thought was that Korea could do nothing but wait until Heaven sought to restore legitimacy to the celestial throne. Until that time Korea had to maintain correct relations with its neighbor, and carry the burden of being the sole inheritor of the Way of the Sages. As a result the idea came about among Koreans that since China was ruled by a dynasty of questionable legitimacy, and since its rulers were not fully civilized, Korea remained the last true bastion of civilization (that is, of course, Confucian civilization). Yŏngjo reflected on this idea that China under the Qing was itself part barbarian when he stated that "the Central Plains [China] exude the stenches of barbarians and our Green Hills [Korea] are alone."[2] Such an idea was reinforced by the reports that in China the teachings of Wang Yangming and other "heterodox" thinkers were widely accepted. Only Korea remained firm in its adherence to "orthodox" Confucian teachings as transmitted by Zhu Xi. All this gave the Korean elite a feeling of distinctiveness or separateness from China as well as a sense of cultural superiority even if their country was militarily weak.

Korea also maintained neighborly relations with Japan. Despite the destruction and loss of life caused by Hideyoshi's invasions, Chosŏn sought to establish peaceful relations with the new government of the Tokugawa shogunate that was established after 1600. In 1606, Seoul sent an embassy to the new ruler, Tokugawa Ieyasu, in Edo (Tokyo). In 1609 a treaty was established with the So clan of Tsushima across the Korea Straits. This allowed Japanese ships to trade at Pusan. A special walled compound was built outside that city, the *Waegwan* (Japan House), where Japanese merchants could reside and trade. From the early seventeenth century to the 1870s about five hundred Japanese lived in Japan House.[3] The two societies carried out a modest but not insignificant trade with each other. Korean merchants sold a variety of Korean goods and some Chinese products in exchange for Japanese porcelain, crafts, and especially silver. Japan's biggest import from Korea was ginseng. In the seventeenth century when the shogunate debased the coins, it minted a special silver money primarily to buy ginseng. Trade between the two lands declined somewhat in the later eighteenth and nineteenth centuries but was never insignificant. In addition to trade, Koreans occasionally sent embassies to Edo. Eleven were sent between 1606 and 1793. These were huge affairs including hundreds of members who traveled by ship and over land visiting cities and towns. A number of Korean scholars accompanied these embassies, where they met Japanese scholars and artists. As a result of these embassies Korean scholars had some influence on Japanese art and philosophy, and they sometimes came back impressed by Japan's prosperity and commercial development.

Despite the trade at Pusan and the occasional embassies with their friendly meetings between Korean and Japanese scholars, the Koreans remained distrustful of their island neighbors. The Chosŏn government refused requests by the Bakufu government to send embassies to Seoul, and the Japanese merchants at Pusan were confined to their walled compound. A sensitive diplomatic point was the refusal of Koreans to acknowledge the Japanese ruler's title of Emperor. This would place the Japanese on equal terms with the Chinese emperor, totally unacceptable in the Korean view of the world. It would also place Korea in the diplomatically inferior position. The Tokugawa shoguns dealt with this problem by simply avoiding any reference to the Japanese emperor in their diplomatic exchanges. In their dealings with Chosŏn the shoguns assumed the title for themselves of *Taikun* (Great Prince). This term was picked up by Westerners when they came to Japan and is the origin of the English term "tycoon."

On their northern border, the Qing had incorporated Manchuria into the Chinese Empire, which meant that Koreans no longer had to worry about Central Asian invaders. In fact, as the result of the use of firearms and artillery by the Chinese and by the Russians in the west, the power of the nomads had been broken. But a new threat slowly emerged from the northwest: the Russians in the seventeenth century conquered Siberia and began to approach the frontiers of Korea. The full force of this new threat, however, would not be felt until the nineteenth century. During their embassy visits to Beijing in the seventeenth and eighteenth century Koreans had their first encounters with Westerners. Initially these contacts were no more than curiosities for Koreans, but toward the end of the eighteenth century Western ideas began to influence a small circle of intellectuals (see chapter 9).

KOREAN TRAVELERS TO CHINA AND JAPAN

Koreans continued under the Qing to send three tribute missions a year. All totaled up, about seven hundred missions went to Beijing during the two and a half centuries from the inauguration of the Qing dynasty in 1644 to the end of the tributary system in the late nineteenth century. The typical mission consisted of about thirty officials who along with their scribes, translators, servants, and porters added up to about two hundred to three hundred persons. They followed a prescribed land route that took up to eight weeks each way and stayed in Beijing for about two months in the Hall of Jade River in the south part of the city. Although technically these were diplomatic missions, the members privately engaged in trade with merchants along the way and in the Chinese capital. Upon arrival there were official functions to attend and the audience with the emperor to prepare for, but much of the time was spent seeing the sights, meeting with Chinese and the occasional foreigner in Beijing, and of course shopping. Other than translators who held the humble status of *chungin* few Koreans could speak Chinese, but they could read and write it. They therefore communicated with their Chinese counterparts in what they called "brush talk," that is, through writing.

For most Koreans the trip was a once-in-a-lifetime opportunity and they tried to make the most of it. Many educated members wrote travel accounts when they got back. About forty of these travel diaries from the Ming, usually called *Choch'ŏnrok* (*Audience with the Emperor*), and five hundred from the Qing, called *Yŏnhaerok* (*Travel Records to Beijing*), have survived. They provide a glimpse into how Koreans saw themselves as well as what they saw in China. By the eighteenth century these travel diaries became a vehicle to critically compare Korea with China, generally with the aim of pointing to the need for reform in their society. This school of critical writing became known as *Pukhak* (Northern Learning), the north being a reference to

Beijing. Thus a uniquely Korean literary form combining travelogue with criticism emerged that had no counterpart elsewhere in East Asia. The diarists were impressed by the level of commercial activity in China. Markets were open all day and night, every day, unlike in Korea where markets generally opened only on market days. And their size and variety were impressive. One observer writing in 1828 wrote, "The lengths these people will take to make a living are really ingenious. There are some who will even cut other people's hair, others will administer baths, still others will cut people's fingernails. And there is a gadget for everything, even for picking paper out of privies or for carrying horse manure."[4]

Korean travel diarists used their works to criticize their own society. Among the important travel diaries was Hong Tae-yong's *Yŏn'gi* (*Beijing Record*). Accompanying an uncle to Beijing as a military aide in 1766, Hong wrote of the order and prosperity of China under the Qing Qianlong emperor.[5] Pak Chi-wŏn's *Yŏrha ilgi* (*Jehol Diary*) saw China's wealth as a model for Korea. China possessed good roads, canals, and canal locks, and made use of carriages, baggage wagons, and wheelbarrows. Korea had a mountainous terrain, Pak noted, but even China's mountainous regions had good roads. Why not Korea? he asked. He was also aware of the less rigid class distinctions in China and the greater ability of men of talent to rise to high office without belonging to elite families. Another famous critique is Pak Che-ga's *Pukhak ŭi* (*A Proposal for Northern Studies*), a memorial to King Chŏngjo in which he argued that Korea must emulate China's technology and commerce.

Korean travelers to China, however, also found much to be critical of. They commented on the subservience of the Chinese to their "barbarian" Manchu rulers. While Koreans proudly wore Ming-style fashions, such clothes were prohibited to their hosts. Especially notable was the custom by which Chinese men shaved the front part of their scalps and tied their hair in the back of their heads into queues. This practice, ordered by the Manchus to distinguish the Chinese from themselves, was to many Koreans a shameful sign of subservience. They could not help contrasting this to their own proud adherence to the practices of the venerable Ming dynasty and their own freedom from domination by a foreign ethnic group. Hong Tae-yong, while engaging in a "brush talk" with a Chinese scholar, for example, was explaining the Korean custom of showing respect for the former dynasty by leaving a blank line before writing the name Ming. The Chinese scholar upon seeing the character for Ming quickly tore up the paper before authorities could see it.[6] Thus, while Koreans increasingly admired the Qing, especially under the Kangxi and Qianlong emperors, they also became acutely aware of their differences, including their greater ideological purity.

Koreans also journeyed to Tokugawa Japan on the twelve missions to that country between 1607 to 1811. Travelers to Japan also wrote diaries and noted the differences between their society and Japan. Since such missions were fewer and held less prestige than those to China, these diaries never developed into a Japanese equivalent to the Northern Studies literature. They do, however, provide insights into how Koreans contrasted themselves with the Japanese. Korean envoys were impressed by the prosperity of Tokugawa Japan, by the size of their cities and their cleanliness. Osaka was larger than Seoul, but almost entirely devoted to commerce with a vast number of shops. There was no equivalent commercial center in Korea. Travelers also commented on the high quality of Japanese craftsmanship and the sophistication of agricultural technology. The cities and towns were clean and bustling, the countryside was prosperous, and the people were well dressed. Japanese steelmaking, in particular, was of a high standard. They also commented on Japan's military strength.[7]

Yet there was much they did not admire about Japan. Japanese moral standards were woefully inadequate. Men and women socialized too openly, and the women were flirtatious. Prostitution and brothels were everywhere, and people of the same surname married. Most shocking was the sight of men and women bathing naked together. Although Koreans themselves had once practiced this custom, in Yi times this was scandalously in violation of propriety. The principle of segregating men and women was not practiced; boys and girls played together, and were not separated at the age of seven as in Korea. Also disturbing was the practice of homosexuality, which confused the distinction between men and women, a cardinal Confucian virtue. Koreans found the level of civilization in Japan to be lower than in their own country. Japanese scholarship was inferior to their own, since the Japanese showed less mastery of the Confucian classics. They had internalized less of what they did know. There were no altars to Confucius and no ritual robes at funerals, nor did the Japanese properly carry out the rites to their parents or ancestors. Koreans were unimpressed by Japanese literature. Their lack of propriety between men and women, their inferior knowledge of Confucian literature and ritual, and their practice of blackening their teeth were all signs of their semibarbarian nature. Patronizingly some Koreans noted the Tokugawa state sponsorship of Neo-Confucianism, commenting that they were making some progress. Koreans could point out with pride that the Zhu Xi school of Neo-Confucianism had been introduced to Japan by a Kang Hang (1567–1618), a Korean scholar who had been taken to Japan as a prisoner of war. Kang worked with Fujiwara Seika, the Japanese scholar who helped establish Neo-Confucianism as an officially sponsored school of thought during the Tokugawa period. Visitors also noted that Yi T'oegye was studied and admired in Japan. Yet visitors from Seoul also noted that Confucian scholars were lower in social status than warriors.[8] Overall the level of learning in Japan, Koreans felt, was much inferior to their own. A few scholars, notably Tasan, took Japanese scholarship seriously enough to study it. But for many the Japanese were "barbarians like the beasts and the birds."[9]

TAXATION AND REFORM

The Chosŏn court, the central bureaucracy, the local government officials, the military, and the many scholars and officials supported by the state derived their income from a complex system of taxes. The Chosŏn state was more successful than its predecessor in raising revenue; still, it struggled to get adequate support. Revenue came from the collection of land taxes, tribute payments in which individuals and localities were required to supply specialized products, the use of corvée labor from commoners, and the forced labor of government slaves. The state also imposed a vast array of supplementary taxes. Since Korea was an overwhelmingly agricultural society, taxes from commerce and industry made up only a small portion of the revenue. Most of the tax burden fell on the peasants.

A major source of revenue came from tribute taxes that consisted of tribute of local specialties to the *chinsang* (royal family), to the *kongmul* (central government departments), and to the *sep'ae* (Chinese emperor). Provincial governors and magistrates were required to supply tribute articles to the king, and these of course were exacted from the commoners and slaves under their jurisdiction. The state kept *kongan* (tribute ledgers) to keep track of payments. The ledgers were based on populations of different districts; however, they were not periodically revised to account for changes in population or in the local economy that may had once but no longer produced a certain product. This resulted in unreasonable levies in some areas. Special levies of tribute could be issued, and sometimes tribute was collected years in advance. *Chinsang* was especially burdensome because it could be levied frequently and unexpectedly. Tribute contracting (*taenap* or *pangnap*) became increasingly more common. Tribute contracting involved middlemen who collected rice or cloth as a substitute for tribute payments from district magistrates or from commoners and used them to purchase tribute goods. Many royal family members and high officials engaged in contracting, and sent their personal aides or slaves to forcibly collect tribute if necessary. By the seventeenth century the tribute system was, in practice, replaced by the direct purchasing of goods through contractors. As a result most peasants and officials simply paid their tribute in the form of rice, cloth, or cash.

Peasants were also burdened by uncompensated labor service. This involved transporting grain taxes and tribute items from villages, and the transportation of them to collecting points. It also included manufacturing boats; mining; gathering husks, straw, coal, and firewood; and hunting game. It could also involve digging for coal; fishing; tending horses; building dikes, dams, city walls, and bridges; and supplying goods on demand. Peasants also had to bear the expense of putting up foreign envoys, officials who were on government business, and the king and his entourage when they were on the expeditions. These expenses could be unannounced and burdensome. Besides this formal tax system, peasants and other commoners were regularly forced to pay bribes and unauthorized fees to officials who often depended on these unofficial charges to support themselves.[10]

The inequity of the tax system and its unsystematic nature troubled many officials, who suggested a variety of reforms. Since as good Confucianists Koreans looked back to the time of the ancient sages of China for models, officials from time to time suggested various reforms based on their understanding of ancient Chinese practice. One popular idea was the well-field system of ancient Zhou China in which the state owned all the land and distributed it to the peasantry, dividing allotments into eight family plots with a ninth plot to be harvested for the state. The interesting fact is that scholars often viewed private ownership of land with suspicion. If only the state owned and could redistribute the land, some argued, the extremes of wealth and poverty would be eliminated and a prosperous peasantry could adequately support the state by paying uniform and fair land taxes. A more practical reform was the *taedongpŏp*, the new tribute replacement tax. The new tax, introduced in the seventeenth century, was designed to replace the old tribute tax. A percentage of the harvest was collected in rice, but this could also be paid in cotton cloth or in copper cash. This was carried out, first in Kyŏnggi province and then gradually throughout the country, over the next century. The land tax fostered the accumulation of commercial capital by *kongin* (tribute men). It also contributed to the emergence of independent artisans producing the products needed by the state. The *taedongpŏp* reduced the cost of arbitrary exactions of officials and clerks, reduced the costs of government expenses in collecting tribute, enormously simplified the tax system, made it more uniform, and prohibited all sorts of irregular levies not authorized by law. Compulsory labor was replaced by paid wages. While an improvement, the new land tax did not eliminate the burdens and inequities of the tax system. Officials could still levy tribute for some items, and governors could demand rare or specialized items from their areas for use by prestigious visitors. The main problem with the reform was that regular periodical land surveys were not carried out, leading to inequities in the land tax system.

Another burden for commoners was military service. Later in the Chosŏn period local levies of peasant-soldiers were replaced by paid recruits and an annual military tax of two bolts (*p'il*, each one equaling two by forty feet) of cotton cloth. In 1750 a *kyunyŏkpŏp* (Equalized Service Law) was enacted in an attempt to levy the tax peasants paid in lieu of military service more equitably. The law reduced the tax to one bolt of cotton and added a grain surtax of about one sixth of 1 percent of the harvest. It also imposed a number of miscellaneous taxes on fish traps, salt production, and fishing and trading vessels. This unfortunately caused a great burden on coastal communities dependent on income from fishing and salt flats. Many reformers saw a uniform household cloth tax as equitable and as a way of ensuring a secure source of revenue for the military. But there was a controversy centered on whether to tax the yangban. While taxing the yangban would enhance state revenues, it would give them the stigma attached to military service. When Yŏngjo levied a tax on the small number of yangban who did not register for school, about twenty-four thousand, this resulted in great protests.[11] Young yangban avoided the tax by registering as students. Sometimes yangban participated in collective village cloth payments, but this was done only occasionally and voluntarily. The burden of this tax remained on commoners. Villagers formed *kye* to share the tax burden. The *kye* is an association in which members pool their money so an individual can then withdraw from this pool when he or she is in need. It is still common today as a way of raising or borrowing money. The unfairness was increased by the fact that the quotas were not adjusted after 1750 to account for changes in the number of adult males in the districts. Neither did the military tax prove an adequate substitute for military service. It became merely another tax, while the military was allowed to deteriorate.

The grain loan system also provided the state with revenue. The state sought to stabilize prices and prevent famine by adopting the Chinese practice of buying and storing grain and then using these stocks to provide grain loans for famine relief and to tide farmers over during the spring hunger season. In the fifteenth century a move was made toward adopting Zhu Xi's *sach'ang* (village granary system), which would be in the hands of local leaders, not officials. But in Korea this was supervised by the magistrates. Although there was an aversion to charging interest, in practice a *mogok* (wastage charge) was levied that was, in fact, interest. The state had in effect become a moneylender. By the seventeenth century grain loans became an important source of revenue for the state and subject to abuse. The state also had *Sangp'yŏngch'ang* (Ever-Normal Granaries) in major market towns for price stabilization. These too lent grain at interest, profiting the officials who managed them. The total value of loans increased in the late eighteenth century. Poor peasants were seldom able to repay the loans on time, keeping them in constant debt, and the accumulated interest payments became in fact another tax. The greatest hardship was on the poorest, who were most likely to need to borrow grain. Overall the tax system, despite reform efforts, was complex and inefficient, reinforced yangban privilege, and placed the heaviest burden on the poor.

AGRICULTURE

Chosŏn society was based on agriculture. At the start of the dynasty this base was strengthened by bringing in land for cultivating and by introducing new agricultural methods. Despite some setbacks such as those caused by the Japanese and Manchu invasions, agriculture continued to expand. The most important development in agriculture was the expansion of wet rice cultivation. The advantage of wet rice was its high yields per acre; it yielded twice as much grain per acre as wheat or barley on dry land. A number of irrigation projects such as building dikes and polders enabled new areas to be brought under paddy. Waterwheels were built to bring water from nearby streams, and the building of reservoirs allowed lowlands far from streams to be converted to paddies. Another important change that accompanied wet rice cultivation was the practice of growing rice in seedbeds and then transplanting them into the paddy. This was more efficient than broadcast seeding. Wet rice and transplanting led to a increase in food production. This more productive method of farming spread in some southern areas during the first two centuries of Chosŏn, and then expanded quickly again in the late eighteenth and nineteenth centuries. Although most heavily concentrated in the south, it was practiced in all provinces except for P'yŏngan in the north.

Intercropping became more important in the eighteenth century, especially in the southern provinces where a winter crop of barley was common. Other intercrops included soybeans, red beans, millet, buckwheat, and root vegetables.[12] Lighter ploughs and hoes also increased productivity. Other agricultural advances included the greater use of fertilizer and a move away from the use of fallow fields. It is not clear if these improvements actually made life more prosperous and comfortable for most peasants. Wet rice cultivation required intensive use of labor and careful attention to irrigation works. Transplantation was also risky, since a drought during the crucial transplantation time could spell disaster for the whole crop.

Evidence clearly indicates that the population of Korea expanded during the Yi dynasty, an expansion that was made possible by agricultural advances; but it is less clear if there was an increase in agricultural productivity. Korean agriculture became more sophisticated and yields per acre were higher than in Western Europe or most other parts of the world. They were not, however, as high as in late Tokugawa Japan or in the more productive regions of late Qing China. Historians debate over whether these agricultural changes led to an increase in agricultural surplus or simply meant more labor was needed. The lack of large urban centers and the rural nature of the population suggest that gains in productivity were modest. Some farmers did benefit by the greater use of cotton and tobacco as cash crops, and the introduction in the eighteenth and nineteenth centuries of New World food crops such as potatoes and sweet potatoes acted as an extra insurance against famine.

COMMERCE AND TRADE

Korea never developed a flourishing commercial economy such as Western Europe, China, and Japan had. Korea remained an overwhelmingly rural, agricultural society. There were no major cities besides Seoul, which was a government center reaching perhaps two hundred thousand in population in the eighteenth and nineteenth centuries. Nor was there a large vigorous commercial class. Korea was also slow to develop a money economy. Coins were minted by Koryŏ and during the Chosŏn period, but only sporadically. One reason for this was that in the fifteenth century the Ming demanded gold and silver as tribute. Koreans then avoided mining the precious metals for fear it would only encourage the Chinese to ask for bullion as tribute. But mining in general was also discouraged since it was thought that it drew peasants away from farming. Some copper was mined and the chief type of money was copper cash, produced regularly from the seventeenth century. This came in the form of Chinese-style round coins with square holes in the center that were placed on strings. Prices of large items were calculated in standard "strings of cash" commonly numbering a thousands coins. Without gold or silver coins or paper money, large-scale transactions could be cumbersome. Partly for this reason, these coins never replaced bolts of cloth such as silk or cotton that continued to be used as mediums of exchange. The state further discouraged a money economy before the mid-eighteenth-century by collecting tribute in kind rather than monetary payments. The Chosŏn state also contributed to the lack of commerce by discouraging navigation and shipbuilding as part of its isolation policy (see chapter 9).

One reason often given for the lack of commercial development was that in the Chinese-Confucian worldview merchants had a low social status. Wealth was thought to be derived from the land while trade and business only diverted people from productive work. Although some commerce was needed, it was considered by the officials to be a necessary evil. Since it was held in contempt, the yangban were forbidden to engage in trade. Such attitudes were hardly conducive to trade, yet they do not appear to have prevented a flourishing commercial sector in China. Korea was not on any major international trade routes, but neither was Tokugawa Japan with its vigorous commercial economy, nor did international trade account for more than a small proportion of China's commerce.

The most fundamental factor contributing to the lack of a vigorous commercial sector was geography. China was a vast continental empire with regions that could specialize in producing particular products. Japan was a long if narrow archipelago with varied climatic regions that could specialize in crops best produced there. Korea by contrast was a smaller land with less regional specialization. More importantly, China had an impressive inland waterway network centered around two great rivers and a canal system that linked them, and Japan had the Inland Sea, a convenient highway linking the major population centers. In Korea there were no great waterways that linked regions. The most obvious avenue for trade was along the coasts. But there were problems, since the western coast had some of the world's highest tides and treacherous sandbars, making navigation tricky. The eastern coast had few harbors and was away from the population centers. Korea's mountainous terrain, while not formidable enough to seriously hinder communication, made the transport of goods expensive. Consequently, roads were merely footpaths and goods were carried overland on the backs of pedlars and porters.

The merchant class was small and their activities were carefully regulated. In Seoul commerce was restricted to *sijŏn* (licensed shops). There were two agencies to control them: the *Kyŏngsigam* (Directorate of Capital Markets), which regulated prices, attempted to prevent cheating and thievery, and collected merchant taxes; and the *Ch'ŏngjegam* (Directorate of Sanitation), which maintained sanitation. Outside of Seoul there were fewer shops. Instead trade was conducted primarily at periodic markets whose location and frequency were fixed by law. Most trade was conducted by *pobusang* (itinerant peddlers) who traveled from periodic market to market. The state also employed artisans to make weapons, clothing, furniture, and a variety of items for the court and officialdom. This eliminated the need for merchants to buy and sell things to the state. Most foreign trade was limited by law to diplomatic missions. After 1442 private trade was allowed among the envoys in their embassies to China, but this amounted to a very modest level. Imports from the official trade included silver, copper, tin, sulfur, swords, sandalwood, alum, sugar, pepper, water buffalo horns, sappan wood, licorice root, and elephant tusks. Some of these were of Southeast Asian origin. Exports were Korean cotton cloth, rice, hemp, ramie, ginseng, floral design pillows, sealskins, and books. Trade along the Yalu river border with China was prohibited, although smuggling existed. Imports consisted mostly of luxury goods for elite. Trade with Japan flourished for a while in the seventeenth century. Koreans imported Japanese copper and silver in exchange for ginseng, medicine, and a variety of goods. There was also a small-scale trade with Okinawa through which Southeast Asian spices were imported. But trade with Okinawa and Japan declined in the eighteenth century.

Late Chosŏn reformers sometimes criticized their land's lack of commercial development and unfavorably compared Korea with the vigorous commercial cities of China and Japan. Some saw commerce as promoting prosperity, not distracting peasants from their farming or yangban from their studies. Commerce began to grow somewhat in the eighteenth century partly as a result of tax reforms. The *taedongpŏp* reform legalized state direct purchases from merchants, and this stimulated trade. Cash was minted more regularly, and the state began to buy goods rather than have them manufactured by government artisans. Artisans, as a result, began moving toward independent production for the market. The growth of cotton production and the introduction of tobacco, which came to Korea indirectly from the Americas through its Asian neighbors, provided new sources of cash crops for farmers.

Signs of greater independent merchant activity appeared. The pedlars formed a guild in the seventeenth century to protect their interests, and some were able to accumulate capital and achieve some prosperity. In the eighteenth century the government gradually gave up opposition to unlicensed merchants. In 1791, the government restricted the monopoly privileges of the authorized Seoul shops and allowed unlicensed merchants to sell any other product not covered which represented a modest move toward freer trade. As the state shifted from collecting tribute to buying goods, wholesale merchants called *kaekchu* or *yŏgak* emerged. They were intermediaries between peasants and the craftsmen and merchants in town. Wholesale merchants became involved in warehousing, consignment selling, and transport. They also ran inns for traveling merchants and provided banking services. Unlike the *kongin* (tribute men), some *kaekchu* served as middlemen in the international trade after 1876 and prospered. A few like Pak Sŭng-jik and Pak Ki-sun became successful entrepreneurs and pioneers of industry in colonial Korea.[13] So in some ways Korea was developing into a more commercialized economy in the eighteenth and early nineteenth century. Nonetheless, except for some scholars such as Pak Che-ga, the Confucian disdain for merchants and trade continued; and Korea remained less commercially developed than its neighbors.

CULTURAL FLOWERING OF LATE CHOSŎN

Korean culture flourished at both the elite and popular levels during the late eighteenth and early nineteenth century. Although the influence of Chinese models in literature and the arts remained strong, there was an elaboration on indigenous forms of aesthetic expression and a focus on Korean subject matter in literature, history, and painting. For example, while the yangban continued to write poetry and essays in classical Chinese, the seventeenth and eighteenth centuries saw the emergence of a literature written in the *han-'gŭl* script. This included novels, a literary form that was very popular in the eighteenth century. The subject matter of novels varied. Some were military adventures, and some of these reflected the interest in Korea's history by heroizing those who resisted foreign aggressors. An example was the novel *The War with Japan;* another, *General Im Kyŏng-ŏp,* was based on the exploits of a general who fought the Manchus. More popular were love stories. An example of the latter, and the most famous of all Korean tales, was *The Story of Ch'unhyang.* This was an eighteenth-century tale of a young lady who falls into the clutches of an evil local official but is eventually rescued by her lover.

While novels were popular in the late Chosŏn, poetry retained its hold as the prime form of literary expression. *Sijo* remained popular. In the eighteenth century a modified form of the *sijo,* the *sasŏl sijo,* became common. This maintained the basic format of the *sijo* with its fifteen-syllable first line and third and final line, but with a middle section that could be expanded by having additional lines added. This ended the tight restriction of the form that had been so prized, and allowed for elaboration and digressions. In the nineteenth century, *Sasŏl sijo* were written by *chungin* and commoners as well as yangban. They tended to be more down-to-earth and often coarse and comic. Most were anonymous. Many historians see in the growth of popular novels and in the newer, freer, and less aristocratic poetry signs of social change as nonyangban began to give voice to their feelings and taste in written literature. However, late Chosŏn literature was still dominated by the yangban. Indeed most authors of novels and expanded verse poetry were yangban who, out of propriety, remained anonymous.

An interesting genre of literature in the eighteenth century and early nineteenth century was the satirical stories written by scholars. These used humor to criticize the inequities and stupidities of Korean society. The outstanding examples came from Pak Chi-wŏn (1737–1805). An innovative writer, his best-known tales are still popular. Many are found in his *Yŏrha ilgi* (*Jehol Diary, 1780*), the record of his trip to China. In the *Hŏ saeng chŏn* (*The Story of Master Hŏ*), a yangban who takes up useful work goes into business, prospers, and offers practical solutions to social and economic problems, but finds the yangban elite unwilling to take up reforms. The *Yangban chŏn* (*Yangban's Tale*) is about a lazy yangban who is a parasite on society. He studies but does not do any useful work and is scolded by his own wife. In *Hojil* (*A Tiger's Reprimand*) a hungry man-eating tiger decides to eat Puk Kwak, a yangban scholar with a reputation as a moral exemplar. But encountering the tiger, the yangban falls in excrement after fleeing the house of a widow with whom he is having an affair. Consequently, he stinks so much that the tiger does not eat him.[14] Another story in this genre is Chŏng Yag-yong's (1762–1836) *Ch'ultong mun* (*On Dismissing a Servant*). In an anonymous story titled *Changkki chŏn* (*The Story of a Pheasant Cock*) a pheasant hen rejects her submissive role as wife. The story thus satirizes fundamental Confucian notions about the relations between husband and wife.

An interesting legacy of Chosŏn was women's literature. In recent years scholars have rediscovered much of this large body of feminine writing. The percentage of women who were literate was small, since even yangban girls were discouraged from learning. Nonetheless, a small number of women became quite accomplished in letters. Lady Yun, mother of Kim Man-jung, is said to have tutored her two sons to pass the civil exams. Lady Sin Saimdang, mother of Yi I (Yulgok), was reported to have been very learned. Hŏ Nansŏrhŏn, a beautiful and highly intelligent daughter of a high-ranking official, was so talented as a youth that she attracted the attention of well-known poets who tutored her. Tragically she died at the age of twenty-three and destroyed many of her poems before her death. Her famous brother Hŏ Kyun collected what remained. These proved to be enough to earn her a reputation as an accomplished poet. *Kisaeng* such as Hwang Chin-i were often accomplished poets as well.

As in Japan, Korean women wrote primarily in indigenous script while men stuck to the more prestigious Chinese characters to express themselves. Women, if they learned to write, generally wrote in *han'gŭl*, which was regarded as fitting for them. *Han'gŭl*, in fact, was sometimes referred to as *amgŭl* (female letters). Women, following cultural expectations, generally wrote about family matters. But within these restrictions Korean women produced *kyuban* or *naebang kasa* (inner room *kasa*). These originated in the eighteenth century and were largely anonymous. They included admonitions addressed to daughters and granddaughters by mothers and grandmothers on the occasion of a young woman's marriage and departure from home. Young brides would arrive with these *kasa* copied on rolls of paper. They would pass them to their daughters with their own *kasa* added. Other inner room *kasa* dealt with the success of their sons in taking exams, complaints about their lives, and seasonal gatherings of women relatives.[15]

Another genre of women's literature was palace literature written by court ladies about the people and intrigues of court. A large body of this literature, much of it still not well studied, survives. Among the best known are the anonymously authored *Kyech'uk ilgi* (*Diary of the Year of the Black Ox*, 1613), the story of Sŏnjo's second queen, Inmok. Queen Inmok is portrayed as a virtuous lady who falls victim to palace politics and jealousies. She struggles to protect her son and is imprisoned by Kwanghaegun. It ends when the doors of the palace where she is imprisoned are suddenly opened following Kwanghaegun's overthrow.[16] Another work, *Inhyŏn Wanghu chŏn* (*Life of Queen Inhyŏn*), tells the virtuous life of Queen Inhyŏn, who married King Sukchong in 1681. She too is victimized at the hands of the evil rival, Lady Chang. Today the most read of these palace works is the *Hanjungnok* (*Records Written in Silence*) by Lady Hyegyŏng (1735–1815). This is the autobiography of the wife of the ill-fated crown prince Changhŏn. Written in the form of four memoirs, it is a realistic and in most respects accurate story of her mistreatment at court, the tragedy of her husband's mental ill-

ness and death, and the sufferings of her natal family by their political enemies. Her memoirs are a literary masterpiece, and because of their honesty
and her astute insights, they are a valuable window into court life in the eighteenth century. Biographical writings by women in East Asia are very rare,
and one by a woman of such high intelligence so close to the center of political life is especially important.[17]

In painting, Korean artists in later Chosŏn tended to focus on Korean
landscapes rather than on scenes from Chinese literature, and departed from
earlier conventions with bolder strokes, spontaneity, and liveliness. In the
seventeenth century Kim Myŏng-guk (1623–1649) developed a distinctive
style with strong Sŏn (Zen) influences. The eighteenth and early nineteenth
centuries was an especially creative period in Korean painting. Chŏng Sŏn
(1676–1759), for example, considered one of the greatest masters, painted the
mountains of Korea. He is especially famous for his paintings of the Diamond Mountains located near the east coast of what is now North Korea.
Sim Sa-jŏng (1707–1769) created a number of paintings from landscapes to
animals characterized by a spontaneity, simplicity, and liveliness. A new
genre of painting appeared in the eighteenth century that had no counterpart
elsewhere in East Asia. These were playful scenes of everyday life depicting
yangban socializing, peasants' merrymaking, or just everyday activities.
Among the genre painters was Sin Yun-bok (1758–?), an artist from the
chungin class who depicted beautiful women and yangban enjoying the company of kisaeng. The subjects of his *An Album of Genre Scenes* are girls on
seesaws, housewives washing clothes in streams, women selling wine, and
women and men flirting. Sin's paintings deviated too much from Confucian
propriety and he was expelled from the Tohwasŏ. Another genre painter,
Kim Tŭk-sin (1754–1822), painted ordinary people at work and play.

The most famous of the genre painters was Kim Hong-do (1745–ca. 1818).
He painted peasants working in their fields, harvesting, working in their
shops, performing music, and engaging in *ssirŭm* (Korean wrestling)
matches. A versatile artist, he also created landscapes, portraits, and bird and
flower paintings. But it is his genre paintings that are most treasured today.
Although he died destitute, Kim Hong-do is recognized today as one of
Korea's greatest artists. These genre paintings with their playfulness and
often humor have no counterpart elsewhere in East Asia. They are not only
instantly charming and appealing, but are also a vivid record of everyday life
in late-eighteenth- and early-nineteenth-century Chosŏn. Genre painting
was an example of the trend among Korean artists, writers, and musicians
of drawing upon their own folk traditions to develop new forms of artistic
expressions. A tradition of erotic art existed as well. Well-known painters
sometimes discreetly created albums of these explicit works for their
patrons.

In addition to the formal art of official artists and yangban amateurs, a rich tradition of art flourished that dealt with folk customs and beliefs. This folk art was "popular among all classes."[18] Unlike the more formal yangban art paintings, *minhwa* (folk paintings) were characterized by bright colors and a sense of spontaneity and vitality. They contained symbols from Buddhism, shamanism, and folk religion traditions. Many such paintings showed scenes from ordinary life, especially festive occasions such as birthdays and New Year's celebrations. Other folk paintings depicted landscapes, tigers, and other wild animals. Another folk art tradition was the mask dance-drama. Mask dance-dramas were performed in Silla times if not earlier. In Koryŏ times they were sometimes performed in court. During the Chosŏn period they were characteristic of village culture. The masks, generally of wood, were highly stylized. Black masks represented old men, red ones young men, and white ones young women. Some stories hint of ancient fertility festivals in which youth/summer triumphs over age/winter. Many satirized the yangban and monks, and provided an irreverence that bordered on social protest. Mask dances were generally performed during festivals such as at the first full moon of the year, Buddha's birthday, Tano (a summer festival), and Chusŏk, the autumn moon festival. Puppet plays were popular and also served as social satire by poking fun at the yangban.

A uniquely Korean art form that emerged in late Chosŏn was *p'ansori*. In a *p'ansori* performance a singer delivers a folk tale while a drummer accompanies him or her, setting the rhythm to the singer's tale and encouraging the singer by shouting out from time to time. The singer conveys the story not only by singing but also through a series of body expressions and dance-like movements. *P'ansori* combines music, drama, and dance in a unique style. It has its origins in eighteenth-century Chŏlla province, and it emerged by the nineteenth century as a popular entertainment performed in villages and towns by traveling performers.[19] In the marketplace a singer would start with an unrelated song, a *hŏduga*, to draw a crowd. Then the performance itself could take up to eight hours, although usually only parts of a *p'ansori* work were performed. Originally there were twelve *p'ansori* works or *madang*; today only six remain. The stories were derived from folktales with many embellishments added. Among the most popular were the *Tale of Ch'unhyang* and the *Tale of Hŭngbu*. The latter is the story of selfish, greedy, cruel Nolbu and his kind, unselfish, but also unpractical younger brother Hŭngbu. Unable to provide for his huge family Hŭngbu asks Nolbu for help, but his elder brother is too selfish to assist. The contrast between the two provides great delight. The story ends happily when a magical swallow that Hŭngbu has helped provides him with money. His greedy brother mistreats the swallow to gain wealth only to be ruined. *P'ansori* has become a great art form and singers spend years of training, traditionally strengthening their voice by practicing over the roar of a waterfall. It has enjoyed a revival in contemporary Korea and has gained a small but growing international following.

The eighteenth century was a great period of historical writing in Korea. Accompanying the trend toward drawing upon local sources for artistic and literary inspiration, historians focused on the study of their own country. An Chŏng-bok (1712–1791), a disciple of Yi Ik, wrote the *Tongsa kangmok* (*Abridged View of Korean History*), the first comprehensive history of Korea from Kija to the fall of Koryŏ by a private scholar. An was concerned with the importance of legitimacy and loyalty. Touching a theme that was to inspire later nationalist historians, An was also concerned with Korea's struggle against foreign invaders. He praised the achievements of those who resisted them such as Ŭlchi Mundŏk, Kang Kam-ch'an, and Sŏ Hŭi-as and less well known heros. Illustrating his professionalism, his addenda discussed historical problems and assessed the reliability of sources. Another scholar, Hong Yang-ho, in 1794 wrote the *Haedong myŏngjang chŏn* (*Biographies of Famed Generals*). It mainly focused on those who fought foreign invaders. Another private history, *Haedong yŏksa* (History of Korea) by Han Ch'i-yun (1765–1814), covered the history of Korea from Tan'gun to the fall of Koryŏ. Both An and Kang used Chinese histories as models, but their subject matter dealt with Korea's own historical development. Han used hundreds of sources, including Japanese as well as Chinese and Korean ones. He compared and evaluated them, showing the sophistication of Korean historical scholarship. His work, not quite finished upon his death, was completed by his nephew Han Chin-sŏ.

Another important history was Yi Kŏng-ik's *Yŏllyŏsil kisul* (*Narration from the Yŏllyŏ Study*), a history of the Yi dynasty from its founding to the reign of Sukchong (1674–1720). The first part deals with the various reigns and the second part with a number of special topics such as institutions, diplomatic relations, taxes, marriage customs, penal systems, and astronomy and natural phenomena. Yi, unlike most Korean historians, refrained from presenting his personal views. Instead he often presented verbatim quotations from his sources, four hundred in all, in an effort to be objective and letting "fact speak for itself."[20] Another work of significance was the *Parhae ko* (*Study of the Parhae Kingdom*), published in 1784. The author, Yu Tŭk-kong (1748–1807), challenged the idea of a unified peninsula under Silla but rather saw Parhae as part of Korean history. Yu referred to the United Silla period as the period of the "Northern and Southern Kingdoms." A number of geographies were compiled by authors such as Sin Kyŏng-jun (1712–1781), who wrote the *Toro ko* (Routes and Roads) and the *Sansu ko* (Mountains and Rivers), and Chŏng Sang-gi (1678–1752), who produced the *Tongguk chido* (*Map of Korea*).

Some scholars today see the beginnings of Korean nationalism in the renewed interest Koreans showed in their own historical tradition. An

Chŏng-bok and Yu Tŭk-kong, for example, traced Korea's history to early times, essentially making it as old as that of China. Since Koreans had often dated the start of civilization with the coming of Kija from China, dating their history back to Tan'gun before Kija implied that Korea was as old as its neighbor and not derivative of China, that it had its own distinctive development. While most contemporary historians regard nationalism as a modern concept not introduced to Korea until the late nineteenth century, some scholars see the antecedents of modern Korean nationalism in the writings of these late Chosŏn historians and other writers. Certainly, Koreans in late Chosŏn displayed a strong sense of possessing a distinctive culture even as they continued to identify with the greater world of Chinese-based civilization.

SIRHAK

A large body of critical scholarship emerged in the seventeenth and especially in the eighteenth century. Today this scholarship is often referred to as *Sirhak,* "Practical Learning." This is a modern term used to categorize a number of thinkers who had somewhat different concerns and a lively intellectual curiosity in a wide variety of areas yet who shared a desire to correct social and political injustices. Many of these scholars came from the *sŏwŏn,* private academies that were important centers of learning. By the eighteenth century there were hundreds of these private academies. They were autonomous institutions where private scholars taught, studied, wrote, and commented on public issues. Different academies became associated with different political factions, so that they were as much as centers of factional politics as scholarship. Nonetheless, they provided an institutional basis for nonofficials to scrutinize society.

One of the earliest of these practical learning scholars was Yu Hyŏng-wŏn (pen name Pan'gye, 1622–1673). His major work, *Pan'gye surok,* completed in 1670, systematically examined the landowning system, education, the institutions of government, and the military. As he did, he carefully pointed out weaknesses and suggested reforms. Among his proposals was a sweeping land reform based on the "Tang equal-field system" in which the government would take possession of all land and then assign equal plots for cultivation to all the peasants. Yu was not a total egalitarian. As with almost all Korean thinkers he accepted the idea of aristocratic privilege and social hierarchy. Under his proposals the state would provide modestly larger shares of land for yangban and bureaucrats according to their rank. But his goal was to create a society that avoided great disparities in wealth and poverty, and that would strengthen both the state and society. He also advocated the replacement of the civil examinations with a new recruiting system in order to reinvigorate the government. Yu was hardly a progressive in the modern sense. He was a conservative reformer, who wanted to bring Korea closer to what he regarded as the golden age of the past.

In the eighteenth century the number of social and political critics grew. One of the most important was Yi Ik (Sŏngho, 1681–1763), who in the same tradition as Yu presented detailed analysis of economics and politics, suggesting various reforms that sought to return to a simpler, more egalitarian past. A man of broad learning and many interests, Yi was concerned with establishing social justice. He also advocated land reform that would guarantee land to all peasants and create a more equitable and just society. He realistically suggested that land reforms be carried out on a gradual basis.

A number of reformers, Pak Chi-wŏn, Pak Che-ga (1750–?), and Yi Tŏngmu (1741–1793), of the Northern Learning School drew from their travels to China to critique their own society. They differed from thinkers such as Yu Hyŏng-wŏn and Yi Ik in that they did not seek to restore an agrarian past but were influenced by recent trends in Qing thought, commerce, technology, and literary styles. They found fault in the yangban for their idleness, and for their lack of appreciation of the practical benefits of commerce and technology. Pak Chi-wŏn, for example, a member of the *Noron* faction, criticized the scholar-bureaucratic class with his previously mentioned satirical narratives *Yangban chŏn, Hŏsaeng chŏn,* and *Hojil* (Tiger's Rebuke). Hong Tae-yong (1731–1783), who belonged to this school, also wrote on science. He suggested that the earth rotated on its axis, and in general was critical of many of the commonly accepted East Asian views on the natural world.

Perhaps the most original of these thinkers was Chŏng Yak-yong (Tasan, 1762–1836), who suggested that the ancients were not always as wise as scholars thought and that changing conditions mean that new generations had to come up with new ways of dealing with problems. Tasan, also concerned with the disparities between rich and poor, called for communally owned land and an egalitarian redistribution of wealth. He was fascinated by science, and took a deep interest in medicine. Tasan was familiar with some Western science and medicine, as well as with Christianity, and drew inspiration from this new source of learning. As with his many of his contemporaries he was influenced by Qing scholarship. He also greatly admired Tokugawa Japanese scholars such as Ito Jinsai, Dazai Shundai, and Ogyu Sorai (all of the Ancient Learning School) and their examination of ancient texts with a concern for practical information. In a short essay, *Ilbonron* (*Essay on Japan*), he praised the effort of Japanese scholars to critically examine ancient texts. He suggested that the Japanese were becoming less militaristic and more civilized, boding well for the future relations between Korea and its island neighbor.[21] Today, some see Tasan as a modernizer breaking with tradition and calling for radical change in thinking. Yet, for all his wide-ranging interests and his openness to new sources of ideas, Tasan was working within the Confucian tradition. He too saw the works of Confucius, Mencius, and the other Chinese classics as sources of great wisdom and guidance. Like Yu Hyŏng-wŏn and Yi Ik, Tasan was more focused on establishing a more equitable agricultural order than promoting commerce.

Some historians today see in all this intellectual ferment the beginnings of modern thought. According to one interpretation the "seeds of modernization" were being planted in Korea during this time. Many contemporary Korean historians have found the beginnings of a commercial revolution, and the possibility of political and social change leading to a more dynamic modernizing society. They cite the loosening of state restrictions on trade, the growth of a money economy, the new cash crops such as tobacco and cotton, the new ideas on science and medicine, and the criticism of the yangban ruling class. However, despite the growth in commerce and a growing acceptance of the importance of commerce and industry among some members of the educated elite, Korea remained a very rural society. The basic contempt for merchants and business among most of the elite changed little before the end of the nineteenth century. Furthermore, most of the "practical learning" scholars were still operating within the Confucian tradition. Most cited the ancient sages and looked to the Korean or Chinese past to find precedents for their reform ideas. There were some exceptions, but Koreans at the start of the nineteenth century were still confident and proud of the fact that they were the upholders of the ancient line of transmission of civilized values. Koreans saw civilization as always being threatened by barbarism and their land as a bastion of the Way of the Sages. The origins of civilization were in China and its principles were laid down by the ancient sage-rulers. But now that China was ruled by semibarbarian Manchus, Korea was the foremost center of civilized values. Peoples outside of East Asia might have some useful things to offer, but they were outside of civilization, ignorant of the sages and of the Way of Confucius, illiterate in Chinese characters, and unable to appreciate true art and poetry or the principles of Heaven.

EVERYDAY LIFE

Everyday life in Korea did not undergo radical change either. Rather changes occurred within tradition. Rice was the main staple for those who could afford it, although the poor and even more prosperous peasants in times of bad harvests ate "coarse grains" such as millet and barley. Living in a cold country, Koreans pickled vegetables so that they would be available in the winter and early spring. In the eighteenth century chili peppers, of New World origin, were introduced, beginning the Korean love of spicy food that set them apart from their northern Chinese and Japanese neighbors. The national dish of *kimch'i*, pickled cabbages or other vegetables in garlic and fermented fish or shrimp seasoned with chili peppers, acquired its modern form at this time. *Kimch'i* was stored in big crockery jars and became an indispensable part of each meal. Fish and seafood was an important part of the diet, although Koreans were also fond of meat if they could afford it. Rice wine was also consumed in liberal quantities.

Chosŏn Korea was only modestly urbanized. The largest city was Seoul, whose population probably peaked in the late eighteenth century at two hundred thousand. If the two river ports of Map'o and Yongsan and a few other adjoining communities are added, the metropolitan area was about three hundred thousand, about the size of contemporary Berlin in Prussia but far smaller than London and Paris. Seoul in 1800 was less than a quarter as big as Edo (Tokyo) in Japan, smaller than Osaka or Kyoto or the great Chinese cities such as Beijing. Yet serving as the political, commercial, and cultural center of the kingdom it was by far the largest city in Korea. Seoul was a walled city with three main gates: the East Gate (Tongdaemun), West Gate (Sŏdaemun), and South Gate (Namdaemun). Running east to west was Chongno (Bell Street), the main avenue. It was a city of royal palaces, numerous royal shrines, government offices, large tiled-roof houses for the rich and small thatched ones for the poor. It also had two major market areas filled with private shops: Ihyŏn area near Tongdaemun and Ch'ilp'ae ara outside Namdaemun.[22]

Seoul in the late eighteenth century was followed in size by P'yŏngyang and Kasesŏng, each with thirty thousand, and by the southern cities of Chŏnju and Sangju with twenty thousand each. Ten or eleven other towns had about ten thousand people.[23] Kaesŏng near Seoul, Ŭiji on the Chinese frontier, and Pusan, the port for trade with Japan, served as commercial centers. All other cities and towns were administrative centers. Unlike those in Western Europe, Japan, or China, Korean cities, even Seoul, lacked a vibrant urban culture. Partly this was due to the humble status of merchants, the modest scale of commercial enterprise, and the Neo-Confucian emphasis on decorum that inhibited a lively cultural life. In addition, most yangban, even when living in Seoul or another city, identified with their country homes, where they most often returned after retiring from public office. Furthermore, much of learning and scholarship in late Chosŏn centered around the hundreds of scattered, mostly rural *sŏwŏn*.

Most Koreans lived in rural villages and supported themselves through farming. Rural life was difficult. The widespread use of rice transplanting added to the labor-intensive, strenuous nature of farm work. All family members were involved in the tasks that were made more onerous by the fact that farms often consisted of scattered parcels, many on steep hillsides. Festivals, periodic markets, and itinerant peddlers and entertainers, as well as weddings and other special occasions, added variety and diversion to rural life. The craftsmen and laborers in cities and towns may have had more amusements available, but life for them was hard as well. Estimates of the actual living standards vary (see next chapter). Evidence suggests that most late Chosŏn Koreans lived modestly, yet for the most part not in extreme poverty.

Life in small villages was often harsh. People lived in close quarters and disputes over field boundaries or any variety of personal resentments were frequent. Village gossip could create or aggravate these disputes that, when accompanied by heavy drinking, often led to violence. For example, the mere rumor that someone was sleeping with some's else's wife could, and judging by legal records, often did result in lethal assaults.[24] In county seats the most important figure was the country magistrate who served a 1,800-day term. In smaller communities the local yangban generally provided leadership. He gave moral lectures at special occasions and informally adjudicated local disputes. *Yurang chisigin* (wandering scholars), who were poor unemployed yangban, often provided instruction to village children and acted as a means of spreading the dominant Neo-Confucian values to rural areas.

Village life, however, was also enlivened by seasonal festivals. The lunar New Year's and the Autumn Moon Festival were the biggest holidays as they still are today. While the yangban looked down on most sports, archery was popular. Koreans are still great archers and in the late twentieth century often dominated Olympic archery events. Korean traditional wrestling, *ssirŭm*, similar to Japanese *sumo*, was also popular. In *ssirŭm*, at least as it is played today, each player binds his loins and the upper thigh of his right leg with a two-foot-long cloth or *satpa*. Each player grasps the *satpa* in the right hand at the loins and the left hand at the thigh; the first to touch the ground with any part of body other than the feet loses. Kings sometimes sponsored wrestling events awarding honors to winners. Several styles existed but only one style remains today. Another popular game was *yut*, played with wooden sticks thrown up in the air. Various martial arts, including those ancestral to *t'aekwŏndo*, were widely practiced in the Yi dynasty, even among common people. In the late eighteenth century the prominent scholars Yi Tŏng-mu and Pak Che-ga wrote the *Muyedobo t'ongi* (*Illustrated Treatise on the Fighting Arts*), a military and martial arts manual. Although the martial arts tradition was derived from China, the manual shows Korean innovations in techniques as well as in the use of schematic illustrations to indicate movement.[25] *Paduk*, better known in the West by its Japanese name *go* and also as Korean chess or *changgi*, was popular, especially among the yangban. Most physical activities were confined to men; however, seesaws were popular among women.

Korean medicine was derived from Chinese practice and theory. Among the popular forms of treatment were *ttŭm* (moxibustion), *ch'im* (acupuncture), and *hanyak* (Chinese medicine). Koreans practiced four methods of physical observation: observing the face and overall appearance *(sijin)*, listening to the sound of the person's voice (*munjin*), questioning the person about his medical history and symptoms (*munjin* written with a different Chinese character), and feeling the pulse and stomach (*chŏlchin*). There were seventeen pulses, each requiring separate treatment. The standard medical reference was the *Tongŭi pogam* (*Exemplar of Korean Medicine*), first compiled in 1610. It ran to twenty-five volumes and was based on Korean and Chinese treatises on medicine. Eating healthy food was and is still an important part of Korean medicine. Healthful foods included *poshin t'ang* (dog meat stew), *paem t'ang* (snake soup), *paem sul* (snake wine), and above all ginseng, valued for its ability to preserve health and virility. These medical foods and medicines, as is true of many other aspects of popular and elite culture in late Chosŏn, are still part of a clearly defined Korean tradition.

Late Chosŏn Korea, while possessing a rigid class structure, was increasingly a society with common cultural values. The vast numbers of petitions to the monarch by ordinary people suggests a wide identification if not attachment to the dynasty and the state. Village schools, yangban public lectures, wandering scholars, and possibly rising literacy among males assisted in the penetration of Confucian norms among the peasant majority. Folk traditions, sports, medical beliefs, popular literature, the style of homes with their heated *ŏndol* floors, and the ubiquitous kimchi jars were all part of a rich, distinctive, and shared Korean cultural tradition.

REGULATING MARRIAGE

The attempts to bring marriage and the family in line with the ideals of Neo-Confucianism included efforts to regulate concubinage and prohibit the remarriage of widows. Marriage to secondary wives was a common practice among the elite, but the tendency was to make a legal distinction between the offspring of first or main wives and the offspring of secondary wives. Children of secondary wives, called *sŏŏl*, were prohibited from taking the civil exams and serving as officials and had many other legal restrictions. These reforms had become general practice by the eighteenth century. They also attracted the attention of some late Yi scholars, who saw the discrimination against secondary sons to be a tragic and unfair situation. The prohibition against remarriage for widows (not for widowers), however, was generally accepted, since a woman must be a virgin when she marries, and she must be loyal to her husband even after death, and obedient to her son.

On Differentiating Between Main Wife and Concubine[26]

The Office of the Inspector-General memorializes [in 1413] as follows:
  Husband and wife are the mainstay of human morality, and the differentiation between main wife and concubine may be blurred. Embodying

the great principles of the one hundred kings of the Spring and Autumn period, King T'aejo accentuated the boundary between main wife and concubine devised by the scholar-officials and instituted as the law of conferring ranks and land on main wives. The distinction between main wife and concubine has thus become clear and the root of human morality straight.

At the end of the former dynasty, the influence of ritual decorum and morality was not pervasive, and the relationship between husband and wife deteriorated. The members of the officialdom followed their own desires and inclination: some who had a wife married a second wife; others made their concubine their main wife. This has consequently become the source of today's disputes between main wives and concubines.

We have carefully examined the Ming code, which reads: "The one who makes a concubine his main wife while the latter is alive is to be punished with ninety strokes of the heavy bamboo, and the situation must be rectified. Someone who already has a main wife and still gets another one is also to be punished with ninety strokes, and they must separate."

—*T'aejong sillok* 25:13a–b

Prohibition Against Remarriage of Women[27]

Marriage was largely an affair between "two surnames," and, as far as the wife was concerned, it lasted beyond her husband's death. Confucian ideology stressed the woman's devotion to one husband, and this emphasis on the exclusive nature of the marital relationship provided Confucian legislators with the arguments they needed to prohibit the remarriage of women, a custom prevalent during Koryŏ. The first version of the State Code of 1469 apparently barred the sons and grandsons of thrice-married women from advancing into the higher officialdom. The debate of 1477 makes it clear that the majority of the discussants, here represented by Kim Yŏngyu (1418–1494), were in favor of keeping the restriction to third and not extending to second marriages. How sensitive this issue was is documented by the fact that the State Code of 1485 did not directly outlaw remarriage but provided that the sons and grandsons of remarried women would not be eligible for civil or military office and would be barred from taking the lower and higher civil service examinations. The ideological and legal implications thus, in fact, made remarriage for a woman impossible.

—From *Sŏnjong sillok* 82:9b–20a

NOTES

1. See Jahyun Kim Haboush, *A Heritage of Kings: One Man's Monarchy in the Confucian World* (New York: Columbia University Press, 1988), 39.

2. Jahyun Kim Haboush, "Constructing the Center: The Ritual Controversy and the Search for a New Identity in Seventh-Century Korea," in *Culture and the State in Late Chosŏn Korea,* ed. Jahyun Kim Haboush and Martina Deuchler (Cambridge, MA: Harvard-Hollym, 1999), 46–90.

3. James B. Lewis, *Frontier Contact between Chosŏn Korea and Tokugawa Japan* (London: RoutledgeCurzon, 2003), 192.

4. Gari Ledyard, "Korean Travelers in China over Four Hundred Years, 1488–1887," *Occasional Papers on Korea* (March 1974), 1–42.

5. Gari Ledyard, "Hong Taeyong and His Peking Memoir," *Korean Studies* 6 (1982): 63–103.

6. Ledyard, "Korean Travelers," 26.

7. Hur Nam-lin, "Korean Officials in the Land of the Kami: Diplomacy and the Prestige Economy, 1607–1811," in *Proceedings of the 1st World Congress of Korean Studies: Embracing the Other: The Interaction of Korean and Foreign Cultures,* The Korean Academy of Korean Studies (Seoul: July 2002), 82–93.

8. Chai-shik Chung, "Changing Korean Perceptions of Japan on the Eve of Modern Transformation: The Case of Neo-Confucian Yangban Intellectuals," *Korean Studies* 19 (1995): 39–50.

9. Hur Nam-lin, "Korean Officials," 88.

10. James B. Palais, *Confucian Statecraft and Korean Institutions: Yu Hyŏngwŏn and the Late Chosŏn Dynasty* (Seattle: University of Washington Press, 1996), 49.

11. Palais, *Confucian Statecraft,* 567.

12. Hochul Lee, "Agriculture as a Generator of Change in Late Choson Korea," in *The Last Stand of Asian Autonomies: Responses to Modernity in the Diverse States of Southeast Asia and Korea, 1750–1900,* ed. Anthony Reid (New York: St. Martin's Press, 1997), 111–13.

13. Carter Eckert, *Offspring of Empire* (Seattle: University of Washington Press, 1991), 12–13.

14. Kichung Kim, *Classical Korean Literature* (Armonk, NY: M. E. Sharpe, 1996), 177–78.

15. Kim, *Classical Korean Literature,* 123–24.

16. Kim, *Classical Korean Literature,* 99.

17. JaHyun Kim Haboush, *The Memoirs of Lady Hyegyŏng: the Autobiographical Writings of a Crown Princess of Eighteenth-Century Korea* (Berkeley, CA: University of California Press, 1996), 6–10.

18. Portal, *Korea: Art and Archaeology* (London: British Museum, 2000), 143.

19. Marshall R. Pihl, *"P'ansori*: The Korean Oral Narrative," *Korean Studies* 5 (1981): 43–62.

20. Choe Yong-ho, "An Outline History of Korean Historiography," *Korean Studies* 4 (1989) : 1–27.

21. Mark Setton, *Chŏng Yagyong: Korea's Challenge to Orthodox Neo-Confucianism* (Albany, NY: State University of New York Press, 1997), 128–29.

22. Kim Dong Uk, "The City Architecture of Seoul," *Korea Journal* 34, no. 3 (Autumn 1994): 54–68.

23. Hochul Lee, "Agriculture as a Generator of Change in Late Choson Korea," in *The Last Stand of Asian Autonomies: Responses to Modernity in the Diverse States*

of Southeast Asia and Korea, 1750–1900, ed. Anthony Reid (New York: St. Martin's Press, 1997), 122.

24. William Shaw, *Legal Norms in a Confucian State* (Berkeley, CA: Institute of East Asian Studies, University of California, Center for Korean Studies, 1981), 81–85.

25. Andrew Pratt, "Change and Continuity in Choson Military Techniques during the Later Choson Period," *Papers of the British Association for Korean Studies* 7 (2000): 31–48.

26. Peter H. Lee and William Theodore De Bary, eds., *Sources of Korean Tradition,* vol. 1, *From Early Times through the Sixteenth Century* (New York: Columbia University Press, 1997), 312–17.

27. Lee and De Bary, *Sources of Korean Tradition,* vol. 1, 319–20.

9

Korea in the Nineteenth Century

Korea in the nineteenth century was coming to the end of a long tradition. The states of Western Europe and their North American transplants in the seventeenth, eighteenth, and nineteenth centuries had undergone scientific, technological, political, and social revolutions that had transformed them from peripheral players on the world stage to global dominance. Korea, under the Chinese tributary system, away from the major international trade routes, had largely gone unnoticed by the West. Koreans had become aware of Europe in the seventeenth century, but until the end of the eighteenth century it was a remote region of no real interest or relevance to them. Gradually in the nineteenth century this changed.

THE "HERMIT KINGDOM"

All the states of East Asia maintained a policy of limiting contact with outsiders in the seventeenth, eighteenth, and early nineteenth centuries. China limited trade with Europeans to the southern port of Canton where it was strictly controlled. A few Jesuits were allowed in Beijing, and a very restricted trade existed between China and Russia. China and Japan did not maintain direct contact with each other, but indirect contact was sporadically maintained between the two through Korea and Okinawa. Chinese merchants from the south traded with Southeast Asia. Japan maintained limited diplomatic contacts and trade with Korea, and allowed the Dutch to trade at Nagasaki, but forbade its own people from leaving the country. Korea was the most isolated society in East Asia. Wary from their troubled experience with the Khitans, the Mongols, the Manchus, the Japanese, and other invaders, Koreans went even further to keep foreigners out and minimize contact with them. As a result, Westerners in the nineteenth century sometimes called Korea "the hermit kingdom."

In some ways the "hermit kingdom" appellation given to Korea was unfair because Korea remained surrounded by China, the Northeast Asian forests, and the Japanese archipelago, in the center of the interconnected East Asian region. Koreans were proud of being part of the greater cosmopolitan civilization associated with institutions and values that for the most part originated in China. Yet no land pursued a policy of isolation so zealously as late Chosŏn Korea. Koreans were forbidden to travel or even to build large boats lest they sail accidentally abroad. The main exceptions were the diplomatic missions to China. But these involved a small number of trusted officials and followed a strictly prescribed route. Chinese embassies visited Korea periodically, but they also followed a special route. No unauthorized Koreans were allowed to met and talk with them, they entered Seoul through a special gate, and once in the capital they were confined to a special walled compound. Few ordinary Koreans saw them. Koreans sent occasional embassies to Japan, but after the mid-eighteenth century these became fewer and confined to the island of Tsushima. Japanese traders came to the southern port of Pusan, but they were restricted to a walled compound, the Japan House, where only authorized Koreans were allowed to met and trade with them. Because of its distance from international trade routes, few Westerners or other visitors from outside East Asia came to Korea, but those who did were prohibited from entering. Thus, Koreans, confident and proud of being a bastion of orthodox teachings, the most ardent adherents to the true Way, lived in a sort of splendid isolation.

INTERNAL PROBLEMS IN THE NINETEENTH CENTURY

Historians differ on whether or not Korea was entering a period of decline, and of social and institutional crisis, in the nineteenth century. One possible symptom of dynastic decline was the politics of the nineteenth century. After the reigns of Yŏngjo and Chŏngjo, Korea entered a period in which weak kings were dominated by powerful clans related to the monarch through royal marriages. It is sometimes called the era of *sedo chŏngch'i* ("in-law government"). When Chŏngjo died he was succeeded by his eleven-year-old second son, Sunjo (r. 1800–1834). The real power was in the hands of the dowager queen, who appointed Kim Cho-sun of the Andong Kim clan to assist her in governing. From 1801 to 1834 the Andong Kim clan dominated the court. When Sunjo died in 1834 her eight-year-old grandson Hŏnjong (r. 1834–1849) became king. Power now shifted to the P'ungyang Cho clan of the boy king's mother. Upon his death the Andong Kim clan engineered the ascension to the throne of a nineteen-year-old royal relation living on a farm on Kanghwa Island who became King Ch'ŏljong (r. 1849–1864). Ch'ŏljong, a heavy drinker, died an early death, leaving only a daughter. The P'ungyang Cho clan then made an alliance with a relative of the royal family, Yi Ha-ŭng, to put his twelve-year-old son on the throne, who reigned as King Kojong (r. 1864–1907). Kojong was married as a boy to a member of the Yŏhŭng Min clan that through Kojong's wife, Queen Min, came to prominence at the court. This struggle for power among the clans mostly involved the high officials at court, but two bloody purges in 1801 and 1839 also accompanied the changes in power (see below).

More dramatic evidence of a dynasty in decline is found in several rebellions that took place during this period. In December of 1811, Hong Kyŏng-nae, a yangban who had failed to the pass the civil service exams or secure a government appointment, led an uprising in the northwestern P'yŏngan Province. Hong's followers attacked government offices and seized control of a number of towns. Joined by peasants and some local officials, the rebels soon had control of much of the province. After five months government troops put down the uprising, ending with a one-hundred-day siege of Chŏng-ju, a walled county seat. Government forces dug a tunnel under the city walls, set off explosives, and stormed the citadel. Hong and many rebels fought to the death. Nearly three thousand civilians and rebel troops were caught alive; all were executed except women and boys under ten. Remnants of Hong forces continued to rebel before they were finally defeated in 1817. The remoteness of P'yŏngan Province from the central government may have been a factor in explaining the swiftness with which the uprising spread. The rebellion had a distinct regional character; a manifesto issued by the rebels complained of discrimination against people from the northwestern part of the country.[1] But other popular disturbances broke out from time to time. A major riot took place in Seoul in 1833, triggered by a sharp increase in the price of rice. Most of the disturbances were in the countryside. These usually involved attacking the local magistrate's office and burning tax records, and sometimes attacking wealthy local yangban. Most were small scale, but a major uprising took place in 1862 in the southern city of Chinju. Thousands of peasants wearing white headbands murdered local officials and merchants in the city. Shortly afterwards another uprising took place in the town of Iksan in Ch'ungch'ŏng Province. Soon violence and destruction were widespread in all three southern provinces until the uprisings were finally suppressed by government forces in 1863.

A more systematic threat to the social order came with a new religious movement, Tonghak (Eastern Learning), founded in 1860 by Ch'oe Che-u. Ch'oe combined Confucianism, Buddhism, and Daoism in what he claimed was an attempt to counter Catholicism (Western Learning) that was entering the country. It is clear though that his new faith had incorporated some

Christian concepts too. For this reason, and because of his call for sweeping social reform, the court saw the new religion as a threat. Fearing rebellion among his followers, the state arrested and executed Ch'oe in 1864. But the new religion did not die out. It made many converts and thirty years later, in 1894, the Tonghaks led a major revolt.

Was Korea toward the end of the Yi dynasty a society in decline? All of these developments are cited by some historians as evidence that Korea was entering into a time of troubles in the nineteenth century. According to this view, peasant unrest was brought about by rural poverty, while discontent grew among frustrated local officials and "fallen yangban" who had lost their opportunity for access to government office. The domination of court politics by powerful in-law families was another symptom of this decline. Some have argued that Korea was suffering from demographic pressure, as the population grew and agricultural production remained stagnant. In the arts and scholarship as well, the brilliant efflorescence of the eighteenth and the beginning of the nineteenth century was not followed by comparable cultural accomplishments in the mid-nineteenth century. In addition, new, subversive ideas from West, in particular, Christianity, were trickling into to Korea, slowly undermining the cultural unity of the kingdom. Christian ideas can be seen in the Tonghak religion, while a small number of dissident intellectuals became Christians.

Some scholars see a parallel with what was happening in China. In the eighteenth century China had a population explosion that continued into the first half of the nineteenth century. This led to overpopulation and, consequently, an enormous pressure on the land. Population pressure probably contributed to the decline of the Qing and to the massive rebellions of the second half of the nineteenth century that cost millions of lives. Some scholars have argued that Korea too was facing declining living standards in the late eighteenth century and nineteenth century due to population pressures. In support of this view historians can point to a serious famine that took place in 1812–1813, to sporadic reports of hunger, and to the 1833 rice riot in Seoul. If this was the case, then perhaps Korea, as well as China, had a weakened and restless society at the very moment of the Western challenge.

It is not clear, however, that Korea was undergoing a rapid increase in population or a declining standard of living. Regular censuses were taken under the Yi dynasty, but the records are incomplete and their accuracy is not certain. Nonetheless, trying to work with these figures and guessing at the rate of underreporting, one scholar has come up with estimates that bring the population of Korea to 4.4 million around 1400, a number that then more than doubled to 9.8 million in 1592. This dropped to under eight million as a result of the Japanese and Manchu invasions, recovering by 1650. It rose to twelve million by 1693; then a famine from 1693 to 1695 caused it to drop toward the ten million level. The population increased again, reaching thirteen million by 1732. According to this calculation, throughout the eighteenth and early nineteenth centuries the population probably never grew above the thirteen- to fourteen-million range, and was still around thirteen million at the end of the nineteenth century.² Other scholars have placed the growth in population higher, with estimates of eighteen million by 1750 after which it leveled out, and perhaps declined modestly in the first half of the nineteenth century to sixteen million in 1850.³

The growth of population was accompanied by improvements in agriculture. Korea was having a modest "green revolution." The production of rice, barley, millet, and beans increased due to the expansion of paddy land. A great number of reservoirs were built in Late Chosŏn, making irrigation easier. Double cropping of rice and barley fields also increased yields. By the late eighteenth century transplanting had spread everywhere except the northernmost areas. Agriculture benefited from the introduction of new crops: red peppers and tobacco in the seventeenth century, and the potato and sweet potato in the eighteenth century. Tobacco provided a cash crop for farmers, and the potato and sweet potato could grow in hilly areas less suitable for other crops.

Evidence suggests that Korea's demographic pattern was similar to that of Japan rather than Qing China. After a steady rise in the seventeenth and early eighteenth centuries Korea's population probably leveled off in the mid-eighteenth century. Agricultural production kept up with population growth, and the number of famines appears to have actually declined after 1750. Korea in the late nineteenth century was one of the more densely populated lands in the world, but it does not seem to have been overcrowded. In fact, the early Western visitors to Korea sometimes commented on the lack of beggars or signs of extreme poverty. In short, there does not seem to have been any great ecological or economic crisis in Korea in the nineteenth century.

Culturally as well, the traditional arts and letters still flourished, if not with the brilliance that marked the time of Yŏngjo and Chŏngjo. Tasan, one of the dynasty's most original thinkers, wrote much of his work during the reign of Sunjo. Other scholars continued the tradition of eclectic writings. Sŏ Yu-gu (1764–1845) compiled *Sixteen Treatises Written in Retirement* (*Imwŏn simnyuk chi*), dealing with a wide variety of social, economic, and intellectual topics. Yi Kyu-gyŏng (1788–1856) wrote *Random Expatiations* (*Oju yŏnmun changjŏn san'go*), another vast compilation of scholarly treatises on government administration, economics, history, and science. Yi Kyu-gyŏng's work is marked by careful methods of empirical scholarship, reflecting the influence of the Qing school of Evidential Scholarship. Kim Chŏng-ho (d. 1864) traveled all over Korea for years and produced what has become his famous *Detailed Map of Korea* (*Taedong yŏjido*) in 1861. In literature *sijo* were composed in large numbers and *p'ansori* emerged as a new literary and dramatic form. Chang Sŭng-ŏp (1843–1897), a poor orphan who gained employment as a government painter, became regarded as one of the three great masters of the Chosŏn period.

An example of the continued vitality of traditional culture is the life and works of Kim Chŏng-hŭi (1786–1856), better known by his pen name Ch'usa. Kim came from a family of yangban landowners in Ch'ungch'ŏng Province.[4] Many had served as officials. His father passed the civil service examination and held the post of Minister of Personnel. The youthful writings of this child prodigy are said to have attracted the attention of Pak Che-ga and other scholars. In 1809 at the age of twenty-four he passed the civil service exam with a *saengwŏn* degree and in the same year traveled with his father on a diplomatic mission to Beijing. There he studied the art of epigraphy from Chinese masters Weng Fanggang and Ruan Yuan. Returning to Korea he examined inscriptions from the Three Kingdoms period and became the leading member of the Evidential Scholarship school in Korea. His interests extended to Buddhism as well. He made an extensive study of Buddhist texts, and unlike many earlier Chosŏn Confucian scholars he made free use of Buddhist terms in his writings. A noted painter, he specialized in orchids. He became better known as a master calligrapher, developing the "Ch'usa" style, which is still much admired. His reputation as an artist and scholar did not protect him from court intrigue. In his fifties he was exiled to the island of Cheju, where he spent nine years confined to living in a small room in a remote village. While in exile he painted and exchanged letters with friends and relatives on epigraphy, geology, history, art, and Confucian and Buddhist doctrine and texts. Eventually family fortunes in the capital changed and he was allowed to return to Seoul. He retired from political life soon after to spend time tutoring a number of young disciples in a provincial town south of the capital. Kim's life illustrates the continual near monopoly of higher culture by the elite and the vicious political intrigues that made public life precarious. His life, however, also represents the best of the Korean scholarly tradition. It was a tradition that was still capable of producing innovations in art and scholarship.

EARLY CONTACTS WITH THE WEST

The world Koreans inhabited was dominated by China, the vast continental empire that contained one of the world's wealthiest, oldest, and most sophisticated societies. Then there was Japan to the east, a participant in the broader East Asian cultural world but also a warlike and dangerous society. To the northwest were the seminomadic peoples that had so often invaded. Koreans maintained sporadic contact with Vietnamese, Siamese, and other southeast Asian people. Beyond this was the world of distant barbarians that Koreans had little contact with, knowledge of, or interest in. Among these remote peoples were the Europeans. Early in the sixteenth century reports of the presence of "Pullanggi" (Franks) in Southeast Asia reached Korea, and in 1597 a Jesuit, Gregorio de Cespedes, arrived in Korea accompanying the Japanese troops, but there is no Korean record of his presence. Some Korean captives in Hideyoshi's invasions were brought back to Japan and converted to Christianity. One, baptized as Antonio Corea, arrived in Italy in 1606 and married an European woman. Antonio Corea never made it back to Korea to report on what he saw. Not until the late nineteenth century did a Korean visit a Western country and come back to relate his experiences to his compatriots.

Direct contact with the West came in the seventeenth and eighteenth centuries. The Jesuits under the talented polymath Matteo Ricci established a small mission in Beijing at the end of the sixteenth century. While they made few converts, they did attract admiration for their skills in perspective painting and mapmaking, their knowledge of mathematics and astronomy, and their curious mechanical devices, especially clocks. The Chinese emperors employed Jesuits to help them maintain an accurate calendar. Koreans traveling on diplomatic missions encountered these Jesuits and shared the Chinese admiration for their technical and mathematical skills. An early reference comes from Yi Su-gwang (1563–1628), who wrote the *Chibong yusŏl* (*Topical Discourses of Chibong*) in 1614, an encyclopedic work with 3,500 entries. Included in his entries were brief descriptions of Western maps, self-striking clocks, ships, prisms, grape wine, Western religion, and Matteo Ricci. Among his descriptions of the countries of the world he mentioned Portugal, which he placed southwest of Siam, and England, which he confused with the Kirghiz tribe in central Asia.[5]

A number of other scholars and officials on diplomatic missions met Jesuits and picked up some knowledge of Western science and religion. One of these, Chŏng Tu-wŏn, in 1631 brought back with him a telescope, a clock, a Western gun, maps of the world and the heavens, and books in Chinese by Western missionaries on astronomy and world geography. For the most part Koreans were dismissive of Christianity, which they viewed as nonsensical and indicative of the low cultural level of Westerners despite their technical skill. Westerners' skills at calculating an accurate calendar were another matter, since one of the most important functions of a ruler was to be able to determine when his people could plant and harvest crops. Prince Sohyŏn, while being held hostage in Beijing by the Manchus, met Adam Schall, one of the most learned of the Jesuits in China, and invited him to send a Jesuit to Korea. Although nothing came of this, the Koreans did adopt Western calendrical methods to determine the position of heavenly bodies over Seoul and thus make a more reliable calendar. Previously they had relied on a calendar based on the positions of heavenly bodies over Beijing.

In the eighteenth century Korean visitors to China continued to stop by the Jesuit mission, which became part of the standard tour of exotic sights in the imperial capital. Jesuits even complained about the Korean visitors who handled their musical instruments and wandered around the cathedral in Beijing, spitting on the floor, ignoring its sanctity. Some Koreans were impressed by Western painting, especially its mastery of linear perspective. Pak Chi-wŏn in his *Yŏlha ilgi* wrote how he and his companions when entering a Jesuit church stretched out their arms to receive babies falling from clouds on the church ceiling. The clouds looked real, and humans appeared to be alive and moving.[6] Western realism even had some influence on eighteenth-century Korean artists, but as in Qing China, the interest in Western painting techniques was a fad that waned in the nineteenth century.

Few Koreans seemed to take the Europeans very seriously as bearers of a great tradition, rather seeing them as just clever barbarians. One of the early recorded exchanges between a Korean and a Westerner is preserved in the correspondence of Yi Yong-ho, a young Korean diplomat who met Joao Rodriques (1561–1633), in which Yi challenged the Jesuit scholar on his explanation of the universe.[7] China is the center of the universe, Yi informed the Jesuit. Rodrigues replied that there is no center of the world. Western cosmology, he further argued, is far superior to the Chinese view, for the Chinese astronomers did not know why celestial bodies moved but the West had an explanation. The Jesuit then went on to explain Catholic cosmology, linking the knowledge of celestial spheres with the broader cosmology of heaven, hell, and God. Yi was impressed with the Westerner's science, but found his cosmology unconvincing.[8] A few took Western knowledge seriously. Yi Ik, for example, although he never met any Europeans, read Chinese translations and extracts of Western mathematics, geography, and medicine, for all of which he had great respect. Nothing, however, the Koreans learned of the West shook their belief in the superiority of East Asian civilization or their Sinocentric views of the world. In fact, Yi Ik noted that Western world maps show China in the center of the world dominating its largest continent, which he regarded as evidence of China's centrality. Mostly Westerners were strange creatures with round eyes, big noses, and sometimes red hair, who as it was frequently repeated urinated like dogs by lifting one leg.[9]

In 1627, three shipwrecked Dutch sailors washed up on the shores of Korea. They were employed building guns for the Korean military. Two died in the Manchu invasion of 1636; a third, Jan Janse Weltevree, who married a Korean woman and adopted a Korean name, survived to greet the arrival of thirty-six of his countrymen in 1653 when their ship wrecked on Cheju. These Dutch sailors too were forcibly detained in Korea and employed for their technical skills. Eight later escaped, and one, Hendrick Hamel, wrote the first account of Korea in a Western language. An accurate observer,

Hamel provided a useful outsider's view of seventeenth-century Korea. Hamel reported that Koreans treated Westerners as objects of curiosity but that even educated Koreans showed little knowledge or curiosity about Western countries. "When we nam'd some Countries to them, they laugh'd at us, affirming we only talk'd of some town or village; their Geographical Knowledge of the coasts reaching no farther than Siam by reason of the little Traffick they have with Strangers farther from them."[10] After Hamel, no more Westerners are known to have arrived in Korea for nearly two centuries.

EXTERNAL THREATS AND "WESTERN LEARNING"

In the nineteenth century the world around Korea was changing. From early in the nineteenth century, Western nations began to arrive on the shores of Korea. British ships appeared on the coast in 1832. In 1846, three French warships arrived on the coast, sent a letter to be forwarded to the king, and left. In 1854, two armed Russian vessels sailed off the northeast coast and clashed with Koreans. Koreans also were aware of what was happening in China. The British went to war with China in the Opium War of 1839–1842, defeated the Chinese, and forced them to engage in trade on British terms. Britain and France went to war with China again in 1858–1860, inflicting another defeat and extracting more concessions. The Russians advanced south, acquiring territory on China's northern frontier and advancing to Korea's Tumen River border in 1860, while the United States forced Japan to open itself to trade with the West in 1854. Koreans through their diplomatic missions in China kept abreast of these changes. It was clear a new barbarian threat was emerging.

Even before these alarming events took place a small number of Koreans became attracted to Christianity, which became known as *Sŏhak* (Western Learning). It was introduced to Korea rather indirectly through written texts. A handful of Koreans on diplomatic missions to China met with Western missionaries in the seventeenth and eighteenth centuries. Most Koreans were highly dismissive of Christianity for many of the same reasons they objected to Buddhism: it promoted selfishness, honored celibacy, and gave credence to miracles. Even an admirer of Western learning such as Yi Ik dismissed these religious beliefs, which he called the "grains of sand and piece of grit" amidst their scholarship.[11] Only in the late eighteenth century did a few Koreans become genuinely drawn to the religion. In 1784, Yi Sŭng-hun (1756–1801) accompanied his father on a diplomatic mission to Beijing and was baptized by a Western Catholic priest. A small number of yangban converted, mostly from the Namin faction that was out of power and tended to produce dissidents. Some *chungin*, however, converted as well. The converts included the scholar Tasan and his two brothers, Chŏng Yak-chŏn and Chŏng Yak-chong. In many ways Christianity's progress in Korea was unique for it was not spread directly by missionaries, but by intellectuals who were attracted to Catholicism through their readings of Christian tracts in translations and through sporadic contacts with Christians in China. The beginning of Christianity in Korea was thus unusual in world history in that early converts largely converted themselves. Lacking any ordained priest, they even baptized themselves with only a vague idea of how baptism should be performed.

In China the Rites Controversy had weakened the Catholic mission the Jesuits established there in the seventeenth century. The pope had ruled in 1742 that ancestor worship and belief in Christianity were incompatible. This angered the Chinese authorities since the rites to a family's ancestors were central to Confucian practice. As Korean officials became aware of Catholicism they too condemned it. Chŏngjo declared it a heresy in 1785; the following year all importation of books of any kind from Beijing was banned lest they contain Christian writings. In 1791, Yun Chi-ch'ung from a yangban family in the southwestern policy of Chŏlla was sentenced to death for failing to prepare an ancestral tablet for his mother. Four years later, however, the first priest from China, Zhou Wenmo, entered Korea in response to appeals from the small Christian community and began making a great number of new converts. By 1801, there were an estimated four thousand Christians in the peninsula. That Catholicism could grow was in part due to the protection given by Ch'ae Che-gong, a *Namin* who held great influence during King Ch'ŏngjo's last years. But with Chŏngjo's death and the ascension of Queen Dowager Kim (Yŏngjo's queen) as regent for the youthful King Sunjo, suppression of Catholicism resumed. This was intensified when a convert, Hwang Sa-yŏng, sent his "silk letter" to the French Catholic bishop in Beijing. In it he asked the Pope to request that the Chinese emperor require the Korean king to grant religious freedom, and to have Western nations send naval forces of fifty to sixty thousand men to compel the Korean government to do so. It was to be delivered by another convert who was scheduled to go on a tribute mission. This only confirmed what many feared, that Catholicism was a dangerous heresy. Furthermore, that many converts like Hwang were from prominent, well-educated families was alarming. In the Catholic Persecution of 1801 three hundred converts were put to death, including the scholars Yi Sŭng-hun and Chŏng Yak-chong along with Zhou Wenmo. Chŏng Yak-chŏn and Tasan were exiled to remote places. This persecution became entangled in factional disputes, since the *Pyŏkp'a* branch of the *Noron* faction that was coming to power charged its *Sip'a Namin* opponents with heresy. Religion became enmeshed with factional politics.

A few years later, however, with the Andong Kim lineage securely in power the persecution of Catholics eased. Meanwhile, the Vatican had appointed a vicar apostolic for Korea, and in 1836, the French priest Maubant, and in 1837, two others, Chastan and Imbert, surreptitiously entered the country. The number of converts reached nine thousand by the late 1830s. But when the P'ungyang Cho came to power they began the Catholic Persecution of 1839 in which the three foreign priests and seventy-five converts were executed. A few years later the first Korean priest, Kim Tae-gŏn, was ordained in Macao and then smuggled into the country. His arrival was shortly followed by the arrival of three French naval ships to investigate the massacres of 1839. Assuming a connection between Kim and the arrival of foreign ships, the court executed him along with eight converts in 1846. With King Ch'ŏlchong on the throne in 1849 and the Andong Kim in power again, the persecutions let up. Twelve French Catholic priests entered and Catholic books and pamphlets were published. The number of converts reached twenty thousand by 1864. In the nineteenth century many converts were from the urban poor; many were women. Most were from the Seoul area. Christianity was by no means sweeping the country, but the presence of a Christian minority with its foreign links was troubling to Korean conservatives.

REFORMS UNDER THE TAEWŎN'GUN

As Korea faced internal and external challenges a vigorous effort of reform took place under the Taewŏn'gun, who was the father of the young king Kojong and served as his regent from 1865 to 1873. The Taewŏn'gun's program of reform was designed to strengthen the monarchy, weaken the power of the factions and great clans, and enhance the revenue of the state. He appointed members of the four major factions to office. As part of his effort to restore the dignity of the royal house, he rebuilt the Kyŏngbok palace in Seoul and restored royal tombs. One of his most radical measures was the abolition of most of the *sŏwŏn*. These private academies had served as institutional bases for various aristocratic factions and for critics of the court. The *sŏwŏn* also possessed considerable land and slaves that were exempt from taxes. Thus by closing down hundreds of the academies he would be eliminating institutions that challenged royal authority and also bringing agricultural land under taxation. After imposing a number of restrictions on *sŏwŏn*, in 1871 he closed down all but forty-seven.

The Taewŏn'gun carried out important tax reforms, reorganizing the grain loan system to make it more efficient both as a source of famine relief and as a source of government revenue. More significantly he instituted a new household tax that replaced the military cloth tax. What made this reform significant was that it was levied on the yangban as well as on commoners. To pay for his new royal palace and other projects he levied a number of new taxes such as a land surtax and a gate tax on goods transported in and out of Seoul. Not all of his reforms were successful; he issued a new coinage that was arbitrarily given a value far above the worth of the copper itself, bringing about inflation.

Initially the Taewŏn'gun was tolerant of Christianity. But the growing foreign crisis in East Asia fed fears that Christianity was a dangerous Western doctrine that would undermine the political and social order. The connection between Catholicism and the French presence in Asia resulted in a belief that Catholic missionary activities were part of hostile French designs on Korea. The regent launched a major persecution in 1866 on the advice of many of his officials, and the government executed nine French missionaries and many Korean converts in what became known as the Catholic Persecution of 1866. He also vigorously resisted any attempts by outsiders to end the country's isolation policy. The French sent seven ships on a punitive expedition to Korea in response to the massacre of Catholics, including several French missionaries. They were fiercely fought by local defenders and forced to withdraw without accomplishing their aims. In the same year, 1866, the *General Sherman*, an American merchant ship, sailed up the Taedong river to P'yŏngyang to engage in trade in defiance of the Korean ban against foreign vessels. After it refused to follow an order to leave, it was burned and all aboard perished. News of the *General Sherman* eventually reached the Americans in China. In 1871, when the United States sent a punitive expedition, the Koreans fiercely fought back, inflicting enough casualties on the Americans that they decided to retreat. The Taewŏn'gun proudly put up stone signs proclaiming, "Western barbarians invade our land. If we do not fight we must then appease them. To urge appeasement is to betray the nation."[12]

The vigor of the Taewŏn'gun's reforms suggests that the Chosŏn state in the third quarter of the nineteenth century was far from being in an irrecoverable decline. Perhaps if the state was left alone it would have continued to flourish for centuries more. But it was not left alone. East Asia was caught up in the relentless expansion of Western nations. Chosŏn officials watched in alarm as China was humiliated by the British in the Opium War in 1839–1842 and again by the British and French in 1858–1860. In the second conflict the British and French attacked and briefly occupied Beijing. When the Americans forced Tokugawa Japan to open up its ports to Western traders and to establish diplomatic ties with the West, it set in motion an internal crisis that resulted in the overthrow of the shogunate in 1868. The government of the Meiji emperor that replaced it was dominated by reformers quick to adopt Western institutions, ideas, and technologies. When the new Japanese government sought to open relations with Korea in 1869, the Koreans were shocked at its representatives' Western dress and their disregard for the diplomatic forms of the East Asian world order.

In 1876, the Japanese used Western-style gunboat diplomacy to demand that Korea open its ports to Japanese merchants and establish formal diplomatic ties with Tokyo. The young monarch Kojong and his court gave in to the demands. Six years later, on the advice of the Chinese, Korea signed a treaty with the United States opening the country to American missionaries and merchants, and establishing diplomatic relations. Soon a trickle of Koreans were traveling to Japan, to the United States, and to Europe. Koreans proved to be eager students, with many quick to see the necessity and advantage of change. But the nation was not allowed to absorb the flood of new ideas entering the country. Instead, Korea became caught in the aggressive imperialistic power politics of the late nineteenth century. China struggled to maintain its influence in Korea, while other powers, most of all Japan and Russia, intrigued to establish control over the peninsula. Ultimately Japan emerged the victor in this competition, and in 1910 Korea was annexed to the island empire. When the occupation ended Korea found itself the pawn of the world's two great powers of 1945, the United States and the Soviet Union, and was effectively partitioned. Korean conservatives warned that the ending of isolation would result in disaster for the country. They were proved right.

THE LEGACY OF TRADITIONAL KOREA

Korea in the nineteenth century was an ancient land with a proud cultural tradition, a cultural tradition with origins going back several thousand years. As a unified state it was more than twelve centuries old, making it older than any state in Europe. Besides China, that vast continental empire, only Japan, and perhaps Cambodia and Ethiopia, could claim as much political continuity. The boundaries of Korea had not changed radically in almost a millennium. The present borders were established during the reign of Sejong in the fifteenth century. These were the most stable national boundaries in the world. Even the eight provincial boundaries had existed largely unchanged for eight centuries, longer than provincial boundaries of any other country. Politically the aristocratic-monarchical system had undergone some modifications but remained fundamentally the same since the Silla period. And the Yi (Chosŏn) dynasty was the third-longest-ruling dynasty of any major state; only the imperial houses of Japan and Ottoman Turkey among major states were older. Socially most of the great families traced their ancestry back many centuries; some, such as the Kyŏngju Kim clan, had been prominent since at least as early as the fifth century. This was an ancestry several centuries longer than that of any royal or aristocratic family in Europe.

Within this relatively stable political framework a well-defined Korean society, possessing a sense of its own identity as a people with their own culture, had emerged. Korea was an ancient land characterized by change within tradition, a strong sense of continuity, and stability. Politically independent, suspicious of outsiders, and remarkably homogeneous with no ethnic minorities, Korea was a land apart. Yet the Koreans were participants in a great cosmopolitan civilization centered in China. Koreans were aware of their distinctiveness as a people with a language very different from their neighbors and their own style of dress, housing, cuisine, and folk customs. Nevertheless, the elite took pride not in their distinctiveness, but in their adherence to cultural values that had their origin in China. Culturally, in some respects the gap between the yangban and the commoners was greater than that between the yangban and the Chinese literati. But this cultural gap between the elite and the nonelite narrowed as Neo-Confucian norms were absorbed by all members of society. Korea was not a "nation" in the modern sense; it was, rather a clearly defined political, ethnic, and cultural unit within East Asian civilization. But the great civilization that the Koreans were so proud to be a part of underwent a severe challenge in the late nineteenth and twentieth centuries. This challenge would fundamentally alter Korean culture and bring the old order to an end.

Yet the rich and ancient cultural tradition of Korea did not die out as much as it was transformed by the exposure to the Western dominated world of the late nineteenth and twentieth centuries. Just as in the past Koreans had looked to China as a cultural model, they now sought to take the best in the achievements of Western civilization and adopt and adapt them to their culture. Twentieth-century Koreans were to look to Japan, the United States, and Europe. Just as they proved to be China's most studious pupils, they would be among the twentieth century's most ardent and eager students, absorbing and bringing back ideas on society, politics, art, literature, music, science, economics, thought, and fashions. These they developed into a unique Korean synthesis. In North Korea the result of this synthesis was the creation of one of the most totalitarian and oppressive systems of government the world has ever seen. In South Korea this led to the emergence of a vigorous if contentious democratic society with an internationally competitive economy. Thus, even at the start of the twenty-first century the legacy of premodern history would continue to shape Korean society, culture, and identity and the ways Koreans responded to the challenges of the rapidly evolving global civilization that they had joined.

NOTES

1. Anders Karlsson, "Challenging the Dynasty: Popular Protest, *Chŏnggamnok* and the Ideology of the Hong Kyongnae Rebellion," *International Journal of Korean History* 2 (2001): 255–77.

2. Tony Michell, "Fact and Hypothesis in Yi Dynasty Economic History: The Demographic Dimension," *Korean Studies Forum*, no. 6 (Winter–Spring 1979–1980): 65–93.

3. Donald Baker, "Sirhak Medicine: Measles, Smallpox, and Chang Tasan," *Korean Studies* 14 (1990): 135–66.

4. Ch'oe Wan-su, "A Study of Kim Chŏng-hŭi," *Korea Journal* 26, No. 11 (November 1986): 4–20.

5. Donald Baker, "Cloudy Images: Korean Knowledge of the West from 1520–1800," *B.C. Asian Review* 3, no. 4 (1990): 51–73.

6. Yi Sŏngmi, "Western Influence on Korean Painting of the Late Chosŏn Period," in *Proceedings of the 1st World Congress of Korean Studies: Embracing the Other: The Interaction of Korean and Foreign Cultures*, The Korean Academy of Korean Studies (Seoul: July 2002), 576–84.

7. Donald L. Baker, "Jesuit Science through Korean Eyes," *Journal of Korean Studies* 4 (1982–3): 207–29, 213.

8. Baker, "Jesuit Science through Korean Eyes," 217.

9. Baker, "Cloudy Images," 68.

10. Gari Ledyard, *The Dutch Come to Korea* (Seoul: Royal Asiatic Society, 1971), 223.

11. Baker, "Cloudy Images," 63.

12. Ki-baik Lee, *A New History of Korea*, trans. Edward W. Wagner with Edward J. Shultz (Cambridge, MA: Harvard University Press, 1984), 266.

Appendix: Romanization

The Korean language has a rather complex sound system that has posed challenges to romanization. This book follows the McCune-Reischauer system that is used by the Library of Congress and with minor variations in most scholarly texts. Below is a basic guide to the pronunciation of the McCune-Reischauer system used in this book. Note: the Korean sound system is very different than in English so the equivalents below are only rough approximations.

CONSONANTS

ch is as in English but unaspirated, sounding a bit more like a j
ch' is pronounced as in English but more aspirated
k as in English but unaspirated, sounding a bit like a hard g
k' as in English but more aspirated
kk a very tense unaspirated k sound
p as in English but unaspirated and sounding a bit like a b
p' as in English but more aspirated
pp a very tense unaspirated p sound
s softer than an English s, but if followed by i pronounced as sh
ss more tense than an English s
t as in English but unaspirated, sounding a bit like a d
t' more aspirated then in English
tt a tense unaspirated t
tch a tense unaspirated ch sound

Other consonants are pronounced more or less as they are in English.

VOWELS

a as the a in father
ae a bit like the a in cat
e roughly as in English
i between the i of tin and the ee of teen
o as in hope
ŏ between the sound of u in fun and the aw in fawn
oe roughly as "way"
u as the u in tune
ŭ similar to the oo in book
ŭi sometimes as in eh

In 2000 the South Korean government adopted a new official Revised Romanization that is also coming into use. Below are some of the differences.

McCune-Reischauer	*Revised Romanization*
ch	j as initial sound
ch	'ch
k	g as initial sound
k'	k
p	b as initial sound
p'	p
t	d as initial sound
t'	t
ŏ	eo
ŭ	eu

In Revised Romanization hyphens between syllables in names are optional.

Below are some names and terms written in First McCune-Reischauer, then in Revised Romanization and in the Korean alphabet.

1.	ch'ŏnmin	cheonmin	천민
2.	Chosŏn	Joseon	조선
3.	Han'gŭl	Hangeul	한글
4.	kisaeng	gisaeng	기생
5.	Kim Pu-sik	Gim Bushik	김부식
6.	Koryŏ	Goryeo	고려
7.	kwagŏ	gwageo	과거
8.	Paekche	Baekje	백제
9.	p'ansori	pansori	판소리
10.	Silla	Silla*	신라
11.	Tan'gun	Dangun	단군
12.	T'oegye	Toegye	퇴계
13.	yangban	yangban*	양반
14.	Yi Sŏng-gye	Yi Seonggye	이성계

* Note some Korean names and terms are spelled the same in both McCune-Reischauer and Revised Romanization.

Glossary of Korean words

ajŏn local officials, also called *sŏri*
amgŭl "female letters," another name for *han'gŭl* (see below)
anbang "inner room" (see *anch'ae*)
anch'ae the section of the house for women also called the *anbang*
ang changgun grand general, top military post in Koryŏ
Chaech'u Privy Council in Koryŏ later called *Todang*
changgun general called
chapkwa specialized technical exams
ch'arye holiday commemorations to ancestors
chesa rites to ancestors
chesul ŏp Composition Examination in Koryŏ
ch'ilgŏjiak "seven evils," legitimate grounds for divorcing a wife
chikchŏn "office-field" allocated to officials
Ch'ilsŏng Big Dipper, widely worshiped Korean spirit
ch'im acupuncture
ch'in Confucian principle of cordiality or closeness between parents and children
chin'gol true bone or true-bone, hereditary elite of Silla
chinsa literary exam in Chosŏn
Chiphyŏnjŏn Hall of Worthies
Chipsabu Chancellery Office during Silla period
chisa wandering geomancers
Chisin Earth God
cho "progenitor," used as an element in Korean royal names
choch'ŏn tribute missions to China also called *yŏnhaeng*
chok a large descent group in Silla
chokpo books kept by lineages where births, marriages, and deaths were recorded
ch'on villages
chondaeŏ or **chondaemal** Korean speech style for addressing superiors
chong "ancestor," used as an element in Korean royal names
Chŏngbang Personnel Authority political institution during military period of Koryŏ

chŏngbyŏng conscripts
chŏnghye ssangsu twofold training in quiescence [meditation] and activity
chongja first son
Ch'ŏngjegam Directorate of Sanitation
chŏngjŏnje "able-bodied land system"
ch'ŏn'gŏ recommendation system
ch'ŏnmin "base people"
ch'ŏnmyŏng Mandate of Heaven
chŏnsi palace exam
chŏnsi-kwa Field and Woodland, system during the Koryŏ by which officials received fixed incomes from certain lands
ch'ŏp commoner or slave concubine (also called a "secondary wife")
chosang ancestors or ancestral spirits
ch'osi preliminary exam
Chosŏn (Chinese: Chaoxian), lit. "Land of the Morning Calm," name of an early kingdom and of the Korean state from 1392–1910
Chowang Kitchen God, one of the Korean household gods
ch'ugugi system of rain gauges
ch'ulga oein "one who left the household and became a stranger": term for daughter who left her natal home after her marriage
chŭlmun prehistoric comb-patterned Korean pottery (also known as **pitsal munŭi**)
ch'ung loyalty
Chungbang Supreme Military Council
Ch'ungch'uwŏn Royal Secretariat in Koryŏ, later called the *Ch'umirwŏn*
chungin "middle men," a subelite class of technical specialists in Chosŏn
chungsi chief minister in Silla
Chungsŏ-Munhasŏng combined Secretariat-Chancellory in Koryŏ
Chungsŏsŏng Secretariat in Koryŏ
han'gŭl the indigenous Korean alphabet (lit. "Korean writing")
hanmun Chinese characters, also called *hanja*
hanyak Chinese medicine
hojang local headmen
hop'ae identification system using special tags in Chosŏn
hunmin chŏngŭm "correct sounds for the instruction of the people," another term for the indigenous Korean alphabet (*han'gŭl*)
Hwaŏm "Flower Garland," a school of Buddhism
Hwabaek Council of Notables
hwarang lit. "flower boys," military bands of aristocratic youth that served as elite units in the Silla army
hwarangdo the way of the *hwarang*
hyangan local yangban associations
hyangban rural yangban
Hyangch'ŏng Local Agency
hyangga a form of Korean-language poetry
hyanggyo state-sponsored local schools

hyangyak isul   medical prescriptions
hyangni   the local hereditary elite
hyo   Confucian principle of filial piety
hyŏnhakkŭm   "black crane zither," a modified Chinese seven-string instrument
idu or **kugyŏl**   transcription system used to facilitate the reading of the Chinese classics
isagŭm   "successor princes," rulers of early Silla
kadong   house slaves
kaekchu   wholesale merchants in Chosŏn, also called *yŏgak*
kamugwan   a central government office that oversaw rural jurisdictions
kasa   a genre of Korean poetry
kayagŭm   a kind of zither
ki   (Chinese: *qi*), the primal matter-energy of the universe
kije   death anniversary commemorations
kijŏn   format used in official histories
kimch'i   pickled cabbages or other vegetables in garlic and fermented fish or shrimp seasoned with chili peppers
kisaeng   female entertainers
Kyojŏng Togam   Office of Decree Enactment
kobuksŏn   "turtle ship," early Korean iron-clad warship
kogok   "curved jewel," stylized bear claws that served as signs of royal authority in Silla
kolp'um   bone-rank system of Silla
kongan   tribute ledgers
kongin   tribute men
kongjŏn   public land
kongnobi   government slaves
kosa   offerings to household gods
kut   Korean shamanist ceremony
kun-hyŏn   prefecture-county, administrative unit under the Koryŏ
Kukhak   National Academy
kuksok   "national practice," term used to distinguish Korean from non-Korean customs
kun   administrative subdivision of province often translated as county
kun   commandery in Chinese-ruled Korea
kwagŏ   civil service examinations
Kwanggun   Resplendent Army
kwisin   spirits
kye   informal loan associations
Kyo   Textual Buddhism
Kyojŏng Togam   Office of Decree Enactment
Kyŏngjaeso   Capital Liaison Office
Kyŏngsigam   Directorate of Capital Markets
Kyŏngguk Taejŏn   official legal code dating from the fifteenth century
Kyŏngyŏn   Classics Mat
kyuban or **naebang kasa**   inner room *kasa*, women's writings about family life

kyunyŏkpŏp   Equalized Service Law
mansin   another term for shaman
maripkan   a title for early Silla rulers
mimangin   "a person who has not died yet," said of a widow
minhwa   folk paintings
minmyŏnuri   a girl bride
mogok   wastage charge, fees charged by state granaries
muban   military officials
mudang   shaman
muhak   military schools
mumun   plain pottery style of early Korea
munban   civil officials or civil aristocracy
mun'gaek   retainers
Munha-sijung   supreme chancellor
Munhasŏng   Chancellery
munjung   name for ancestral lineages
munkwa   highest level of civil service examinations
Munmyo   National Shrine to Confucius
myoje   graveside commemorations to ancestors
myŏnggyŏng ŏp   Classics Examination in Koryŏ
Namin   "Southerners," political faction in Yi Korea
Nogŭp   stipend villages in Silla
nongjang   landed estates
Noron   Old Doctrine political faction in Yi Korea
oegŏ nobi   out-resident slaves
ŏndol   style of heated floors in Korean houses
ŏnmun   vernacular script (another term for the indigenous Korean alphabet, *han'gŭl*)
oryun   the five ethical norms of Confucianism
Ŏsadae   censorate in Koryŏ
Owi Toch'ongbu   Five Military Commands Headquarters
paduk   Korean name for the game of *go*, also used to designate a style of dolmen in early Korea.
p'aedo   a suicide knife
paekchŏng   outcaste group
paem sul   snake wine
paem t'ang   snake soup
pando   lit. "half island," peninsula
panmal   Korean speech style for addressing inferiors
pangnap   (or *taenap*)   tribute contracting
p'ansori   distinctive Korean form of folk tales presented by a singer/dancer accompanied by a drummer
p'ansu   blind exorcists
pap   cooked rice
pinyŏ   a long pin used by Korean women to tie hair
Pumaguk   "Son-in-law Nation," term used for Korea during Mongol period

pobusang   itinerant peddlers
pon'gwan   clan-seat system under the Koryŏ
Ponhyang Sansin   Mountain God, one of the Korean household gods
Popŏp   Paired Provisioner system
pu   rhyme-prose
Pugin   "Northerners," political faction in Chosŏn
Pukhak   Northern Learning term for late Chosŏn reform minded writers
pulch'ŏnjiwi   "never removed tablets" containing names of ancestors
punch'ŏng   predominant ceramic ware from the 1390s to the 1590s
p'ungsu   geomancy
pyŏl   distinction between husbands and wives
Pyŏlmuban   special military force developed to defend Korea against invading Jurchen
p'yŏngin   "good people" or socially respectable people
p'yŏnnyŏn   annalistic format
Pyŏso Kakssi   Toilet Maiden, one of the Korean household gods
sach'ang   village granary system
sadaebu   derived from the Chinese term *shidafu*, meaning scholar-official
saenae-mu   mask dances in Silla
saengwŏn   classics exam in Chosŏn
Saeng yuksin   Six Ministers Who Lived
Saganwŏn   Censor-General
Sahŏnbu   Office of Inspector-General
Sajŏn   "private land"
sama   lower-level civil service examinations
Sambyŏlch'o   Three Elite Patrols
samgang   "three cords" or basic principles of Confucianism
Samsa   "three institutions," the censorate organs in Chosŏn
Samsin Halmŏn   Birth Grandmother, one of the Korean household gods
Samsŏng   Three Chancelleries term for the three highest administrative organs in Koryŏ
sangdaedŭng   the chief of the *Hwabaek*
Sangp'yŏngch'ang   "Ever-Normal Granaries"
Sangsŏsŏng   Secretariat for State Affairs in Koryo
sangsuri   Silla system of having non-Sillan tributaries send hostages to serve at court in rotation
sanobi   private slaves
Sansin   the Mountain Spirit
sarang ch'ae   the section of the house for men
sasaek   four colors, another term for the major political factions in Chosŏn
sasŏl sijo   later expanded form of *sijo*
Sa yuksin   Six Martyrs
sedo chŏngch'i   "in-law government," term used for nineteenth domination of court politics by royal consort families
Sibi to   Twelve Assemblies, private schools that trained young men for civil service examinations in Koryŏ

Sigŭp   tax villages in Silla

sijo   a "short, suggestive poem" consisting of three lines, each with fifteen syllables

sijŏn   licensed shops

Sillok   Veritable Records, the official history of the reign of a Korean king

sin   Confucian principle of trust between friends

Sinŭigun   Army of Transcendent Righteousness

sip chŏng   ten garrisons

Sirhak   "Practical Learning," modern term for reform minded scholars in late Chosŏn

sŏ   Confucian principle of order between elders and juniors

Sŏbang   Household Secretariat

sŏdang   oath banner Silla military units, see also *sŏjae*

Sŏin   "Westerners," political faction in Yi Korea

Sŏhak   "Western Learning," Korean term for Christianity

sŏja   children born to a *ch'ŏp* (see above)

sok   subordinate prefectures in Koryŏ

sŏjae or **sŏdang**   village schools

solgŏ nobi   household slaves

Sŏn   meditative Buddhism (Japanese: Zen)

sŏnggol   hallowed bone or sacred bone, ruling elite of early Korea

Sŏnggyun'gwan   National Confucian Academy

Sŏnghwang   a local guardian god

Sŏngju   walled towns

Sŏngju   House Lord, one of the Korean household gods

sŏŏl   another term for *sŏja*

sŏri   local officials, also called *ajŏn*

Soron   Young Doctrine, political faction in Yi Korea

sŏsa   general supervisory authority possessed by Censorate

sŏwŏn   private academies in Chosŏn

ssirŭm   Korean-style wrestling

Sumun   Door Guard, one of the Korean household gods

Sŭngjŏngwŏn   Royal Secretariat in Chosŏn

taedongpŏp   tribute replacement tax

taekwa   a name for the highest-level civil service examinations (see also *munkwa*)

T'aep'o   Festival of Wine

t'akja   "table" style of dolmens in early Korea

tan'ga   "short song," another word for *sijo*

tangsanggwan   those of senior third rank and above

tan'o chomsu   sudden enlightenment and gradual cultivation taught by Chinul

tchok   long, braided hair worn by women

teril-sawi   boy child grooms

todŭngnyŏ   "robber woman," said of a daughter

Tohwasŏ   Bureau of Painting

T'ŏju Taegam   Site Official, one of the Korean household gods

Tonghak   "Eastern Learning," nineteenth-century religious movement

Tongin   "Easterners," political faction in Chosŏn

tongnyŏnhoe   classmate organizations
toryŏng   military commander
ttŭm   moxibustion
tup'um   head-ranks, a heredity status system of Silla
ŭi   righteousness and justice
ŭibyŏng   "righteous armies," resistance bands during the Japanese invasions of Korea
Ŭigŭmbu   State Tribunal
Ŭihŭng Samgunbu   Three Armies Headquarters
Ŭijŏngbu   State Council of Chosŏn
ŭm   privilege by which sons received automatic appointment to office
Waegu   term for Japanese pirates
wang   Korean term for king
wŏnhwa   lit. "original flowers," female leaders of the *hwarang*
yangban   lit. "two sides," the aristocratic elite of Korea
yangin   "good people," not slaves or outcastes
Yemun'gwan   Office of Royal Decrees
Yi   (Chinese: *li*), the patterning principle of the universe
yŏl   Confucian principle of distinction between men and women
yŏmbul   recitation of the name of Buddha
yŏnhaeng   mission to Beijing
yuhak   student status that included exemption from military duty and eligibility for taking the civil service exams
yuil   people of merit and integrity, civil service appointees through recommendation system
Yukcho   Six Ministries
Yukpu   Six Ministries
yuktu-p'um   head-rank six, highest of the head-ranks of Silla
Yurang chisigin   wandering scholars
yut   popular game played with wooden sticks

Selected Bibliography

Barnes, Gina L. *State Formation in Korea: Historical Archaeological Perspectives.* Richmond, Surrey: Curzon Press, 2001.

A summary of archaeological and historical scholarship on the early states in Korea from Old Chosŏn through the Three Kingdoms period. More for the serious student of early Korea than the general reader.

Bishop, Isabella Bird. *Korea and Her Neighbors.* New York: Fleming H. Revell, 1897.

The intelligent observations of the wife of a late-nineteenth-century British diplomat, entertaining but also useful for her insights into Korea in the last days of the old order.

Buswell, Robert E. Jr. *Tracing Back the Radiance: Chinul's Korean Way of Zen.* Honolulu: University of Hawaii Press, 1991.

Translations and analysis of the writings of the important Koryŏ Buddhist monk. Contains a lengthy introduction to Chinul's life and thought as well as background information on Buddhism in premodern Korea. Aimed at a fairly high scholarly level.

Buzo, Adrian, and Tony Prince, trans. *Kyunyo-Jon: the Life, Times and Songs of a Tenth Century Korean Monk.* Sidney: Wild Peony Press, 1994.

A translation of the eleventh-century biography of a tenth-century Koryŏ Buddhist monk of the Hwaŏm school of Buddhism. It has a short text with lengthy scholarly annotations and appendices. A rare glimpse into Korean Buddhist hagiography with a useful nineteen-page introduction. Contains translations of the eleven *hyannga* poems for which this work is chiefly famous.

Ch'oe Pu. *Ch'oe Pu's Diary: A Record of Drifting across the Sea.* Translated and with an Introduction by John Meskill. Tucson: University of Arizona Press, Tucson, 1965.

The account of a fifteenth-century Korean official who was shipwrecked off the coast of China, describing his stay in China and his return home. Provides an insight into the values and attitudes of an early Chosŏn Confucianist and his observations about China.

Ch'oe, Yong-ho. *The Civil Examinations and the Social Structure in Early Yi Dynasty Korea: 1392–1600.* Seoul: Korean Research Center, 1987.

A controversial study of the civil examination system that argues that the civil exams were open to commoners and even to some slaves.

De Bary, William Theodore, and Jahyun Kim Haboush, eds. *The Rise of Neo-Confucianism in Korea.* New York: Columbia University Press, 1985.

A collection of essays by scholars analyzing Neo-Confucianism and its impact on Korea. The fifteen essays are of a high standard but are often demanding for the non-specialist. The introduction by De Bary, one of the foremost East Asian scholars, provides a helpful entry into the topic of Neo-Confucianism and its importance.

Deuchler, Martina. *The Confucian Transformation of Korea: A Study of Society and Ideology.* Cambridge, MA: Council on East Asian Studies, Harvard University, 1992.

A detailed examination of impact of Neo-Confucian ideology on Korean society during the transition period from late Koryŏ to mid-Chosŏn. The work focuses on ancestor worship, funerary rites, succession and inheritance, the position of women, the institution of marriage, and the formation of descent groups. This major study argues that a radical social transformation occurred, driven by ideological concerns.

Duncan, John B. *The Origins of the Chosŏn Dynasty.* Seattle: University of Washington Press, 2000.

An important work that analyzes the elite families of the Koryŏ and early Chosŏn to determine the extent of social and political continuities. The author argues that the change from Koryŏ to Chosŏn did not involve a radical change in Korea's social structure. Clearly written with many insights into premodern Korean history.

Eckert, Carter J., Ki-bail Lee, Young Lew, Michael Robinson, and Edward W. Wagner. *Korea Old and New: A History.* Cambridge, MA: Korea Institute, Harvard University, 1990.

The standard English language survey text on Korean history. Especially useful as a survey of Korea since 1876.

Gardiner, Kenneth H. J. *The Early History of Korea: The Historical Development of the Peninsula up to the Introduction of Buddhism in the Fourth Century C.E.* Honolulu: University of Hawaii Press, 1969.

A short analysis of the early history of Korea to the fourth century C.E., based almost entirely on the textual sources. Still useful on the written sources for early Korean history but now dated by the wealth of archaeological evidence that has been uncovered in recent decades.

Griffis, William Eliot. *Corea: The Hermit Nation.* 9th ed. New York: AMS Press, 1971.

Originally published in 1883, the first work on Korea by an American scholar. Interesting as a summary of what was known about Korea in the West on the eve of its opening to Westerners.

Haboush, Jahyun Kim. *A Heritage of Kings: One Man's Monarchy in the Confucian World.* New York: Columbia University Press, 1988.

An excellent study of Chosŏn period politics and society, and especially of kingship, through the study of the eighteenth-century monarch Yŏngjo. Clearly written with a wealth of insights and information.

Haboush, JaHyun Kim. *The Memoirs of Lady Hyegyŏng: the Autobiographical Writings of a Crown Princess of Eighteenth-Century Korea.* Translated and with an Introduction and Annotations by JaHyun Kim Haboush. Berkeley, CA: University of California Press, 1996.

The most readable translation of this fascinating work consisting of four memoirs by an eighteenth-century court lady. Contains a lengthy and informative introduction. Extremely helpful in understanding Chosŏn politics and society.

Haboush, Jahyun Kim, and Martina Deuchler, eds. *Culture and the State in Late Chosŏn Korea.* Cambridge, MA: Harvard-Hollym, 1999.

A collection of informative essays on the politics, religion, and society of late Chosŏn.

Han, Suzanne Crowder. *Notes on Things Korean.* Seoul/Elizabeth, NJ: Hollym International Corp, 1995.

An entertaining, nonacademic introduction to traditional Korean customs, art forms, and crafts.

Han, Woo-keun. *The History of Korea.* Translated by Kyung-shik Lee. Edited by Grafton W. Mintz. Honolulu: University of Hawaii Press, 1974.

A survey history by an eminent Korean historian. Now dated by more recent scholarship.

Henthorn, William E. *A History of Korea.* New York: The Free Press, 1971.

A narrative survey of Korean history to the nineteenth century. Somewhat outdated as a result of recent research and literature on premodern Korea.

Hong (Lady). *Memoirs of a Korean Queen.* Translated and edited by Choe-wall Yang-hi. London: KPI, 1985.

A serviceable translation of the memoirs of Lady Hyegyŏng.

Hoyt, James. *Songs of the Dragons Flying to Heaven.* Seoul: Royal Asiatic Society, Korea Branch, 1971.

An English translation of the fifteenth-century didactic cycle of poems concerning the establishment of the Yi dynasty. This was the first work to be written in the new alphabet, *han'gŭl.* The Korean text is placed next to the English translation. Well annotated with an informative introduction.

Hulbert, Homer. *The Passing of Korea*. Seoul: Yonsei University Press, 1969.

Originally published in 1906, an opinionated description of Korea at the end of the Chosŏn by a Christian missionary who admired much of the culture.

Illyŏn. *Samguk yusa. Legends and History of the Three Kingdoms of Ancient Korea.* Translated by Tae-Hung Ha and Grafton K. Mintz. Seoul: Yonsei University Press, 1972.

Uneven translation but does provides a look at this rich depository of myth, legends, and history from thirteenth-century Korea.

Janelli, Roger L., and Dawnhee Yim Janelli. *Ancestor Worship in Korean Society*. Stanford: Stanford University Press, 1982.

A study of an important aspect of Korean culture by two anthropologists.

Jeon, Sang-woon. *Science and Technology in Korea: Traditional Instruments and Techniques*. Cambridge, MA: MIT Press, 1974.

A comprehensive survey of science and technology in Korea mostly from the Chosŏn period. Includes astronomy, shipbuilding, pottery, metallurgy, printing, papermaking, gunpowder, and weapons technology.

Kalton, Michael. *The Four-Seven Debate: An Annotated Translation of the Most Famous Controversy in Korean Neo-Confucian Thought*. Albany, NY: SUNY Press, 1994.

A translation of an exchange of letters between two sixteenth-century philosophers, Yi Hwang (T'oegye) and Ki Taesŭng (Kobong). Introduction provides a clear analysis of Neo-Confucian thought in Korea.

Kendall, Laurel. *Shamans, Housewives, and Other Restless Spirits*. Honolulu: University of Hawaii Press, 1985.

A work by an American anthropologist on the religious rituals and activities of Korean women. Although her study deals with modern Korea, it provides a good introduction to shamanism and traditional "folk" religion.

Kendall, Laurel, and Mark Peterson, eds. *Korean Women: View from the Inner Room*. New Haven, CT.: East Rock Press, 1983.

Ten essays by anthropologists and historians dealing with Korean women in a Confucian society. Several of the essays are concerned with the Chosŏn period while others deal with women in the twentieth century. Most essays are readable and insightful.

Kim, Key-hiuk. *The Last Phase of the East Asian World Order: Korea, Japan, and the Chinese Empire, 1860–1882*. Berkeley: University of California Press, 1980.

Although this book deals largely with events after 1860, the first chapter provides a good survey of the East Asian world order in late Chosŏn times and Korea's place in it.

Kim, Kichung. *Classical Korean Literature*. Armonk, NY: M. E. Sharpe, 1996.

A series of essays that provide an excellent introduction to the literature of Korea before the late nineteenth century.

Kim-Renard, Young-Key, ed. *King Sejong the Great: the Light of Fifteenth Century Korea*. Washington, DC: George Washington University, International Circle of Korean Linguistics, 1992.

Fourteen short illustrated essays on aspects of Korean culture during the time of or associated with King Sejong. Topics include rites, Confucianism, *han'gul*, innovations in printing, the arts, ceramics, science and technology, and medicine.

Lancaster, Lewis, and Chai-Shin Yu eds. *Introduction of Buddhism to Korea: New Cultural Patterns*. (Berkeley: Asian Humanities Press, 1986)

A collection of articles dealing with the introduction of Buddhism in Korea and its subsequent spread from there to Japan.

Ledyard, Gari. *The Dutch Come to Korea*. Seoul: Royal Asiatic Society, 1971.

A translation and commentary of the seventeenth-century account of Korea by the shipwrecked Dutch merchant Hamel.

Lee, Ki-baik. *A New History of Korea*. Translated by Edward W. Wagner with Edward J. Shultz. Cambridge, MA: Harvard University Press, 1984.

A translation from what has probably been the most widely used college textbook on Korean history in South Korea by one of that country's most eminent historians. Mainly focuses on pre-nineteenth-century Korea. It contains a large number of names and terms that may overwhelm a non-Korean being introduced to Korean history. Perhaps most useful as a reference work.

Lee, Peter H., ed. *Anthology of Korean Literature: From Early Times to the Nineteenth Century*. Honolulu: University of Hawaii Press, 1981.

Translated with useful introductions by a leading scholar and translator of Korean literature. This anthology provides more than one hundred and fifty short poems, songs, and excerpts from biographies and prose tales, essays, and myths. Presents a good overall introduction to premodern Korean literature.

Lee, Peter H., ed. *A History of Korean Literature*. Cambridge, UK: Cambridge University Press, 2003.

Combining a narrative history with criticism, this work offers a learned introduction to Korean literature by leading scholars. Approximately two-thirds of the essays are devoted to premodern literature.

Lee, Peter H., trans. *Lives of Eminent Korean Monks: The Haedong Kosung Chon*. Cambridge, MA: Harvard University Press, 1969.

An annotated translation of the extant chapters of this collection of short biographies of famous monks first compiled by the monk Kakhun in 1215. Contains brief accounts of eighteen Korean and foreign monks from the Three Kingdoms period. A fascinating glimpse into Korean Buddhism in this period with a helpful introduction by the author.

Lee, Peter H., and William Theodore De Bary, eds. *Sources of Korean Traditions.* Vol. 1, *From Early Times Through the Sixteenth Century.* New York: Columbia University Press, 1997; and Choe, Yong-ho and William Theodore De Bary, eds. *Sources of Korean Traditions.* Vol. 2, *From the Sixteenth to the Twentieth Centuries.* New York: Columbia University Press, 2000.

An indispensable collection of primary sources on Korean history, edited and translated by some of the leading scholars of premodern Korea.

Lee, Sang-Oak, and Duk Soo Park. *Perspectives on Korea.* (Sidney: Wild Peony Press, 1998).

A collection of scholarly essays, some providing good insights into premodern Korea.

Lewis, James B. *Frontier Contact between Chosŏn Korea and Tokugawa Japan.* London: RoutledgeCurzon, 2003.

A study of the contacts and perceptions Koreans and Japanese had of each other from the seventeenth to the late nineteenth centuries. Aimed at the specialist, it provides detailed information of the Waegwan near Pusan.

Pai, Hyung Il. *Constructing "Korean" Origins: A Critical Review of Archaeology, Historiography, and Racial Myth in Korean State-Formation Theories.* Cambridge, MA: Harvard University Press, 2000.

Mainly concerned with the use of archaeology, ancient myths, and texts by twentieth-century Korean historians and writers to create various versions of national identity. It is useful for understanding the historiographical issues surrounding early Korean history as well as better understanding the sources that our historical knowledge is based on. Much useful material on the Tan'gun myth.

Palais, James B. *Politics and Policy in Traditional Korea.* Cambridge, MA: Harvard University Press, 1975.

An examination of the reforms of the Taewŏn'gun in the 1860s and early 1870s that provides considerable information on the political, social, and economic problems of the late Chosŏn. Some of this study has been superseded by the author's later work, *Confucian Statecraft and Korean Institutions: Yu Hyŏngwŏn and the Late Chosŏn Dynasty* (see below).

Palais, James B. *Confucian Statecraft and Korean Institutions: Yu Hyŏngwŏn and the Late Chosŏn Dynasty.* Seattle: University of Washington Press, 1996.

This massive study of over one thousand pages uses the writings and concerns of the seventeenth-century scholar Yu Hyŏng-wŏn to examine a variety of political, economic, and social issues debated among the educated elite during the Chosŏn period. A bit unwieldy as a narrative text, this work by one of the leading American scholars of Korea contains a wealth of information and insights on premodern Korea.

Palais, James B. *Views on Korean Social History.* Seoul: Institute for Modern Korean Studies, 1998.

Two essays given by James Palais in 1997 at the Graduate School of International Studies at Yonsei University. Deals with some controversial issues in Korean history.

Peterson, Mark A. *Korean Adoption and Inheritance: Case Studies in the Creation of a Classic Confucian Society.* Ithaca, NY: Cornell University Press, 1998.

Examines adoption and inheritance documents from the fifteenth to the nineteenth centuries for evidence of social change during Chosŏn Korea.

Portal, Jane. *Korea: Art and Archaeology.* London: British Museum, 2000.

Chronological account of the art and archaeology of Korea from the Neolithic period to the twentieth century, primarily focusing on premodern art traditions. Covers a wide sampling of art forms including folk art as well as the art of the elite. Well illustrated with an informative commentary, this book provides a good introduction to Korea's rich artistic heritage.

Pratt, Keith. *Korean Painting.* Oxford, UK: Oxford University Press, 1996.

A survey of Korean painting from the fourth-century tomb paintings to the twentieth century.

Pratt, Keith, and Richard Rutt. *Korea: A Historical and Cultural Dictionary.* Richmond, Surrey: Curzon Press, 1999.

A compact but comprehensive dictionary of names, terms, and topics dealing with Korean history and culture. A handy reference work.

Ro, Young-chan. *The Korean Neo-Confucianism of Yi Yulgok.* Albany, NY: State University of New York Press, 1988.

A somewhat technical study of the important sixteenth-century Korean philosopher.

Setton, Mark. *Chŏng Yagyong: Korea's Challenge to Orthodox Neo-Confucianism.* Albany, NY: State University of New York Press, 1997.

Study of one of late Chosŏn's most important and original thinkers. Contains a clear, insightful explanation of his thought and the Qing and Tokugawa influences on it.

Shaw, William. *Legal Norms in a Confucian State.* Berkeley, CA: Institute of East Asian Studies, University of California, Center for Korean Studies, 1981.

A well informed study of legal theory and practice in Yi dynasty Korea, based primarily on the *Siminrok* a late-eighteenth-century collection of judicial reviews of difficult criminal cases. Contains one hundred of these short reviews of legal hearings.

Shultz, Edward J. *Generals and Scholars: Military Rule in Medieval Korea.* Honolulu: University of Hawaii Press, 2000.

An important study of the often neglected period of military rule in the twelfth and thirteenth centuries by a leading specialist.

Toby, Ronald P. *State and Diplomacy in Early Modern Japan.* Princeton: Princeton University Press, 1984.

An important study of Japanese foreign relations during its "seclusion period" (*sakoku*) from the early seventeenth to the nineteenth centuries, much of it focusing on Japanese-Korean relations.

Stephen Turnbull. *Samurai Invasion, Japan's Korean War, 1592–98.* London: Cassell & Co., 2002.

Well-illustrated account of the sixteenth-century Japanese invasion of Korea, aimed at the general reader.

Wagner, Edward W. *Literati Purges: Political conflict in Early Yi Korea.* Cambridge, MA: East Asian Research Center, Harvard University, 1974.

A detailed study of the four literati purges in the fifteenth and sixteenth century. Contains an outline of the institutional structure of the early Chosŏn.

Yi Chung-hwan. *Yi Chung-Hwan's T'aengniji: the Korean Classic for Choosing Settlements.* Translated with an Introduction by Inshil Choe Yoon. Sydney: University of Sydney East Asian Series Number 12, 1998.

A translation of the influential eighteenth-century text on geomancy. The original text was written to help the yangban find a desirable place to live.

Yi T'oegye, and Michael C. Kalton. *To Become a Sage: the Ten Diagrams on Sage Learning.* New York: Columbia University Press, 1989.

An examination of the diagrams drawn by the sixteenth-century Korean philosopher to illustrate his Neo-Confucian concepts.

Yi Sun-shin. *Nanjung Ilgi: War Diary of Admiral Yi Sun-shin.* Translated by Ha Tae-hung. Edited by Sohn Pow-key. Seoul: Yonsei University Press, 1977.

A translation of the war diary of this now venerated sixteenth-century admiral.

Index

About the Author

Michael J. Seth is associate professor of East Asian and world history at James Madison University in Harrisonburg, Virginia. He received his PhD from the University of Hawaii and his MA and BA from the State University of New York at Binghamton. Dr. Seth has lived and worked in South Korea and is the author of *Education Fever: Society, Politics and the Pursuit of Schooling in South Korea* (2002).